D0251249

INTELLIGENCE

A NEW LOOK
INTELLIGENCE

HANS J.
EYSENCK

Transaction Publishers
New Brunswick (U.S.A.) and London (U.K.)

Library of Congress Catalog Number: 98-14308
ISBN: 1-56000-360-X
Printed in the United States of America

Library of Congress Cataloging-in-Publication Data

Eysenck, H. J. (Hans Jurgen), 1916-
    Intelligence : a new look / Hans J. Eysenck.
        p. cm.
    Includes bibliographical references and index.
    ISBN 1-56000-360-X (alk. paper)
    1. Intellect. 2. Intelligence tests. 3. Nature and nurture.
3. Individual differences. I. Title.
BF431.B97   1998
153.9—dc21   98-14308
                                                                CIP

Contents

Introduction

*"Nothing is so unequal as the equal
treatment of unequal people."*
—Thomas Jefferson.

Why another book on intelligence? There are several reasons. A lot
has happened in the past dozen years or so that has completely changed
our perspective on intelligence and IQ testing. For a beginning, recent
work on much larger and better selected samples has extended our evidence on the hereditarian aspects of intelligence, as well as on the environmental ones, with important consequences. In addition, advances in
molecular genetics have enabled us to discover DNA markers which
can be used to identify a chromosomal region, and, eventually to iso-
late a gene for simple genetic-traits; multiple-gene traits, like intelligence, are just beginning to be investigated by these methods. But
already we have much more detailed and certain knowledge in this
field, and a review seems timely.

There is also much new evidence on the biological *intermediaries*
between DNA and behaviour. Clearly, DNA cannot directly influence
behaviour; it can lead to the development of neurological structures,
psychophysiological mechanism, glandular and hormonal emissions,
transmitter receptors, and many other biological mechanisms the study
of which has thrown a flood of new light on the nature of intelligence,
and measurement of differences in intelligence.

A third line of research has been concerned with ECTs—elementary
cognitive tasks such as reaction-time and inspection-time, offering the
subject tasks which are so easy that even severely mentally retarded
children can carry them out, but where *speed of execution* is the variable measured. Older theories of intelligence predicted a lack of correlation with IQ: the observed positive correlations suggest a return to
Sir Francis Galton's theories of mental speed, theories which also find
support from the biological studies mentioned above.

1

It has been part of the theory of intelligence for over fifty years that in addition to *general intelligence*, measured by IQ tests there are many special abilities (verbal, numerical, visuo-spatial, memory, etc.) which independently contribute to our cognitive behaviour. Recently several authors have begun to talk about "multiple" intelligence, and advocated the notion of "social" or "practical" intelligence; it seemed opportune to look at these new ideas and see whether they had any scientific meaning.

Finally, I include a fairly lengthy study of one of these special factors that interact with general intelligence to produce certain effects in the actual world, and I chose creativity and intuition, and the production of works of art and science by the geniuses of this world. The topic was chosen because of its general interest, because it illustrates the way I believe the relation between IQ and other special abilities and personality can best be studied, and because to many people it is strictly beyond the capability of science to investigate. I do not believe that anything that exists cannot be measured; as Thorndike said memorably, everything that exists, exists in some quantity and can therefore be measured.

These, then, are some of the changes that have taken place in recent years; most have not yet gotten into textbooks; together, they approximate a general paradigm which could form the firm basis for future research—a paradigm not too unlike the one I envisaged in my book, *A Model for Intelligence*. There are, of course, many anomalies and problems still remaining; that is the inevitable fate of any scientific theory. Even Newton's theory of gravitation, one of the most famous of all scientific theories, was riddled with anomalies, and Newton had to fudge and fiddle to get even the most exiguous fit between prediction and activity. But I do feel that things are beginning to hang together, and the next few years should see an even closer coming together of experimental findings and theoretical expectations.

I have not, of course, covered everything that relates to intelligence; this is not meant to be a textbook, but a fairly concise outline of what science has to say about the topic at the present moment. I have been particularly careful to depart as little as possible from the great orthodoxy. What is orthodoxy? One approach is via textbooks that have been highly praised and widely adopted; I have used Nathan Brody's *Intelligence* as an objective survey of the existing literature. Mark Snyderman and Stanley Rothman surveyed the opinions of over 600 experts on certain important and potentially controversial questions in the field of intelligence; I have taken cognizance of the agreements published in their book, *The IQ Controversy*, and while I was a member of the Board of Scientific Affairs of the American Psychological Association, we set up a Task Force, charged with making a report on the present standing of the intelligence concept; I have paid much attention to this report. Finally, the *Wall Street Journal* published a statement by over fifty experts in intelligence testing, outlining the major conclusions they thought were justified about intelligence; its meaning, its measurement, its inheritance, and its social importance. I have reproduced this statement in the appendix. I did not find any particular discrepancies between my account and what these voices of orthodoxy had to say. Where there are slight differences in interpretation (not in facts!), I shall say so and argue the case.

It is important to point out the existence of considerable agreement on the basic facts in this field. What you read in the newspapers, hear on the radio and see on television, is hardly even the truth as seen by experts; it is the wishful thinking of journalists, seen through filters of prejudice and ignorance. What you read in popular books, like S.J. Gould's *Mismeasure of Man*, is a palaeontologist's distorted view of what psychologists think, untutored in even the most elementary facts of the science. (A palaeontologist is an expert in the study of fossils to determine the structure and evolution of extinct animals and plants—hardly the background for a far-ranging critique of the complex field of intelligence!) Would an astronomer accept the criticism of the Big Bang theory offered by a professor of immunology, patently lacking in factual knowledge of astronomy?

I am mentioning Gould as one of a group of politically motivated scientists who have consistently misled the public about what psychologists are doing in the field of intelligence, what they have discovered, and what conclusions they have come to. Readers who may feel that such an indictment is intemperate are invited to compare the contents of the second edition of Gould's book with a lengthy critique of it by P. Rushton that appeared recently, and goes in great detail into the factual content of Gould's book, with devastating results. Gould simply refuses to mention unquestionable facts that do not fit into his politically correct version; he shamelessly attacks the reputation of eminent scientists of whom he disapproves, on completely nonfactual grounds, and he misrepresents the views of scientists who take into serious account the experimental and empirical material available. Readers are invited to look at the writings of these two antagonists, and decide on their own who is more credible.

I have not included a chapter on the "politics of IQ," because I am concerned with facts, not politics. Many critics of IQ testing have concentrated their fire on the alleged political implications and consequences of such work, and have impugned the motives of research workers in this field. Yet far from supporting the status quo, as often alleged, IQ testing has in fact had the result of advancing meritocracy, and destroying the feudalistic and nepotistic world where it matters more whom you know than what you know. As regards motivation, I have known personally most of the scientists who were responsible for the growth of the IQ testing movement—from Charles Spearman, Leo Thurstone, Godfrey Thomson, J.P. Guilford, Ray Cattell, Cyril Burt, and David Wechsler to more recent exponents like Robert Plomin, Paul Klein, Nathan Brody, Richard Herrnstein, John Horn, Robert Sternberg, Howard Gardner, Arthur Jensen, and Douglas Detterman. None of them would recognize the popular picture of the ultra-conservative protagonist of a vanishing feudal type of capitalism. Most were moved by a strong desire to redress the accidents of birth that prevented bright working-class boys and girls from obtaining an education fit for their talents, and quite generally to make their contribution toward an improvement of our educational system for all children. The majority believed that research into intelligence would have greatly beneficial social consequences, as indeed it has had already. All believe in "inquiring into truth," which, as Francis Bacon said, "is the love-making, or the wooing of it, the knowledge of truth, which is the presence of it, and the belief of truth, which is the engaging of it, in the sovereign good of human nature." This belief in the importance of searching after truth is the true motivating factor in the lives of those who have carried out research in this field, not personal profit or political prejudice. It seems worth while to restate this simple fact, so often disregarded and neglected by politically motivated commentators wholly ignorant of the true facts.

For many people, when all is said and done, "intelligence" is still a mentalistic kind of concept, miles away from the reassuring solidity of height and weight, mass and temperature. But of course physics isn't like that any more; now we are dealing with notions much more evanescent and diaphanous than IQ. Consider an example. Stephen Weinberg and Aldus Salam, two well-known physicists, used the concepts of quantum field theory to combine the electromagnetic and electroweak forces, ending up with three new particles. These had no mass, and should have been easy to observe, but could not be detected.

Trying to give their particles some mass, the physicists assumed the existence of hypothetical fields known as "Higgs" fields, after their inventor, Peter Higgs. The result was a specific theory containing four new massive particles, the W+, W–, Zo, and Higgs boson. But nobody has found the Higgs boson so far; the ú1.5 billion Large Hadron Collider is set to look for it. But Hawkins has argued that his solutions and equations derived from combining the system of quantum mechanics and general relativity will make the Higgs boson impossible to detect! I would think the IQ is a lot less evanescent, and more intelligible, than the Higgs boson, even though it may "exist," in its undetectable form! There is little doubt that intelligence is a *meaningful* concept, can be *scientifically measured*, and has a *respectable* theory to contain it. It is the task of this volume to justify these claims.

But what about accuracy of measurement? The incredible degree of accuracy with which we can measure time and distance—hardly a second out in a million years, hardly a yard out in measuring the distance from earth to moon—can surely not be equalled by any form of mental measurement? Well, it depends what you are measuring. Take cosmology, and let us look at the age of the universe. According to the Big Bang theory, this can be measured by reference to the Hubble constant, H_o, that is, the ratio between red shift velocity with which galaxies seemed to move away from the observer of the distance of the galaxies in question. When I was a young student, this constant was estimated at 500; now it is estimated at a tenth of that value, with two major groups debating fiercely whether it is around 30 or around 70! Not much accuracy there. Correspondingly diverse are estimates of the age of the universe, with some of the oldest stars apparently older than the universe! The latest studies suggest that estimates of the age of the oldest stars have been out by as much as seven billion years. Given that the stars are now believed to be between nine and twelve billion years old, that is quite an error! Simple things like time and distance on earth are easily measured with great accuracy; after all we have been working at this for thousands of years. Consider things like the age of the universe, the distance of remote galaxies are much more difficult to measure, and the measurements are much less accurate. Psychological measurement lies somewhere in between. Errors in IQ measurement are quite small, perhaps around five points of IQ. These errors can be reduced by multiple testing, that is, using many tests, with different makeup, and including tests of general ability as well as many specific abilities. For practical use, IQ tests are extremely cost-effective—just a few pence for an IQ estimate! Stellar observations are vastly more expensive, costing billions of pounds or dollars. Given enough money, we could make IQ measurement much more accurate. Psychology has always worked on a pittance, compared with the amount of money poured into physical science. We need much larger set-ups, with facilities including the latest EEG machines, PET scans, magnetic resonance imaging apparatus, etc., together with skilled technicians to work there, and large computers to analyse the data. These facilities should be available in every research department; at present they are available in none! As Winston Churchill said, in a different context: "Give us the tools and we'll finish the job!"

1

The Paradox of Intelligence
and Its Measurement

The concept of intelligence, and its measurement, present us with a curious paradox. On the one hand, we have hardboiled scientists devoting their lives to the exploration of cognitive abilities, and expert in the complex statistics that are involved in testing theories about intelligence, regarding this body of work as an outstanding success of experimental psychology, marking the first triumph in actually measuring, with considerable accuracy, a mental quality. On the other hand, we have journalists, media people, and even the occasional scientist drifting in from other disciplines, not expert, or even knowledgeable in the field, decrying the whole effort as a waste of time, futile busywork, socially divisive, and useless in practice. This surely is an odd situation, particularly when we find that intelligence testing has attracted much political hostility—Hitler banned it because it was Jewish, Stalin because it was bourgeois. (They banned Einstein's relativity theory for the same reasons!)

What are the main criticisms and questions you can hear over and over again in the media? One frequent assertion is that psychologists can't agree on the nature of intelligence, and thus obviously have no idea what it actually is. Another assertion maintains that IQ tests have no practical importance, and measure nothing but the ability to do IQ tests. A third assertion is that the notion that IQ differences are largely due to genetic causes has been conclusively disproved since certain results reported by Sir Cyril Burt have been suggested to have been fraudulent. A fourth assertion states that IQ testing was invented to maintain the "status quo," favouring the ruling class, and helping to suppress the working class. And as a fifth and final assertion we have the notion that IQ testing is a tool of racists to demonstrate the superiority of the white race. These five assertions have achieved great popularity among the uninformed; they share one characteristic in common—they are all completely false. I shall discuss them all in detail in due course, but will begin by briefly discussing each in turn.

1. Psychologists disagree about the nature and definition of intelligence.

In 1988, Mark Snyderman and Stanley Rothman published a book, *The IQ Controversy*, which contained the answers of over 600 experts in the fields of intelligence testing, educational psychology, developmental psychology, behavioural genetics, sociology and education, cognitive science, counselling psychology, and occupational psychology to questions about intelligence, 99.3 percent agreed on the importance of abstract thinking and reasoning; 97.7 percent on problem-solving ability, and 96.0 percent on the capacity to acquire knowledge. This does not suggest a lack of agreement, and indeed these definitions agree well with common sense—we tend to call somebody intelligent who can reason clearly, think well in abstract terms, solve mental problems, and learn rapidly. Why then the notion that psychologists disagree?

Psychologists often describe the many things a high IQ enables us to do. These are indeed manifold, but to concentrate on one or the other does not imply disagreement on the nature of intelligence itself. Physicists may study many different consequences of gravitation—the apple falling on Newton's head, the globular shape of the planets, the creation of the galaxies, the movements of the planets, the occurrence of tides, the existence of black holes, the laws of gunnery. This does not mean that physicians are in disagreement on the fundamental law of gravitation. Similarly, many different consequences can be deduced from the postulation of a factor of general intelligence, but that does not imply disagreement on its nature. There are of course debates about important aspects of intelligence, but then so are there debates about the nature of gravitation—is it a distortion of Einstein's space-time continuum, is it a question of particle interaction, "gravitons" as quantum mechanics would have it, or what? Complete agreement on everything is not necessary to make a concept meaningful.

2. IQ tests measure nothing important, merely the ability to do IQ tests.

Nobody who has even the most passing acquaintance with IQ testing would ever make such an outrageous statement. To take just one or two examples: IQ predicts with considerable precision a child's scholastic achievement, or a youth's success at university. In the famous Isle of Wight study, for instance, all five year olds on the island were IQ tested, that is, *before* they even went to school. Their final school grades at the age of sixteen years were predicted very accurately by their IQ, and when the IQ was reassessed at the same time, it had changed very little. In other words, IQ *predicts achievement*; it is not something you are taught at school. Similarly, IQ predicts success at university, law school, medical college, or indeed any advanced teaching unit more successfully than anything else, including interviews or special examinations. Within a given job, occupation or profession, IQ almost invariably correlates with performance. I will give more detail later, but it will already be obvious that IQ tests measure something very important indeed.

3. The notion that differences in IQ are largely determined by heredity has been disproved.

Quite the contrary is true. It has been known for many years that heredity contributes more than environment to differences in IQ, but recent years have brought forth a veritable flood of evidence to support and strengthen this early finding. We have also experienced a tremendous improvement in the very complex statistical reasoning and modelling underlying any estimate of the relative weights to be given to nature and nurture, and we now understand much better than before just what it means to say that IQ differences are largely genetic, and what consequences follow from such a statement. Much of the criticism heaped on psychologists stating the simple facts of genetic determination derives from a completely erroneous perception of just what such a statement means, and what its consequences are. A major purpose of this book is to spell out these consequences in some detail.

4. IQ testing was invented to maintain the "status quo," and strengthen the ruling classes.

Such a statement is not only untrue, but contrary to the facts. In the first place there is no way in which IQ could be said to maintain the "status quo"; by identifying bright working-class boys and girls, and pushing them up the educational ladder, IQ testing leads towards a meritocracy, that is, a state of affairs in which leadership positions and access to the professions depends on ability, not nepotism, family connections, or whom you know. It is the great leveller that disregards feudal claims, parental status, and family influences. It was introduced originally precisely in order to enable bright working-class youths to obtain an education suitable to their talents, and not to be held back by examinations that favoured the rich, attending the better class of school, and kept back the child coming from an inner-city school. I knew many of the pioneers who introduced these tests, and they were all outraged by the handicaps suffered by deprived children of the poor, and determined to do what they could to make the playing field more even. The evidence supports the view that they succeeded; many more working-class children achieved a better education when IQ tests played a part in selection.

5. IQ testing was introduced to bolster the claims of the white race to superiority.

Tests are essentially colour-blind, and give an objective estimate of intellectual ability. If anyone fancied, or hoped, that they would prove the superiority of the white (Caucasian) race he would have been bitterly disappointed. The races showing the highest IQ are the mongoloid races—Japanese, Chinese, Korean; whites are certainly not at the top. The highest scores go to the Jews who probably should not be counted as a race but as a religious sect; nevertheless, it will hardly gratify racist groups to find Jews at the very pinnacle of intellectual achievement!

All these criticisms tend to have a political context, as one might have anticipated from the dislike expressed towards IQ testing by Hitler and Stalin, brothers-in-arms to ban any signs of objectivity from the political landscape. Modern writers who seek to castigate IQ testing often sail under the flag of Marxism; this would include people like Steven Rose, Leon Kamin, and R.L. Lewontin, whose book, *Not in Our Genes,* received much favourable attention from journalistic reviewers in the media, and severe criticism from experts writing in scientific journals. The same was true of Stephen Jay Gould, whose book, *The Mismeasure of Man,* has more factual errors per page than any book I have ever read. Actually these writers, and many others who had added their voices to the Marxist choir, have not even been able to quote Marx and Lenin accurately. Here is a definitive statement from Lenin that should clear the air: "When one says that experience and reason testify that men are not equal, then one understands under equality the equality of *abilities* or the equivalence of bodily strength and mental capacities of men. It is quite obvious that in this sense men are not equal. No single reasonable man and no single socialist ever forgets this."

Lenin goes on to characterize as an "absurdity" the idea of extending equality into these spheres and concludes by saying, "When socialists speak of equality, they understand thereby *social* equality, the equality of social position, but not at all the equality of physical and mental abilities of individual persons." Even the *Communist Manifesto* asks "from each according to his abilities," postulating differential abilities even after the communist heaven has been achieved!

I will not deal with political arguments any further. I am a scientist, not a politician, and while it is obvious that scientific findings may have social and political implications, these are never apparent, and the uses made of scientific findings depend more on one's value system than on the facts discovered. When you find that a given person, or groups of persons, has a low IQ, you may say, "Let them sink to the bottom where they belong," or you may say, "Let us do whatever we can to allow them to develop whatever gifts they have to the utmost of their ability." Facts are objective, decisions subjective. We may not like the facts, but they are stubborn; facts are the products of nature, and scientists are merely the messengers who seek and pass on the messages nature has for us. Don't shoot the messenger, he is doing his best!

The notion is quite popular that the concept of "intelligence" is very modern and was invented by psychologists less than 100 years ago. It is also often said to be purely Western, and geared to capitalist economics. But of course *intellegentia* was used by the ancient Romans in much the same way we use the term "intelligence," and even earlier the Chinese elaborated ideas about intelligence that are very similar to our own most modern views. Thus almost 2,500 years ago this concept was clearly defined by Confucius. He and his followers regarded it as being related to having a "top brain" and a quick mind, a reference to speed of mental functioning that we shall find amply supported by the most recent experimental studies. He also emphasized sensory discrimination, that is, the quality of eyes and ears to take in information, and use it to discriminate between different precepts. Again, the idea was used by Charles Spearman in 1904 to construct tests of intelligence which later work showed to correlate quite well with IQ tests. Confucius categorized people into three types: superior, medium, or inferior—"as stupid as two spring worms," as the Chinese put it. This classification, of course, reminds us of Plato's men of gold, of silver, and of brass, again referring to differences in mental ability.

Confucius laid it down that all people should be taught regardless of their ability, but type of education should be according to their ability. This again agrees well with modern achievement doctrines, as does his distinction between general ability and specific abilities, which we shall come across later on in its modern form. Finally, Confucius made the distinction between *tian zi*, the mental ability given by heaven, and *shuan chang*, the result of learning through training and education, an adumbration of theories of nature and nurture. The Chinese had no doubt about the importance of heredity in this context. They phrased this notion in terms of intelligence being a "gift from heaven"; thus an intelligent person is described as being *de thian du hou*, meaning "getting a uniquely big share from heaven."

It would be equally wrong to imagine that intelligence tests are of modern vintage. Over one thousand years ago, the Chinese elaborated a test called the "Seven Coincidence Boards," or wisdom boards; these closely resemble the Form Boards used in modern nonverbal intelligence tests. The wisdom boards can be manipulated to form a variety of figures, as shown in figure 1.1, thus testing visuo-spatial perception, divergent thinking, and creativity, although of course they did not form part of a psychometrically tested, explicit theory of mental ability. But implicitly China relied for 2,000 years on a civil service selected objectively by means of examinations open to all, and almost certainly correlating quite highly with IQ, this produced the longest period of existence for any civilized society the world has ever known, and also led to the discovery of many scientific and technical facts and inventions thousands of years before Europe was able to emulate the Chinese sages. As these few lines show, this tendency to outpace Europeans in scientific discovery extends even to the field of intelligence; here too the Chinese have anticipated most of our theories and practices, but as in physics, chemistry, medicine and astronomy, without putting their findings into an explicit theoretical context, or elaborating them into a properly organized practice.

Before going into detail about IQ measurement, it may be useful to say a few words about the concept of intelligence, if only because it is often used in different ways by different people, or even by the same person in different contexts, and this often causes confusion. One might even say that most of the confusion that is often apparent in public debates is due to simple misunderstandings that could easily be avoided

FIGURE 1.1
Chinese Seven Coincidence Board (wisdom board)

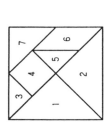

(a) Designed in Song Dynasty (960-1277)

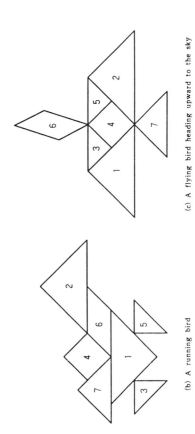

(b) A running bird

(c) A flying bird heading upward to the sky

Nine-hundred-year-old intelligence test used in China. The task is to use the seven pieces in (a) to construct meaningful figures, as in (b) and (c).

with a little care. Let us start with a historical note. Our term "intelligence" comes from two Latin words: *intellegentia* and *ingenium*. The former, when you consider the ways Cicero used the term, means something like "understanding" and "knowledge"; the latter "natural disposition" or "ability." These are two meanings of our term, intelligence, that have always adhered to it. Fundamental to intelligent behaviour is an underlying disposition that enables us to reason, to think abstractly, to learn. The greater this ability, the more we are likely to learn, and to know. This knowledge is thus itself a sign of high intelligence, although in a sense derivative. Raymond Cattell, one of the famous names in intelligence research, labelled these two aspects of intelligence "fluid" and "crystallized ability." "Fluid ability" refers to the dispositional concept, the ability to acquire many kinds of knowledge. "Crystallized ability" refers to the knowledge already gained. Scientists will recognize the same sort of difference as that between potential and kinetic energy. Fluid ability is often written g_f, crystallized ability g_c, where g refers to general intelligence.

These two aspects of intelligence are of course closely related. A vocabulary test is one of the best measures of intelligence because it is obviously a test of g_c, the number of words acquired by listening and reading is a function of g_f provided the environment contains a sufficient supply of spoken and written words. Tests of g_f contain no material that would not be familiar to everyone of a given age; the problem in each case cannot be solved by acquired knowledge. For example, the sequence of numbers:

$$2 \quad 4 \quad 7 \quad 11 \quad 16 \quad ?$$

obviously requires for an answer the number 22, but this has to be worked out. The elements, simple numbers, are known to everyone. Of course this is a very simple test of g_f, but it will illustrate the point. Even tests like this demand some small amount of knowledge, and if that is not forthcoming the test will be meaningless. People who construct tests of IQ are very careful to construct these with a specific audience in mind, and make sure that for that audience questions are appropriate, and all the elements well known (or equally unknown, as in non-verbal tests). This is an example of a non-verbal test item.

How do we know that items such as these actually measure intelligence? Our vague notions of intelligence are built up from experience over the centuries; the ancient Greeks and Romans found, just as we do, that people differ in their ability to learn, think, reason, solve prob-

FIGURE 1.2
Nonverbal IQ Test Item

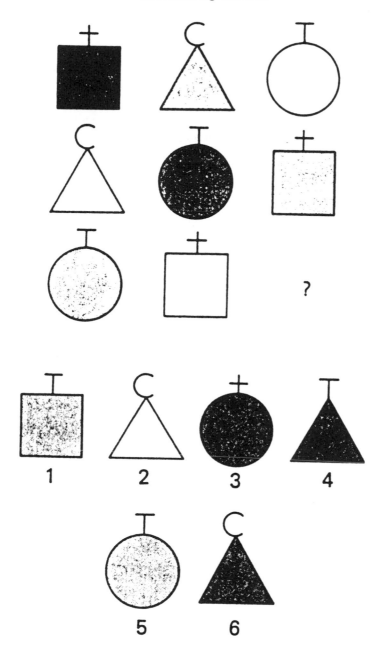

lems, and generally get the right idea. If our tests did not on the whole agree with such commonsense notions, we would hardly agree to the proposition that they measured intelligence! In the same way we have commonsense notions of hot and cold—snow is cold, sun is hot. Thus our notions of temperature arose from experience; if thermometers did not agree with these experiences, we would not trust them as measures of temperature! IQ tests and thermometers are more reliable, less subjective, and more valid than personal judgments based on experience, and furthermore they are capable of infinite improvement; yet there is a continuous line from the most elementary subjective notions to the most complex measuring instrument. Of course we have advanced further in our understanding and measurement of intelligence; but we are on our way, and as we shall see; we have done quite well so far.

2

Origin and Meaning of the IQ

The person most directly responsible for making intelligence a scientific and measurable concept was a Victorian polymath and genius, Sir Francis Galton, born in 1822, a half-cousin of Charles Darwin; he made seminal contributions in a variety of fields—exploration and geography, metereology, photography, classification of fingerprints, genetics, statistics, anthropometry, and psychometry. His major contribution to differential psychology arose from his conviction that all human characteristics, both physical and mental, could ultimately be described quantitatively—"when you can, count!" He conceived of intelligence as a general ability, largely inherited, and best measured in terms of speed of mental processes, as for instance the speed of reaction to a sudden stimulus. He died in 1911, still firmly convinced that general cognitive ability was by far the most important influence on a person's life achievements.

Alfred Binet was born much later than Galton (1857), but died in the same year. A professional psychologist, he was appointed a member of a commission by the French minister of public instruction to recommend what should be done about the education of subnormal children in the schools of Paris. In response he developed a test which became the first scale for the measurement of intelligence; it appeared in 1905, with later revision in 1908 and 1911. He is the father of all modern tests of intelligence, but his views differed in many ways from those of Galton, as we shall see. Binet argued that there were three methods for measuring intelligence. The first was the *medical* method, which looks at the anatomical, physiological, and pathological signs of inferior intelligence; this has recently been resurrected, as we shall see, to explore links between DNA and behaviour. The second is the *pedagogical* method, which relies on school-acquired knowledge to measure intelligence, which is regarded as the sum of acquired knowledge. The third is the *psychological* method, which attempts to rely on direct observation and measurement of intelligent behaviour. How can this be done?

What Binet did had the simplicity of genius written all over it. He argued that as children grow up, they function more efficiently as far as intelligence is concerned. If you present a child of five with a problem he cannot solve, he will suddenly be able to do so when he is six, or seven, or eight. Taking a certain problem, say a circular drawing with a break somewhere, you would tell a child that this represents a park in which he had lost a ball. Starting at the entrance (the break in the circle), how would he set about looking for his ball? Any regular search (going up and down, going in ever decreasing circles) is counted as a correct answer. Vaguely rushing about is wrong. If the average child can solve this problem at the age of five, but not at four, then the age-level of the problem is five years. Any child that can solve the problem then is said to have a *mental* age of (at least) five, whatever his chronological age. Of course you would use many more tests like this, and you would measure his M.A. (mental age) in months as well as in years, but in essence this is what Binet did to construct his scale. The concept of mental age is the crucial insight here; if you compare a child's mental age with his chronological age (C.A.), you can tell whether he is bright (M.A. greater than C.A.) or dull (M.A. lower than C.A.) The German psychologist William Stern brought the two together in the simple IQ formula:

$$IQ = \frac{M.A.}{C.A.} \times 100.$$ (The 100 is introduced to get rid of the decimal point.)

If an 8-year-old has an M.A. of 10, his IQ is:

$$125 = (\frac{10}{8} \times 100), \text{ but}$$

if a 12-year-old has an M.A. of 10, his IQ is;

$$83 = (\frac{10}{12} \times 100).$$

this ratio does not change to any extent from the age of five (when IQs can be meaningfully measured) to the age of sixteen or so. After sixteen mental growth ceases gradually, so that M.A. does not increase, hence after that age we cannot use the formula any more. If we did a person with an IQ of:

$$133 \text{ at } 12 = (\frac{16}{12} \; ' \; 100).$$

would have an IQ of 50 at 32 $(\frac{16}{32} \; ' \; 100)$, and

would have an IQ of 25 at 64 $(\frac{16}{64} \; ' \; 100)$!

How do we calculate IQ for adults? When we measure children's IQ, they are distributed in the shape of a normal r Gaussian curve (named after the famous mathematician Karl Friedrich Gauss who discovered its formula.) This is shown in figure 2.1. At the bottom are shown IQ levels from 60 to 140; the curve shows that few children have very high or very low IQ, with 50 percent between 90 and 110. Only 4 in a thousand (0.4 percent) have an IQ above 140, or below 60. (This is actually not quite correct; in addition to the 0.4 percent of very dull children, we have a fair number of children whose birth injuries have destroyed important parts of the brain, leaving them at a much lower intellectual level than expected.)

A similar distribution is arrived at if we simply give each child a score, made up of the total number of correct answers he gives on a test. We can then translate the score into an IQ—the average score corresponds to an IQ of 100, and so on. We can thus use the normal curve to translate scores into IQs directly, for adults as well as for children, and that is what is now done practically universally. The statistical niceties need not detain us; note just that modern IQs are not really quotients of any kind, but have merely retained the name IQ although arrived at by an alternative formula.

Another feature of the bell-shaped curve is called the *standard deviation* (S.D.) which denotes the amount of spreadoutness of the whole curve. If the brightest child had an IQ of 120, and the dullest one of 80, the curve would have been much more compressed, as indicated by a much smaller S.D. These two figures, mean and S.D., are sufficient to describe the curve completely mathematically; it will become clear presently why I have introduced the S.D. here. Usually 3 S.Ds. either side of the mean includes practically all of a given population, with only a very small proportion outside these limits. For the IQ, the S.D. is usually reckoned to be about 15.

What does a given IQ mean, in social terms? The average person of course has an IQ around 100, by definition. To do reasonably well at an

FIGURE 2.1
Curve of Distribution of IQ

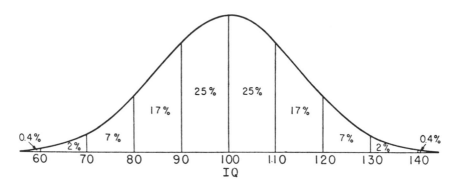

English grammar school, or a German gymnasium, or a French lycée, a child would need an IQ of 110 or better, although with hard work he might succeed to stay at the lower end of his class even with a slightly lower IQ. To enter a (good) university, an IQ of 115 would be pretty well the lowest limit, leading to a modest lower second or even third-class degree. For a first, something like 125 would be required at a minimum. Professors would clock in at 130 or above. Table 2.1 gives the average IQs of members of various middle-class, skilled, and semi-skilled working-class occupations. These are pretty similar from country to country, and from time to time.

There is one interesting thing about this table, other than the obvious relationship between IQ and social status. Note that the S.Ds. of the occupational groups increase dramatically as you go down in social status. Nearly all the middle-class occupations have S.Ds. below 15, which is the population standard. This makes sense; to become an accountant, or lawyer, or teacher, you are required to take examinations that need a high IQ in order to be successfully passed; hence low-level IQ people have been automatically excluded. The skilled working-class occupations are near or slightly above the general level in IQ and also

TABLE 2.1
IQs of a Number of Different Professions,
Together with Their Standard Deviations

	Mean:	S.D.	
Accountant	128	11.7	
Lawyer	128	10.9	
Auditor	125	11.2	
Reporter	124	11.7	Middle class
Chief clerk	124	11.7	Occupations
Teacher	122	12.8	
Draughtsman	122	12.8	
Pharmacist	120	15.2	
Bookkeeper	120	13.1	
Toolmaker	112	12.5	
Machinist	110	16.1	
Foreman	110	16.7	
Airplane Mechanic	109	14.0	Skilled working
Electrician	109	15.2	class Occupations
Lathe operator	108	15.5	
Sheet metal worker	108	15.1	
Mechanic	106	16.0	
Riveter	104	15.1	
Painter, general	98	18.7	
Cook & baker	97	20.8	
Truckdriver	96	19.7	Semi-silled
Labourer	96	20.1	Working class
Barber	95	20.5	Occupations
Lumberjack	95	19.8	
Farmhand	91	20.7	
Miner	91	20.1	
Teamster	88	19.0	

in S.D.; in other words, there has been little selection as far as these occupations are concerned. But when we come to the semiskilled working-class occupations, we find very high S.Ds.! In other words, here we have people with high IQs in the same occupations as people with very low IQs. Statisticians call such a triangular distribution *heteroscedastic*: IQs are compressed at the high end and extended at the low end.

Clearly, a high IQ is a necessary but not a sufficient condition for getting into one of the professional, high salary/high status groups!

Why we have this large reservoir of underused ability is not really well known. Some are neurotic or otherwise psychologically impaired; some are alcoholics, some are incurably lazy. Many are just unlucky, one way or another. Should society not try and enable them to use their God-given abilities? That of course is for society to decide; it is one of the functions of IQ testing to draw attention to such oddities, and raise questions. The least that the figures in table 2.1 do is to demonstrate once and for all that IQs have social relevance; there is a very close correlation over groups between IQ level, social status, and income. Whatever we may say about equality, clearly as a nation (and that is true of all other nations where IQ testing has been carried out) we do value very highly whatever IQ tests measure. Binet clearly hit on something that proved to be both scientifically important and socially relevant.

It is important to realize that Galton and Binet failed to agree on important aspects of intellectual functioning. These points of disagreement have effectively given rise to many arguments over the years, and much research. We know much more than we used to in respect to the points at issue, thanks to that research, and we have found that mostly both were right in what they emphasized, and wrong in what they denied. We can hopefully go on from there, but a brief review of the problem involved will still be useful because many echoes can still be heard from their far-off battles, and many surviving warriors still long for the sound of combat.

The first point concerns the question of *the one or the many*. Is there only one intelligence, as Galton thought, or are there many intelligences? Binet thought of intelligence in much more comprehensive ways: "We must make known the meaning we give to this vague and very comprehensive word 'intelligence.' Almost all the phenomena that occupy psychology are phenomena of intelligence." Thus he included under the term "intelligence" a variety of faculties, like suggestibility, volition, attention, and emotion. He was convinced that intelligence is embodied in the total personality, and in fact regarded "intelligence" merely as the average of a large number of faculties, such as memory, verbal abilities, numerical ability, etc., that were relatively independent, and should be measured separately. Hence he opposed the notion of an IQ, and it is in a sense paradoxical that he should be regarded as the father of intelligence testing when he actively opposed the notion that intelligence was a meaningful scientific concept, and tended to regard it more or less as a statistical artefact. Unfortunately, Binet died before he could put his ideas into some coherent order; much of what he said is incompatible with what he did.

Galton and Binet were arguing along philosophical lines, but soon their successors joined combat on a more factual battlefield. Galton's paladin was Charles Spearman, professor of psychology at University College, London (and incidentally one of my teachers!); Binet's paladin was Leo Thurstone, professor of psychology at Chicago (and incidentally one of my friends!). Both came to psychology from the "hard" sciences. Spearman had been an engineer in the British army; Thurstone had worked in Edison's laboratory. Both were statistically sophisticated and used their knowledge to turn the verbal argument into a mathematical and empirical one. Both started with a concept originated by Galton, namely that of *correlation*. This expresses the degree of similarity between two tests or measures, of whatever kind, and ranged from 1.00 for perfect agreement to 0.00 for no agreement at all. Take the various teams in the premier division of the English football league and try to predict the order in which they will emerge at the end of the season. You will hardly be completely successful, but neither will you fail completely. Most people who know something about soccer will rank them in an order that correlated around between 0.60 and 0.70 with the true, final order. (The same is true of American football, or of cricket and baseball). The correlation between height and weight in a group of people will be around the same level. Correlate an IQ test with another and you will get correlations around 0.80. Correlate an IQ test and a measure of personality, and the correlation will be around zero—they are simply different concepts.

What did Spearman and Thurstone do with this statistical formula? Spearman argued that if you administered a whole series of tests to a group of children, and calculated the correlations between the tests, the table of intercorrelations (called a matrix) should form a certain *pattern*, identified by mathematicians as being of rank one. Thurstone argued along similar lines that the matrix would be much more complex, and hence of a higher rank, corresponding to being generated by a fair number of separate and independent factors, like verbal ability, numerical ability, memory, spatial ability, and so forth. Both performed the experiment, and both found their theories supported. How was that possible?

Spearman argued that all the tests used should be *very different* from each other. If you included two vocabulary tests, then they would correlate together so highly as to destroy the pattern. Thurstone argued that one should include several different tests of the same faculties— verbal, or numerical, or memory. Else how could you discover these factors? When large matrices of correlations were finally published, it became obvious that both were right. There was a very strong general intelligence factor, embracing all the tests involved, but in addition there were a number of special factors as demanded by Thurstone—verbal, numerical, spatial, and so forth. Intelligence seems to be made up like a hierarchy—at the bottom many thousands of test items. These correlate to form separate groups or factors, measuring different faculties. And finally these factors all correlate together to produce the all-embracing general intelligence factor called "g" by Spearman. This is the widely accepted compromise between Galton and Binet, Spearman and Thurstone. I talked to both at the height of the controversy, and found that while they very much respected each other, each still hankered after his own model. But the statistics dictated the compromise, and you can't argue with statistics!

The other two major arguments between Galton and Binet will form the substance of the next two sections. The first relates to the question of *nature and nurture*—Galton arguing for the importance of nature, Binet as an educationalist being more concerned with nurture. The second relates to the best way of measuring intelligence—Binet's IQ tests, or Galton's notion of biological measures. Again we shall see that both were right in what they asserted, and wrong in what they denied. As often in science, great scientists are not usually wrong in what they say, but they may be one-sided. Science always provides the necessary counter-balance in the shape of opposing theories, attempts at experimental proof, and finally synthesis of opposing claims. Light is neither corpuscular, as Newton thought, nor a simple wave, as Huygens asserted; it turned out to be both, however implausible that once appeared. Let us see what research made of the opposite views of Galton and Binet.

Before doing so, however, it may be useful to discuss some of the disadvantages of IQ testing. Ideally, a scale of measurement should have a true zero-point and identical intervals. Length or weight measures have these properties—you can have zero length and weight, and one inch or gram is like any other. Heat measure now has a true zero (absolute zero) at $-273.16°C$, and we have equal interval scales. Scales of hardness lack these advantages, and so does IQ. There is no absolute zero, and a 10-point difference may carry different meanings at different points of the scale. This limits the kinds of mathematical manipulations that can be performed; an IQ of 140 is not twice an IQ of 70 just as a temperature of $100°C$ is not twice as hot as one of $50°C$! Experts of course are well aware of what can and what cannot be done with scales of this limited (ordinal) kind, and are not likely to transgress the inexorable rules of mathematics!

Like length, time, and mass, IQ is dependent on when and where it is being measured. As Einstein showed, a body moving near the speed of light changes its length relative to a stationary observer, and time flows less speedily, while mass increases. IQ is defined by giving the *average* person a score of 100, but as a performance scale the average person in 1950 may not give the same score as the average person in 1990. James Flynn has shown that the average person now, in the leading capitalist countries, does rather better than the average person twenty or more years ago. This means that on a test standardized twenty years ago, the average person would now have a score of 106 IQ, rather than 100 IQ, suggesting the need for restandardization of the test. The average gain is about 3 IQ points per decade, (depending on the country, and the type of test used), though the meaning of such an increase is not altogether clear. Certainly there has been no corresponding gain in school achievement, suggesting that it is not intelligence as such that is increasing, but merely a not perfectly accurate measure of it.

What might be the reason? We do not know but a number of hypotheses have been put forward. One is *test sophistication*—people are now much more familiar with IQ-type tests, and practice is known to have a positive effect. *Cultural differences* are another possibility; daily life and occupational experience both seem more "complex." There is greater communication; television is exposing us to more information; children stay in school longer. Finally, there have been improvements in *nutrition*; large nutrition-based increases in height have occurred during the same period as the IQ increases. I shall later on discuss the relevance of nutrition to IQ differentiation.

Possibly, indeed probably, all of these explanations play a part. Let me single out test sophistication, because it is well documented and presents practical problems for school selection and other practical applications of IQ testing. If we take the Wechsler test, an individually administered test having eleven subtests, and widely regarded as the gold standard of IQ testing, we find that giving a person the test a second time, his or her IQ score will on the average increase by 9 points—partly due to remembering what was done the first time, partly due to knowing better just how to do IQ tests. This test sophistication increases still more on doing the test a third time; indeed, it also assists in doing other tests of IQ, but only up to three repetitions. After that test sophistication helps very little.

Clearly this fact holds important lessons for practical applications, as for instance in school or university selection procedures. What is being recommended is that all the children or adults in question should be given three trial tests before the crucial one; after that, very special tuition or practice has little effect on the outcome. All have had sufficient practice to be able to put their best foot forward. IQ tests are not perfect, but knowing their weaknesses and disadvantages makes it possible to take counter measures, and neutralize these disadvantages.

In the measurement of IQ we encounter certain problems that often perplex the layman, and may give rise to undeserved criticism. We may use speed or power tests, for instance, or some combination of both. In the former the problems are rather easy, and given enough time most subjects could probably solve most if not all correctly. However, there is a tough time limit, set so that nobody can solve all problems in the time given, and the score is the number correctly solved.

In power tests, the problems increase in difficulty, and many are so difficult that only a few subjects can solve them. It used to be thought that these two types of tests measured different aspects of intelligence, but they were found to correlate so highly together that this notion was abandoned, and many tests combine the features of both, being limited in time, and increasing in difficulty. Critics often look at test items and say: "These are ridiculously easy; they can't measure intelligence!" They found that subjects have very little time to find the solution, and the more intelligent find the solution more quickly.

We also have the difference between what are called "culture fair" tests, and tests requiring knowledge. Test 1.2 is culture fair; no specialized knowledge is required. A test of vocabulary knowledge would not be culture fair, because it demands specialized knowledge that may be differentially acquired by members of different ethnic groups, or members of different socioeconomic groups. As already mentioned, the former tests measure fluid intelligence (ingenium), the latter crystallized ability (intelligentia) and superficially these two concepts seem very different. In reality g_f and g_c correlate quite highly together in most countries that have a uniform education system, for the simple reason that g_f measures *ability to learn,* while g^c measures *amount learned*; obviously the amount learned depends crucially on one's ability to learn. This is particularly true of such bits of knowledge as are represented by a person's *vocabulary,* which is picked up not only in school, but in daily conversation, in reading newspapers, in listening to radio and watching television, and a thousand different ways. Hence for many practical purposes tests of g_c may be acceptable as measures of intelligence, but they obviously present problems that are not shared by tests of g_f which are usually preferable if an unbiased estimate of intelligence is required.

If tests using information are utilized, it is necessary to specify the population on which they are to be used, for example, town or country children, children of a specific ethnic group, and so on. The necessary qualification is similarity of educational experience. But we cannot rely on expectations of what might differentiate given populations. It used to be thought that black children would be handicapped in g_c tests like vocabulary, but in actual fact they do better in such tests than on g_f tests. Chinese and Japanese children, on the other hand, do better on g_f tests than on g_c tests. Selection of tests to be used must always depend on the *purpose* of the test, and experimental knowledge of the relevant variables. *A priori* criticisms, which are not based on detailed knowledge, are of little use, and only confuse the picture.

The same is true of criticisms often heard of individual items in the test. Thus the word "cow" in a vocabulary test for young children is sometimes objected to because inner-city children would be less familiar with cows than country children. There are two answers. Test constructers usually balance items, for example, by including the word "bun" with which inner-city children would be more familiar than country children. Even more important, they would do a *statistical analysis* of any observed differences between country and inner-city children, or between white and coloured children, or whatever, to discover the existence of such extraneous factors, and remove the offending items.

Statistical analysis of the results is very important in deciding on questions relating to the *validity* of intelligence tests, that is, the question of whether such tests really measure "intelligence." There are two ways of coming to a decision. I have already mentioned the first; test results must bear a reasonable relation to social criteria implied in the notion of "intelligence." High IQ children and adults must do better at school, at university, in their jobs; they must learn complex material more quickly, solve problems more quickly, have more good and successful ideas. They must rise in the social scale, while low IQ children and adults must fall in the social scale. They must earn more than low IQ men and women. These predictions all have been shown to be true in every case. Personality, health, alcoholism, luck, and many other factors confuse the picture to some extent, but not sufficiently to obscure the major trends.

I have no wish to quote thousands of articles that render these generalizations safe; *The Bell Curve* has amassed and discussed much of this material. I will just quote one study which looked at the household income of 4,376 middle-aged American men. The ordinate shows income, the abscissa IQ, from the highest percentile to the lowest. It will be seen that there is a perfect linear relation; with every increase in IQ there is a corresponding increase in earnings!

One has to be vigilant, of course, in looking at the evidence. Some critics have looked at the average earnings of thirty-year-old men, and found no difference between bright and dull. This is true, but one must remember that professional men (and women) have a long and ill-paid apprenticeship; their true earning only comes into effect after their thirtieth birthday. Working-class jobs, on the other hand, pay maximum earnings much earlier; proper comparisons should be made at age fifty or so.

This, then, is the first criterion; it is an *external* one. The other is *internal*, dependent on the lawful behaviour of test results. I have already mentioned the major items of internal evidence, namely the fact that all cognitive tasks however simple or however complex, correlate positively together, generating a "positive manifold." In other words, something like general intelligence is all-pervasive. It follows from this that our choice of tests is not arbitrary, as is often asserted. We would be well advised to pick tests that correlate most highly with all the other tests, and shun those that correlate poorly. And when we sort out tests in this fashion, we find that those correlating most highly in the rest are tests that employ abstract thinking, cognitive problem solving, and speedy learning of abstract material! Thus our notion of what intelligence is, is based on sound empirical evidence. It is this agreement between external and internal evidence that makes the conclusion reasonable that our tests measure intelligence, and that intelligence can be rationally defined and measured.

The objection may be discussed here, namely that the relations I have noted between worldly success and IQ is due to the fact that *both* are in turn dependent on socioeconomic status of one's family. This is not so, the correlation of IQ and success is usually higher than that between socioeconomic status and success. Even within the same family, the brighter children rise, the duller ones fall. There is some effect of socio-economic status, but it certainly fails to account for the observations relating IQ to success.

3

Nature and Nurture: The Great Partnership

It should be clear even to the meanest intelligence that a debate over nature or nurture must be quite pointless; to produce anything, nature and nurture must co-operate. Without the genes to produce our brain, our bones, our muscles, we are nothing. And without an environment to nourish us, and allow us to grow, we are nothing. Yet philosophers, psychologists, sociologists, anthropologists, and many others have fought Tweedledum and Tweedledee battles over this lost cause for many years. It is of course not a question of either-or, but of how much of each. Contrast the considered statements of Galton and of J.B. Watson, the father of behaviourism. According to Galton, "There is no escape from the conclusion that nature prevails enormously over nurture when the differences of nurture do not exceed what is commonly to be found among persons of the same rank in the same country." Watson, on the other hand, maintained that "the behaviourists believe that there is nothing within to develop. If you start with the right number of fingers and toes, eyes, and a few elementary movements that are present at birth, you do not need anything else in the way of raw materials to make a man, be that man a genius, a cultured gentleman, a rowdy or a thug," and to make sure we understood him correctly, he said, in what is probably the most widely quoted sentence in all psychology: "Give me a dozen healthy infants, well-formed, and my own specified world to bring them up in and I'll guarantee to take anyone at random and train him to become any type of specialist I might select—doctor, lawyer, artist, merchant-chief, and, yes, even beggar-man and thief, regardless of his talents, penchants, tendencies, abilities, vocations, and race of his ancestors."

Do we here have two equally absurd extremes, asserting immoderate and egregious nonsense? Not quite. Like the ski resort full of girls hunting for husbands and husbands hunting for girls, the situation is not as symmetrical as it might seem. No psychologist, geneticist, or biologist has ever asserted that nature was all, and nurture played no part, even Galton's somewhat extreme statement merely asserts that nature is more important than nurture. Watson, and behaviourists generally, ruled out genetic influences *completely*; they asserted in all seriousness that nurture is all, and that by creating the right environment we can produce any result we want as far as human behaviour and intelligence are concerned. (Not all behaviourists were quite as benighted, and even Watson occasionally grudgingly admitted some small role to heredity).

Galton's belief was based on observed similarities in intellectual achievement between different members of a family; his particular interest being members of the most eminent families. But of course that horse won't run; such similarities could just as well arise from environmental factors. Eminent parents give their children a good environment, send their children to the best schools, enable them to go to university—all that may be enough to ensure the future eminence of the children. Oddly enough, it is the opposite finding that argues most strongly for the inheritance of outstanding ability. Genes from father and mother are randomly allotted to the offspring; this segregation of genes is a lottery in which an occasional winning ticket can be had even by the offspring of intellectually very mediocre parents. Indeed, given that such mediocre parents are the great majority, we might expect that most geniuses would come from parents not themselves eminent. This is indeed so; Newton's parents were peasants, as were the parents of Gauss; if you look at the families of the two dozen most famous mathematicians over the centuries, you will only find very ordinary people, only one or two eminent, and none a genius.

Or take Michael Faraday, perhaps the most outstanding physicist of the nineteenth century; his father was a blacksmith who could hardly support his family—Michael was allotted one loaf of bread which had to last him a week. His elementary education was almost nil, and he sought work as an errand boy. He never went to university, but was apprenticed to a bookbinder. Hardly the environment Watson would have prescribed for one of the most famous scientists who ever lived.

For Watson, as for Marx, science was not to understand things, but to change them. It did not occur to Watson (or to Marx) that understanding must precede any successful efforts at change. The hell of Stalinist Russia is a testimony to the evil that uninformed change mania may do. Behaviourism of the kind preached by Watson and Skinner has fortunately been less able to do harm, but by encouraging neglect of biological studies of brain mechanisms, and a one-sided emphasis on hypothetical environmental determinants it succeeded in setting back scientific study of intelligence some fifty years.

Geneticists never made the same mistake of plugging just one of the two interacting forces that shape our destiny. The reason is a very simple one. The fundamental formula of behavioural genetics is: $V_P = V_G + V_E$, meaning that the total phenotypic (observed) variety of behaviour is a function of genetic *and* environmental factors. That means that we cannot study the one without the other, and hence behavioural geneticists have always been honour bound to look at both heredity and environment. Most psychologists failed to heed this imperative, and published papers in countless numbers (and still do!) that equated correlation with causation. There is a very high correlation over the first fifty years of this century between the export of iron ingots from Pittsburgh, and the number of registered prostitutes in Yokohama, but the one did not cause the other! So if you find a quite moderate correlation between the tendency of parents to hit their children, and the tendency of the children to go to court for doing grievous bodily harm, you cannot argue that the hitting *caused* the offence of doing grievous bodily harm.

It is possible (and indeed likely) that the genes causing the parents to hit the children were inherited by the children and caused them to commit grievous bodily harm. On the data given, you simply cannot decide between the alternatives; quite possibly both sets of causes are involved. Or perhaps unruly and obstreperous children create such havoc that their parents see no alternative to hitting them. To interpret correlations in causal terms requires special independent evidence that can only be obtained by taking *both* sets of factors into account, and that can only be done by following the lines of modern behavioural genetics.

Behaviouristic environmentalism was one of the forces that shaped the antigenetic movement that was so predominant in the United States until quite recently. The social egalitarianism movement, recently sanctified as "politically correct," forcefully pushed in the same direction, along the lines of a (misunderstood) declaration that "all men are created equal!" This equality, as in the quotation from Lenin given earlier, refers to equality before the law, social equality, not equal endowment; yet it has fed numerous hopes and aspirations firmly denied by nature. It is nature, not psychologists and geneticists, that has created the laws under which we function, yet many people blame psychologists and geneticists for nature being what it is. "Illogical," as Mr. Spock would have said (the one with the pointed ears, not the absurd psychoanalyst who advised parents to do whatever their babies wanted them to do—only to repent after the damage has been done!)

In spite of the pressures to deny the importance of genetic factors in producing differences in intelligence, there was enough evidence of a strictly scientific kind available in 1941 to enable Professor R.S. Woodworth, doyen of American psychologists, to write a monograph at the request of the American Psychological Association in which he surveyed the available evidence and concluded that differences in IQ were due 70 percent to genetic causes, 20 percent to familial (between-families, or "shared" environment factors), and 10 percent to within-families or apparently accidental causes that might differently affect children in the same family. Some forty years later I carried out a similar survey, together with David Fulker, a professional geneticist, dealing with the much larger amount of evidence available then; we came to the same conclusion. We omitted completely the work of Sir Cyril Burt because he had been accused of fraudulence. Now, another twenty-five years later, much more, and much better work is available, but it does not essentially alter the picture, although it does enable us to bring the picture to a sharper focus. Thus *professionally* the facts have always been known, even though for political and social reasons they have often been denied, usually by people not expert in these fields.

Let us consider some of the different lines of research that have established these facts.

1. First, and most important, are investigations that look at identical or monozygotic twins (MZ), that is, twins originating from a fertilized ovum that splits in two parts, both of which grow into separate individuals, having identical genes. Occasionally the twins are separated at birth, or a little later, and grow up in different environments. When that happens, genetic factors and environmental factors are artificially separated, and we can ask how similar the grown-up twins are to each other. If environment is all-important, the correlation should be zero; if heredity is all-important, it should be around 0.90 (not quite 1.00 because the measuring instrument is not perfectly reliable). There are five major studies of this kind. These studies gave heritabilities from .68 to .78; they involved adults from Europe and the U.S. This may serve as a reasonable estimate of heritability, but certain criticisms have been made of these data. The major ones are that some twins were separated later in life than others, and that some twins were brought up in fairly similar environments. Both have been looked into, but both have been found to exert very little influence in the final estimate. We may say

with some confidence that a figure of around 70 percent for IQ heritability is not unreasonable. Actually it is a *minimum* figure. The actual values are somewhat higher, as we have added the unreliability of the measuring instrument to the environmental factors. If we make the necessary statistical correction we would have an estimate of heritability nearer 0.80, that is, 80 percent. Perhaps Galton was not so far off after all!

2. Our next method is to compare MZ twins with dizygotic or fraternal twins (DZ). These are the product of two ova simultaneously fertilized by two spermatozoa, and thus genetically no more alike than siblings, that is, 50 percent on the average. If genetic factors are important, then MZ twins should be more alike than DZ twins, if each pair is brought up together. The correlations found in some thirty-four studies were 0.86 for MZ twins, and 0.60 for DZ twins. Note that the reliability of the test used was 0.87; in other words the MZ twins were as like each other in IQ as it is possible to be given the errors of measurement of the test used. When we take into account assortative mating (like marrying like), which is quite considerable, the estimate of heritability would be even higher. Newer studies, published after these summaries were made available, gave even bigger differences between MZ and DZ twins. Altogether the data are not far off an estimate of 0.70.

A criticism sometimes heard is that parents may treat MZ twins in a more similar manner than DZ twins. This is true, but the behaviours involved, such as dressing the twins alike, are trivial and have been found quite uncorrelated with IQ. This is not, therefore, a serious criticism.

One important point is seldom discussed, namely the accuracy of twin diagnosis. How do we *know* which pair of twins is monozygotic, which dizygotic? DZ twins vary around the 50 percent identical heritability mark, depending on random segregation of genes; some pairs may be very near to being identical, others very dissimilar. An almost infallible procedure, called simple sequence repeat length polymorphism (SSLP), consists of highly informative markers, typed using the polymerase chain reaction. While a noninvasive method of DNA extraction is used, the method is expensive, time consuming, and necessitates personal contact. Dermatoglyphic analysis; also needing personal contact, uses fingerprints. Finally, questionnaires asking questions about observable similarities of height, features, etc. are easy to use, cheap, and do not require personal contact. Dermatoglyphic analysis is only 87 percent correct; this is clearly not good enough. Lengthy questionnaires are 97 percent accurate; short four-question ones are only 92 percent accurate. While these estimates are only approximate, they do indicate that the most widely used method, namely short questionnaires, is not anywhere near perfect, and this obviously must have repercussions on data collected and analysed using this method. There is a very important general law in statistics that says that if data contain valid information, random errors reduce the apparent validity. In other words, true differences are smudged and appear less marked than they really are. In genotype analysis a possible error of 2x8 percent, that is, 16 percent, is quite large, and would reduce the heritability estimate. (The actually observed error of 8 percent must be doubled because the error *range* is from 50 percent accuracy (chance) to 100 percent accuracy! The error is not quite random, but sufficiently so to reduce estimates of heritability to an unknown extent. Thus the figures quoted are minimal estimates, the true values are likely to be higher. Hopefully, future studies will use the SSLP measures. This could be done easily and cheaply by only doing the SSLP analysis on cases most doubtful on the questionnaire basis.

   3. A complimentary type of study to the separated MZ twins is the investigation of adopted children. If the adoption takes place shortly after, even immediately after birth, then the child's heredity is contributed by his *biological* parents, his environment by his *adoptive* parents. Taking a large group of adopted children, we can then correlate their IQs with the IQs of their biological and their adoptive parents. Which will be higher? All correlations are quite small when the children are very young, because accurate measurement of IQ is not yet possible, but for older children the correlations are considerably higher for biological than for adoptive parents. And, a rather unexpected finding, correlations of a child's IQ with his adoptive parents *decrease* over time, while those with his biological parents *increase* over time. In other words, the longer he lives in the environment provided by his adoptive parents, the more like his biological parents he becomes! This is a finding that seems to go counter to all expectation; the longer a child is exposed to a given environment, the greater should be the influence of that environment. Readers may like to think about the solution of this riddle. I shall give my preferred interpretation later on.

   Another way of studying the effects of adoption is to compare biologically unrelated siblings growing up in the same family, for example, two adopted children, or an adopted child and one belonging biologically to that family. The outcome is quite clear; such children show little or no similarity in IQ, in spite of the common environment. The number and complexity of adoption studies makes any thorough review impossible, but the major results are as outlined. A possible criticism might be that adoption may not be random, with what appear the brightest babies going to the families with high socioeconomic status. But it is difficult to estimate the IQ of a newborn child, and if there is any such selective placement it would work in the direction of increasing the similarity between children and adoptive parents! However that may be, the correlation between unrelated children reared together in adoptive families is approximately zero for adolescents.

4. The genetic relatedness of family members should be reflected in the degree of similarity shown by their IQs. Thus, parent offspring correlations should be similar to those between siblings, higher than those of half-siblings, lower for cousins, and so forth. Over 100,000 pairs of relatives have been studied, and over 500 familial IQ correlations reported in the literature. The general outcome has been an astonishingly faithful agreement between the two sets of data; the closer the genetic similarity of family groups, the higher the correlation between their IQs. Thus for parent-offspring the correlation is around 0.42; for cousins it is 0.15. This is an easy but powerful method of analysis, with an obvious theoretical rationale; it clearly supports the other methods described already in suggesting a strong genetic influence on IQ differences.

5. We can manipulate the environment for certain groups of children so as to *minimise* environmental differences. If we made the environment for all the children in a group as identical as possible, then we would expect the S.D. of the distribution of IQs to shrink—provided environmental forces were important. If the environment was really equal for all the children—same teachers, same books, same food, same entertainment, same medical attention, same games, same everything, then the differences between the brightest and the dullest should be much reduced, or even eliminated. Two types of experiments have been done along these lines.

One used an orphanage where all the children were treated as alike as is humanly possible. Yet when their IQs were measured the S.D. for this group was pretty much the same as in the outside world—reduction to vanishing point of all the environmental differences that are supposed to reduce intellectual variability had no discernible effect on the children; there were still bright and dull, as well as average. Similarly, an experiment was done in Warsaw where the government, in its infinite Stalinesque wisdom, housed a large group of people in identical houses, paid them identical wages, sent the children to identical schools, provided identical medical treatment, and quite generally eliminated as far as possible all differences in the environment, physical and mental. Yet the children when tested proved just as diverse as children elsewhere—IQs ranged all the way from very high to very low, with the majority in the middle. Clearly manipulation of the environment to eliminate differences in IQ is no easy matter!

6. There is a well-known effect called *inbreeding depression*, which manifests itself through the general physical inferiority of children whose parents have mated incestuously—father/daughter, brother/sister, or at a more remote distance first or second cousins. Such children are likely to be sickly, suffer all sorts of medical troubles, and also show neurotic and other psychiatric disorders. The reason, briefly, is that all individuals carry in their chromosomes a number of *depressive* genes, that is, genes which depress IQ, health, etc., these genes are almost always recessive, so that they have no effect on their phenotype unless by rare chance they mate up with another such gene at the same locus on a homologous chromosome. That, of course, is much more likely when the parents are related. Since such genes are depressive, they will tend to degrade the phenotypic expression of the characteristic in question, whether physical or mental. Hence IQ would show inbreeding depression if it were inherited along similar lines of inheritance as the other characters studied.

There have now been a number of studies, usually involving cousin marriages (which are permitted in some cultures, e.g., Arabic). The expected effect has indeed been found; in each study the IQs of the children from cousin marriages were several points lower than expected from the known parents' IQs. Results of father/daughter, or brother/sister pairings are usually quite catastrophic, with the child showing a very much lower IQ than expected. Here again biological laws are clearly observed in the transmission of IQ.

7. The opposite of inbreeding depression is hybrid vigour, the effect of interbreeding between members of two unrelated groups, or different races. This is called *heterosis*, and produces superior offspring in that the matching of recessive genes is less likely in such different gene pools. It is well-documented in relation to physical characteristics; in relation to IQ there are few studies, but these do support the view that heterosis can be observed with respect to IQ. Matings between Chinese and Caucasian, for instance, produce children who on the average are several points of IQ higher than expected. This deduction from the genetic theory, too, is thus confirmed.

8. I have left one final proof to the last because it leads into a discussion of the *meaning* of genetic determination, and a demonstration that

FIGURE 3.1
Erroneous Conception of the Way IQ Inheritance Works

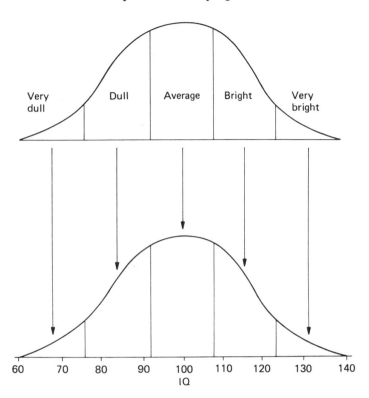

the social consequences of such (partial) genetic determination are not at all what most people expect. When I give a lecture and tell people that IQ is 80 percent inherited, they nearly always have in mind a picture like that shown in figure 3.1. In this the very dull parents (at the top) have very dull children (at the bottom), very bright parents have very bright children, and so on. We are apparently dealing with a caste society in which our children are forever destined to continue in the class of their parents. This is not a pretty or acceptable picture for most people, and it is responsible for much opposition to the genetic model.

It also happens to be completely false. What the laws of heredity predict, and what we actually find, is that IQ obeys the law of *regression to the mean*—a law, incidentally, discovered by Galton. What this law says, essentially, is that the children of very bright parents will on the average be bright, but less so than their parents; they will regress to the mean. Similarly, the children of very dull parents will be dull, on the average, but not as dull as their parents. They, too, will regress to

FIGURE 3.2
Correct Conception of the Way IQ Inheritance Works

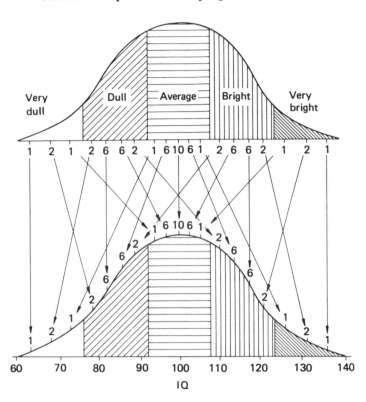

the mean. Figure 3.2 illustrates what is happening; it will be clear that this is very different from the depressing picture given by figure 3.1. There is constant change, up and down the IQ ladder, from one genera- tion to the next. The lottery of the segregation of genes at conception pushes one up, the other down. There is no fairness about it all; nature does not play cricket!

This turmoil should have important social effects; in particular one would expect a great deal of *social mobility* in countries not imposing an artificial caste system, as in India. And this is precisely what we find. Table 3.1 shows social mobility data for 36,000 white American sons aged 25–46; their fathers' status is shown on the left. There is some agreement, but not much between fathers and sons. A father in the higher manual category is as likely to have a son in the higher white-collar category as in the higher, or lower manual category. Even the sons of lower manual workers have a good representation in the

TABLE 3.1
Social Mobility of 36,000 White Americans, Aged 25–46

Father's status	Son's status					
	1	2	3	4	5	None
Higher White Collar (1)	*54*	15	12	12	1	6
Lower White Collar (2)	45	*18*	14	15	2	6
Higher Manual (3)	28	12	*28*	24	1	7
Lower Manual (4)	21	12	23	*36*	2	7
Farm Worker (5)	17	7	20	29	*20*	8

higher white-collar category. Regression is clearly a most important *biological* law determining *social* behaviour, and not in the way most people would think.

There are many studies of this important effect, and they obey a general formula; the amount of regression is a function of the degree of heritability of the trait. If heritability is 100 percent, there is no regression! We can determine the heritability of intelligence by looking at the amount of regression, and we find that 70 percent heritability (uncorrected) fits perfectly.

The belief in some sort of caste system, being implied by the fact of genetic determination of IQ is only one of a series of mistaken assumptions that bedevil any genuine understanding of the true meaning and implications of "heritability." One of the worst errors is to regard heritability as a fixed, immutable constant. It is not. What it is is a *population statistic*. In other words, it characterizes the position of *a given group*, at a given time—say, British people around 1990. The figure for heritability might have been quite different in England at the time of Good Queen Bess. The reason for this, of course, lies in the fact that environment plays a part in determining IQ, and that environments differ. In Great Britain education is universal, and sufficiently similar for rich and poor to provide the minimum essentials for everyone to understand the rules of IQ testing, and know the alphabet and the numbers needed to solve the IQ problems constructed in these terms. In India now, and in Good Queen Bess's day, that was not so, and many children had no teaching at all, and were essentially illiterate and innumerate. Progressive educational methods are doing their best to return us to those days, with illiteracy and innumeracy being characteristic of more and more school-leavers, both here and in the United States, and if that trend continues no doubt we will see a lower heritability.

A recent experiment will illustrate what I mean. Educational achievement, being largely mediated by IQ, of course, also shows a healthy degree of heritability. In Norway the educational system has changed over the past forty years from a privileged, unequal system to a very egalitarian one. It was predicted that comparing the scholastic achievements of twins at the beginning and at the end of that period, heritability would be much higher at the end than at the beginning, and so it turned out. *Changing the degree of inequality in the educational system in the direction of greater equality led to a greater influence of heredity on achievement.* It follows that our estimate of 80 percent heredity, 20 percent environment only applies to certain national groups studied in the past, like English, North American, Middle European, and Scandinavian populations, Russians, Australians, and Canadians; it may not apply to Indians, Malays, or African countries.

One important consequence of the fact that heritability is a population statistic is of course that *it does not apply to individuals*. It is meaningless to say that your IQ is determined to the extent of 80 percent by heredity, just as we cannot say that because the average height of English males is 5 ft. 10 ins., therefore your height will be 5 ft. 10 ins. Heritability is a concept that only applies to groups, not to individuals. Once we succeed in identifying individual genes making for high IQ, we may go one step further and say something specific about individuals but, although a beginning has been made with the advent of *molecular genetics*, it will be a long time yet before anything of the kind will be possible.

An interesting picture of what is meant by an adult heritability of 80 percent is given in figure 3.3. In both parts of the figure, the cross-hatched curve represents the actually found distribution of IQ, as shown in figure 2.1. The superimposed curve at the top illustrates the distribution we would find if everyone had identical heredity for intelligence, and all differences in IQ were entirely due to environmental causes. In the bottom illustration the superimposed curve shows what the distribution of IQ would be like if all contributions by environmental factors were eliminated, and only genetic factors active. It will be clear that while neither condition would reproduce the actual distribution, the bottom figure is much closer to reality than the top one.

Some people feel that experiments and statistics like those discussed here are all very well, but they would prefer something more tangible.

FIGURE 3.3

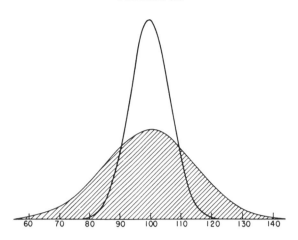

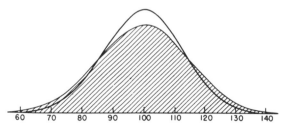

The cross-hatched curve shows the distribution of IQ actually found. The top figure shows by contrast the hypothetical distribution of IQ if it were determined entirely by environmental factors. The bottom figure shows by contrast the hypothetical distribution of IQ if it were determined entirely by genetic factors, given a heritability of 80 percent.

The new molecular genetics bid fair to actually identify some of the genes responsible for the high heritability of intelligence. What we are concerned with are not one or two major genes, but multiple genes of varying effect size, usually referred to as quantitative trait loci (QTL). Using what is known as "allelic association strategy," researchers have already succeeded in identifying two markers for high IQ, and within the next ten years a great deal of progress will undoubtedly be made in the field, and we will gain a much deeper insight into the nuts and bolts of the biological basis of intelligence. We now know how to do it, and have already begun to do it, with positive results. To deny the genetic basis of intelligence is simply no longer a tenable choice.

I have so far spoken of *the* heritability of IQ. But strictly speaking that is not correct because *heritability estimates vary with age*. It is lowest in young children (around 40 percent) and highest in adults (around 80 percent). Why is that so? The answer lies in the equivocal nature of the term "environment." We normally assume (wrongly) that this is objective, fixed, and measurable. We can specify a family's earnings, social position, the provision of books and newspapers, television sets, types of education provided, and even, through questionnaires and observation, the type of discipline used by the parents—strict, loving, or whatever. But there is a problem. Children, as they grow up, increasingly *choose* their environment; this choice itself is driven by genetic factors. And they *interpret* their environment in terms of their genetic contributions. Ask sets of twins about the nature of their upbringing, and they will by no means show complete agreement. MZ twins agree significantly more than DZ twins; in other words, similar parent behaviour is interpreted differentially by the children, agreement being much higher in children with identical heredity.

Let us return to Michael Faraday, who came from a very poor family and had practically no schooling. He chose to apprentice himself to a bookbinder in order to be able to read, and study books on science. Having achieved a remarkable level, he went to public lectures by Sir Humphrey Davy, the famous chemist. He wrote up these lectures in summary form and sent them to Davy, who was impressed and made him his assistant. In other words, Faraday *created* his environment, driven by his genetically determined needs and abilities. The environment is not something objectively given, we create our environment in large part ourselves. If our peer group seems to determine much of what we do, what made us choose this particular group to associate with? We could have chosen a different group, with different interests and aims. Our environment is *structured* by ourselves, on the basis of genetic drives.

This fact, now well-established, may help to explain why heritabilities for IQ are so much higher for older people. Children have little choice as far as their environment is concerned, and hence the influence of the environment is comparatively great. As they get older the variety and availability of choices increases, and if these choices are at least partially determined by genetic factors, the influence of environment is thereby diminished. We *force* all children to learn to read; adults *choose* if and what they want to read. The same reasoning may serve to explain the odd finding that as adopted children grow up, their IQ correlates less and less with that of their adoptive parents. When the child is young, he is living in an environment that is almost wholly determined by his adoptive parents; this leads to some correlation between his IQ and theirs. But as he gets older he becomes more and more free to make his own choices, based on his heredity, and that will lead him away from conditions imposed on him in his extreme youth by his adoptive parents. This seems a reasonable explanation for an otherwise inexplicable result.

It also explains another age-related fact, namely that environmental influences of the family-related kind (shared environments) are strong for young children, but fade as the child grows up and drops to almost zero in later adolescence and maturity. In discussing heritability and the kind of environmental influence that is important, we must always bear in mind the age-group we are talking about; as age increases, heritability *increases* and familial influence *decreases*. General estimates disregarding age differences are meaningless. The conclusion Woodworth came to, in respect to the relative importance of heredity, familial and nonshared environment, quoted at the beginning of this chapter, clearly require replicating, taking age into account. Shared environment as a causal factor is powerful in young children and adults.

Finally, let me briefly discuss two related beliefs that are highly pessimistic but quite erroneous as far as hereditary influences are concerned. The first is that heredity fixes certain behaviours, abilities, or personality traits once and for all. The second is that because of this fixedness there is nothing that can be done to change things, a notion of therapeutic nihilism.

In our discussion it is most useful to start out with the distinction made by geneticists between genotype and phenotype; the former refers to the totality of factors that make up the genetic complement of an individual, while the latter refers to the totality of physically or chemically observable characteristics of an individual that results from the interaction of his genotype with his environment. (Environment is here more widely defined than is perhaps usual, and includes not only intra-uterine and post-natal conditions but also a variety of molecular factors acting within and between the embryonic cells.) Different genotypes may give rise to the same phenotype (in different environments) and different phenotypes may be shown by the same genotypes.

That complexity is well shown by some often-quoted examples. Himalayan rabbits reared under ordinary conditions have a white body with black feet; when reared in a warm cage, they do not show any evidence of black colour, although genetically identical (same geno-type, different environment). Even more interesting and relevant is an-other study which investigated the interaction of heredity and environment in four breeds of dogs. Half of each litter was reared un-der "indulgent" conditions, the other half under "disciplined" condi-tions. (The litters were genetically pure, that is, of practically identical heredity). At eight weeks of age, the puppies were tested in a situation where the person who had reared them conditioned them not to eat, by swatting them over the rump whenever they approached the food dish. The effectiveness of the conditioning was then tested by the trainer leaving the room and observing the behaviour of the puppies. Basenjis, who are natural psychopaths, ate as soon as the trainer had left, regard-less of whether they had been brought up in the disciplined or the in-dulgent manner. Both groups of Shetland sheep dogs, loyal and true to death, refused the food, over the whole period of testing, that is, eight days! Beagles and fox terriers responded differentially, according to the way they had been brought up, indulged animals were more easily conditioned, and refrained longer from eating. Thus conditioning has no effect on one group, regardless of upbringing, and affects two groups differentially, depending on their upbringing. Clearly interactions can be complex and difficult to disentangle, although in humans there is little likelihood of finding such marked differences in different ethnic strains as in these highly inbred litters of dogs.

A final experimental illustration which is directly relevant to our main theme is provided by a study by Cooper and Zuback, who took two strains of maze-bright and maze-dull rats, bred for this characteris-tic over thirteen generations. (In other words, some learned running a maze quickly, others learned it slowly.) Members of each group were reared in either a normal laboratory-rat environment, in an enriched environment (in which slides, tunnels, bells, balls, and other objects were provided, as well as complex visual stimuli), or in an impover-ished environment, (only food boxes and water pan being provided). At sixty-five days of age the rats were tested on a standard maze, and their errors in running this maze counted (which is a reasonable intelli-gence test for rats). Findings were as follows: The enriched environ-ment produced a considerable improvement over the natural habitat performance in the dull, but not the bright rats. Conversely, a restricted environment pushed up the error score of the bright rats, but left the dull ones unaffected. Note this interaction effect, but note also that, in contradistinction to human conditions, the rats were assigned to conditions; they had no chance to select their preferred environment. This is an important difference.

Now let us consider therapeutic nihilism. If something is innate, people are prone to argue, then there is by definition nothing you can do about it; let us rather concentrate on those aspects of the problem which we can affect in some way, that is, the environmental ones. But this notion is mistaken; it assumes that what is true in one particular environment is universally true. As we have seen, that is not so; change the environment in ways relevant to the problems, and you may change the phenotypes in ways previously unexpected and impossible to predict without the requisite knowledge of just what it is that is being inherited. Consider phenylketonuria, a well-known disease which affects about one European child in forty thousand (it is, interestingly, much rarer among Africans). This disorder causes mental defect, and it has been found that about one in every hundred patients in hospitals for severely mentally handicapped children suffers from it. This disorder is known to be inherited and is, in fact, due to a single recessive gene. The great majority of children suffering from it have a level of mental performance which is usually found in children half their age. These children can be distinguished from other mentally handicapped or from normal children by testing their urine, which yields a green-coloured reaction with a solution of ferric chloride due to the presence of derivatives of phenylalanine. Here we have a perfect example of a disorder produced entirely by hereditary causes, where the cause is simple and well understood, and where the presence of the disorder can be determined with accuracy.

Does this discovery imply therapeutic nihilism? The answer is definitely no. Let us go on to demonstrate in what ways the gene actually produces the mental effect. It has been shown that children affected by phenylketonuria are unable to convert phenylalanine into tyrosine; they can only break it down to a limited extent. It is not clear why this should produce mental deficiency, but it seems probable that some of the incomplete breakdown products of phenylalanine are poisonous to the nervous system. Phenylalanine, fortunately, is not an essential part of the diet, provided that tyrosine is present in it. It is possible to maintain these children on a diet which is almost free of phenylalanine, thus eliminating the danger of poisoning to the nervous system. It has been found that when this method of treatment is begun in the first few months of life, there is a very good chance that the child may grow up without the mental handicap he would otherwise have encountered. In other words, by understanding the precise way in which heredity works, and by understanding precisely what it does to the organism, we can arrange a rational method of therapy which will make use of the forces of nature, rather than try to counteract them. Thus we are led to the paradoxical situation where *environmental* manipulation (withdrawal of food containing phenylalanine) becomes effective once the *hereditary* nature of the disorder is recognized, and a precise understanding of its mode of working has been achieved. These children live literally in a different environment, an environment not containing phenylalanine; in such an environment they are not handicapped and are equal to all other children.

Genetic studies can serve to throw light on problems that have usually been attacked by means of statistical analyses, such as the "the one and the many" problems discussed in a previous chapter. We found there that in addition to a general factor of intelligence there are several *special abilities* independent of g. These specific abilities also show genetic determination to varying degrees. Thus verbal and spatial ability are more heritable than, for example, memory and processing of speed, but too little research has been done in this field to be certain of this finding. Research in this area is relatively recent, and much of interest remains to be discovered.

What does seem fairly definitive is the fact that *the same genetic factors largely influence different cognitive abilities*—just what we would expect if the notion of a general factor of intelligence was correct. Multivariate genetic analysis has been responsible for this important piece of information. The method used is simple—instead of correlating one twin's verbal ability with his co-twin's verbal ability, we can correlate one twin's verbal ability with his co-twin's spatial ability. Genetic influence on what is common to the two abilities is indicated when such cross-twin correlations are greater for identical than for fraternal twins. The fact that multivariate analysis shows that there is genetic overlap among cognitive abilities is one of the strongest arguments in favour of g. This can also be expressed in another way: the more strongly a particular test loads on a factor of general cognitive ability, the higher is its heritability.

The same argument can be applied to the relationship between intelligence and scholastic success. I have already pointed out that scholastic success has a strong genetic component. Multivariate genetic analysis shows that genetic effects on scholastic achievement overlap almost completely genetic effects on intelligence—leading to an interesting converse. Given the observed correlation of around 0.50 between intelligence and scholastic success, *discrepancies* between intelligence and school achievement are largely environmental in origin! This is an interesting example of the important fact that environmental influences can be detected and quantified only by genetic experiments.

Genetic analyses also enables us to tell *which* environmental factors are influential in determining a person's measured intelligence. I have already mentioned the difference between *shared environment*, that is, the family influence on twins or siblings growing up in the same family, and nonshared or *specific* environment, that is, environmental influences that affected one twin or sibling only, but not the other (having a good or bad teacher, falling ill or not falling ill, etc.) I have mentioned Woodworth's estimate of 20 percent shared environment, 10 percent specific environment, but recent work has shown that the position is more complex.

These figures may be true for young children, but change over time. In a follow-up study extending over ten years, 181 adoptive siblings were studied. At the average age of eight years, their IQ correlation was 0.26. However, ten years later, their IQ correlation was 0.01, suggesting that shared family environmental effects on IQ decline to zero after adolescence. This result is of course in good agreement with the finding, already mentioned, that as adopted children grow up, their IQs grow more and more to resemble those of their biological parents, and less and less those of their adoptive parents.

Thus for adults, we would have to amend Woodworth's statements to read: 80 percent genetic factors, 20 percent nonshared (specific) environments. Interestingly enough, the same lack of influence for shared (family) environment has been found for personality factors—we have to forget about the old notion of the family shaping the personality of children, as well as the Freudian notion of the importance of the first five years—these are not the influences that determine our personality or our intelligence!

These are just some of the complexities of the nature-nurture co-operative venture. The discussion will have made it clear why no serious scientists will argue for one or the other being singly responsible for human or animal behaviour. Both are always involved, and interact in complex ways. Only long-continued scientific study and experimentation can unravel these complexities; political slogans are unlikely to be helpful!

4

Intelligence, Reaction Time, and Inspection Time

We must now turn to the third difference between Galton and Binet. Binet, as we have seen, tried to measure intelligence (or rather the different facets of intelligence) by means of everyday life problems (like the ball lost in the park), or by verbal and numerical problems that made use of school knowledge (at a rather low level), or that directly examined such faculties as memory and suggestibility. All our modern tests are based on the same principles. But what of Galton's view that simple tests of biological functioning, like reaction time and simple perceptual discrimination tasks, could tap the fundamental biological underpinnings of intelligence? Such views were anathema to a behaviouristic orthodoxy that did not believe in genetic factors determining intelligence and refused to look at physiological intermediaries between DNA, the basic genetic material, and behaviour.

Many psychologists in the between-war years, and the years that followed Hitler's downfall, vulgarized Binet's thinking into arguing that parental teaching and school learning in fact produced all the observed differences in IQ between them. Behaviourists, like B.F. Skinner, explicitly told psychologists that what went on in the brain was to remain a black box, and should not concern psychologists! This absurdity—we don't want to know about the actual working of the brain, thank you very much, we just study behaviour—must stand beside Watson's claim to be able to make any child into anything he fancied, as the most famous statements to render psychology ridiculous in the eyes of serious scientists. Fortunately, we have recovered our minds and brains in recent years, but for many years the Zeitgeist was very much opposed to Galton.

But were there no experiments to support Galton? Is it not a fact that if a theory is true, then experiments will show it to be so? Things don't always work that way, even in the best-regulated scientific families. In 1901, Clark Wissler published a very important experimental paper in which he apparently succeeded in showing that intelligence and reaction time were not correlated at all—if true, a definite disproof of Galton's theory. S. Sharp, even earlier, also published some negative results. These studies were taken very seriously at the time, and effectively closed all minds against Galtonian theories, although they were among the worst experiments ever carried out by psychologists. (They achieved this distinction against some fierce opposition!)

Why were they bad? In the first place they were carried out on highly intelligent university students, thus only tapping a very small range of ability. Two tests might correlate quite highly when applied to a random set of people, with IQs from 70–140, say. But if their IQs ranged from 125–135, there is not much room for any correlation! But Sharp and Wissler didn't use any proper measure of intelligence anyway; they used students' grades, which in such a group are known to correlate very little with IQ. Even so a large population might have produced interesting results; Sharp only used seven subjects! And finally, to get a meaningful score on a reaction time RT test, we need about a hundred repetitions of the signal-reaction sequence in order to cancel out the variability always observed in such tests. Wissler used three to five repetitions! This is known to give a very inaccurate estimate of a person's RT. Take all these factors together, and you get completely meaningless and uninterpretable results. Helen Peak and E.G. Boring actually found in 1926 an almost perfect correlation between RT and IQ, again on a small number of subjects only, and several others found significant correlations also, always showing the brighter subjects giving the shorter RTs, but nobody was willing to listen. "Don't confuse me with facts, my mind is made up!" seemed to be the general outlook.

I became convinced that there was something important to be found in this area as the result of some tests that Desmond Furneaux was doing with me at the time (in the 1950s). I was dissatisfied with the usual habit of correlating tests, in which the number of correct solutions constitutes the score on a given test. It seemed to me, on the basis of much work with such tests, that different persons can obtain the same score without ever solving the same problems! Consider three people, Adam, Brown, and Cyril. On an abbreviated IQ test, here are their performances on a number of test items, increasing in difficulty— C stands for correctly solved, A stands for abandonment, and W stands for wrong answer:

						Score:
Adam	C	C	C	W	W	W	3
Brown	W	A	W	C	C	C	3
Cyril	A	A	C	C	A	C	3

All three have a score of 3, but Adam has 3 items wrong, Cyril has abandoned 3 items. Different children solve different items. Can we really maintain that all are exactly alike as far as performance is concerned? Doesn't Cyril give up rather easily on items he might have tackled successfully? And isn't Adam rather impulsive, getting items wrong he might have got right if only he had persevered and checked his answers?

Thinking back on Galton's theory that perhaps intelligence was an important consequence of *mental speed*, we began to measure the time taken over each problem. Now that is easy when you are dealing with one child at a time, but what happens when you are giving group tests? Desmond solved the problem by suspending a device in front of the class that had three numbers from 0 to 9; these thus made a three-figure number which changed up by one every second. The subjects wrote down the setting of the device *before* and *after* solving each problem, by subtraction it was then possible to work out the duration of the solutions. The problems used were all IQ test favourites, namely letter sequence items, somewhat like this:

a   c   f   j   o   ?

with "o" the obvious answer. The experiment worked very well, we discovered that while *speed* was the major factor involved in getting a good score, there were two other factors: Persistence, that is, not giving up too easily, and error checking, that is, avoiding wrong answers.

Furneaux was dissatisfied with our timing mechanism. As he said, it takes some time to look up, register the setting of the device, look down again, and write down the setting. The time taken might not be the same for everybody, and should be subtracted from a person's total time for a given item, leaving only the actual time spent on the solution of that item. So he got the subjects to simply write down the setting of the device, and, lo and behold, they showed great differences in the length of time required for that simple task! And lo and behold again, when the time taken just noting down settings was correlated with an independent IQ test, *the correlation was just as large as that of the letter sequence test!* In other words, you don't need a genuine intelligence test like the letter sequence task; you can do just as well with measurements of the speed of simple perceptual (reading the setting) and motor (writing down the setting) responses. We never published the results, but I was determined in due course to resurrect the "speed" theory of intelligence. In 1967, I was asked to write an article on the theory of intelligence assessment in which I quoted some recent work done by German-speaking psychologists that had given impressive evidence in favour of a speed-intelligence theory. I sent a copy to my old friend, Art Jensen, who decided to make the issue his major research concern, and has been pursuing this line of work ever since. It is largely due to him that RT studies are now taken seriously, and that we have gained an enormous amount of information on the true relationship between IQ and RT.

Figure 4.1 shows a diagram of the apparatus used to measure RT. Eight green jewelled lights (black squares) are distributed in a half circle, each with a bell-push (white circles) in front. In addition, there is a "home" button in the centre of the console. The subject rests his finger on the home button. When one of the lights goes on, he transfers his finger as quickly as possible from the home button to the button in front of the light that has just come on. We measure two things. One is called the *decision time* (DT), which begins with the coming on of the target light, and ends with the subject removing his finger from the home button. Next we have the *movement time* (MT). which begins when the subject removes his finger from the button, and ends when he depresses the target button. DT + MT = RT. Experimentally, we can measure *choice reaction time*, where any one of several lights can come on in a random sequence, or we can measure *simple reaction time*, where only one and the same light comes on each time. Fifty to a hundred repetitions are needed to get a *reliable* measure, using the average of all the measures. We can also measure the width of distribution of these 50 or 100 measures, indicating how closely their DTs and MTs cluster around the mean; as we shall see, that is an important predictor of IQ. The measure used is of course the S.D. (standard deviation) we have encountered before.

Sometimes more complex stimuli than simple lights flashing on and off are used. Consider the odd-man-out experiment in which three lights come on simultaneously, two close together and one (the odd-man-out) at some distance. Subjects are required to press the button adjacent to the odd-man-out light. Other types of test (probe recognition test) present

FIGURE 4.1

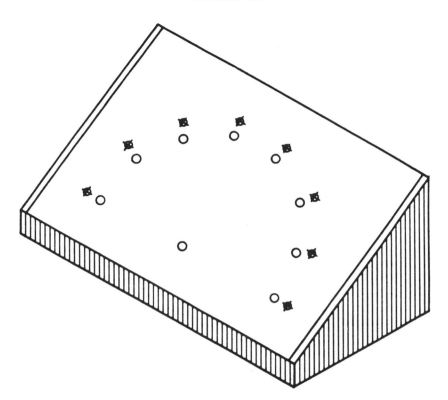

Console used for reaction-time experiment. Push buttons indicated by circles, green jewelled lights by black squares. The "home" button is in the lower centre.

a list of three, four, or five letters or numbers; this is then replaced by a single letter or number which is the stimulus. Subjects have to say whether it was or was not one of those shown originally. Or, conversely, we can show one letter or number, and then a set of three, four, or five, asking for a decision whether this set contains the original letter or number. This test involves short-term memory (STM)

A test involving long-term memory (LTM) is typified in the following test. The subject is shown two percepts, say A and a, or A and B, and has to press either a Yes or a No button to say whether the two percepts are, or are not, identical alphabetically, or, in another version, are both capital letters. Such more complex tests tend to give higher correlations with IQ than simple or choice RT, for reasons to be discussed presently.

All these, and the other tests mentioned in this section, are often called measures of *elementary cognitive tasks* (ECTs), meaning by elementary that they are so simple that even mentally deficient patients, with IQs well below 50, can solve the "problems" presented, and do so without any errors; they just do it very slowly. Usually such tasks take much less than one second, and require a minimum of thought, for most people they are quite automatic. How do these ECTs relate to IQ? On the assumption governing research for most of the past, there should be no correlation at all; there is little knowledge involved, no past learning, no problem solving, and no abstract thinking in the Binet sense. If there were to be a correlation, these ECTs might be testing, as Galton thought, the speed of mental functioning that underlies high IQ performance.

A recent quotation from Steven Ceci will illustrate what the environmentalist theory of IQ, stemming from Binet, really tried to say:

> The processes associated with schooling influence performance on IQ tests through a combination of *direct* instruction (e.g., it is in school that most children learn the answers to many IQ questions such as "In what continent is Egypt?" "Who wrote Hamlet?" and "What is the boiling point of water?") and *indirect* modes or styles of thinking and reasoning (e.g., schools encourage taxonomic/ paradigmatic sorting and responding, rather than thematic/functioning responding, and this happens to be the valued form of responding on IQ tests. (Emphasis in the original)

Such a view is obviously untenable (remember the Isle of Wight experiment, where IQ tested prior to entry to school predicted very accurately success at school), but environmentalists seldom pay much attention to such well-documented facts. The long series of experimentally controlled ECTs may in due course have some lasting effects.

What are the findings? The major one is that both decision time and movement time are significantly correlated (negatively) with IQ—high IQ predicts shorter DTs and MTs. (DTs are usually more informative than MTs.) With *simple* RTs correlations average around –0.10, for *choice* RTs around –0.20 to –0.30. Most of these studies used students, with the inevitable restriction of range of IQ, thus lowering the observed values. Oddly enough, variability of RT was correlated with IQ even higher than RT itself; the brighter the subject, the narrower the band of RT values around the mean. Typical correlations with IQ are around –0.30. When we combine several different types of tests we get correlations around –0.50. The odd-man-out and the probe recognition tests give higher correlations than simple choice RT tests, varying from –0.40 to –0.60, with variability correlating about the same with IQ. Thus the most complex ECTs give rather better results than the most simple—presumably they give speed of mental processing a better chance to manifest itself. But the correlation of *variability of performance* with IQ cannot be explained by relying on theories of speed of mental functioning, and I will attempt an explanation later on.

Just how can we explain in detail why more complex RT tests correlate more highly with IQ than less complex RT tests? Anticipating the theory developed in a later chapter, we may find a more fundamental explanation of RT differences in the idea that people differ in the probability that *errors* will occur in the transmission of information through the cortex, and that the greater the number of errors, the slower will be the reaction to a given stimulus. (Just why this will be so will be discussed later.) Now if this is true, then measurement of RT is essentially an indirect measure of errors occurring during the transmission of information. But such a measure would be expected to be more accurate the larger the sample of neurons and synapses involved. More complex RT tasks involve very much larger samples of interactions between neurons than do simple RT tasks. Simple RT tasks may involve hundreds of neurons, choice RT takes thousands, odd-man-out or probe recognition tasks tens or even hundreds of thousands of neurons. Consequently the chances of getting an accurate measure of the likelihood of errors occurring during a test is much higher for complex than for simple tasks.

If this is true, then why is it that RT tasks only work if times are relatively short—500 milliseconds is about the longest time for an RT test to give reasonable correlations with IQ. The answer is probably that for longer tests it is not a question of reaction time that decides performance level. Individuals begin to use different methods of working, use experience, memory, knowledge to structure their responses, and generally transform the RT nature of the tests into a closer and closer resemblance of an ordinary IQ test.

IQ tests can be divided into timed (often called speed) and untimed (often called *power tests*). In speed tests you give subjects so many fairly easy items to solve that none can do them all in the time given; number correctly solved is a function largely of speed of solution. Power tests rely on containing items so difficult that the less able cannot solve them at all, however long they may try. (Most tests, as I have explained earlier, combine the two methods, using items of different difficulty, and imposing a time limit.) It used to be thought that speed tests measured a rather superficial kind of intellect, power tests a more profound kind, but the two correlate so highly that it is clear that they both measure the same underlying "g". Critics have suggested that RT tests might correlate better with speed than with power tests, but although the suggestion is intuitively appealing, it has not proved correct. RT tests correlate just about the same with speed as with power tests!

RT tests measure the speed of reaction to a very simple stimulus. How about the speed of apprehension, that is, the time taken to correctly recognize a stimulus presented only for a very short time? This is in the realm of the inspection time (IT) technique. What is done is to show the subject a very simple display, usually two parallel lines with one much shorter than the other; he is then required to say whether the longer one was on the right or on the left side, and press a button accordingly. The task is of course so simple that even a mentally defective person can carry it out without error, but the duration of presentation is so short (from 200 milliseconds down to 20 milliseconds) that it becomes progressively more difficult to decide. The experimenter explores the presentation times, and discovers for each person the level (the shortest time of presentation) at which he is 97.5 percent successful. There is no RT involvement; the subject has all the time he requires to think about what he has seen, and respond. What is found is that high IQ goes with low thresholds; in other words, the better you are at recognizing the presentation at very high speeds, the greater your IQ; correlations range around 0.50, perhaps a little higher. Instead of visual presentation, we can present a series of sounds, varying in pitch; here too the ability to recognize which of the two was higher, was highly correlated with IQ.

The measurement of IT is a little more complicated than this brief account indicates. Thus we usually follow the presentation of the stimulus with a presentation of a "mark," that is, set of lines overlapping the long and short lines completed, thus making the appearance of an after-image impossible. Even under those conditions, some 20 percent of subjects report noticing a kind of movement of the shorter line, caused by its replacement by the longer line making up the marks. Use of such may constitute a different *strategy* to that apparently required, but such use does not correlate with IQ. When individuals using it are omitted, the correlation between IQ and IT increases markedly. There are ways of using more complex marks that make use of this strategy impossible, and we may expect correlations with IQ to react and possibly exceed .60.

Another way to improve correlations is probably the use of more complex stimuli, in exactly the way more complex problems in RT experiments have given much higher correlations with IQ. Can we pinpoint the kind of more complex stimuli that would work best? Let us go back to Spearman. He suggested three major laws of reasoning that cover all the uses of abstract thinking. The first was the *Law of Apprehension*, that is, the fact that a person approaches the stimulation he receives from all external and internal sources via the ascending nerves. Simple reaction time and inspection time would seem to measure this elementary aspect of mental functioning, and sensory discrimination would also seem to fall into this field.

Next we have the *Education of Relations*. Given two stimuli, ideas, or impressions, we can immediately discover any relations existing between them—one is larger, simpler, stronger or whatever than the other. And finally, we have the *Education of Correlates*—given two stimuli, joined by a given relation, and a third stimulus, we can produce a fourth stimulus that bears the same relation to the third as the second bears to the first. Examples will make this clearer. The word "high" is directly apprehended. The words: "high" and "low" give rise to the relation of oppositeness. And given "high," and "low," and "big" as the third stimulus, we can use the fundament, "big," and the relation of oppositeness to arrive at the correlate, "small."

If Spearman is right, then tests constructed on these principles, that is, using apprehension, education of relations and education of correlates, should be the *best* measures of g_f; that is, correlate best with all other tests. This has been found to be so; the Matrices test, using material such as the figure in figure 1.2, has been found to be just about the *purest* measure of IQ, and more verbal measures, such as illustrated by the item: High : Low = Big : ? have been equally successful. Thus we can test Spearman's ideas, and they have been found strongly supported by results. The Matrices test was constructed *explicitly* by following Spearman's rules, and has probably been more widely and successfully used than any other group test.

In constructing the odd-man-out RT test, I used these principles explicitly; you have two lights close together, and one some distance apart. Apprehensions furnish you with these data, that is, the fundaments (the three lights) and the relations between them (nearness); you then apply these relations as instructed. We could add the Education of Correlates and again offer three lights as before but require the subject to press the button in front of a fourth light that bore the same spatial relation to the third light as the second light did to the first. I would be surprised if this test did not correlate with IQ even more strongly than the odd-man-out!

Oddly enough, RT tests have seen this development from simple to choice to complex presentation, but IT has stuck with the simple comparison of two lines. It seems very likely that more complex presentations would give higher correlations with IQ. Thus we might use three lines, all differing in length, and respond by pressing one of three buttons to indicate its position of the middle-light line. Or we might have two or more collections of dots, and indicate which had the largest number of dots. It must be the task of future research to raise the IQ-IT correlations well above the .5–.6 level, but it seems certain that it can be done.

It will be obvious that if several different techniques all correlate to some extent with IQ, then an estimate of ECT based on the sum of several such tests would correlate even better with IQ. This is what has been shown in several experiments; correlations in excess of 0.70 have been found. This is around the lower level of correlations found between one IQ test and another. Clearly Galton was right, we can approach a measure of intelligence by using ECTs in various combinations, and produce results not very much different from those produced by ordinary IQ tests. This has certainly proved astonishing to adherents of the environmentalist-learning school, but the results are too decisive to argue against. Furthermore, some ECT tests have been tried out on MZ and DZ twins, and have been found to have substantial heritabilities. It is difficult not to conclude that these data support some such notion of intelligence as being based on *speed of cortical processing of information.*

Spearman, in his theoretical and experimental working out of Galton's theories, used the notion of discrimination of visual, auditory and tactile stimuli as being fundamental to the notion of intelligence; he found good evidence in its favour. This type of ECT also fell into disrepute, but has been rescued recently. Modern research, inevitably much better organized and methodologically superior to the work done by Spearman in 1904, found highly significant correlations in the 50s between a person's efficacy in discriminating between stimuli and his IQ. This notion of sensory discrimination has in fact led to the construction of a test that will help to measure the IQ of a baby just two to six months old. The specific method used employs the concept of *habituation* defined as a decrement in attention following the repeated presentation of a stimulus. You present to the child two pictures, one to his right, the other to his left. One is novel, the other he has seen before. There is a tendency for the baby to look at the novel picture, and the brighter he is (as determined when he is old enough to be given a proper IQ test), the more he will tend to do so. Obviously, discrimination is basic to this behaviour; the infant must be able to discriminate between a picture previously seen, and one that is novel.

ECTs are of theoretical rather than practical interest; why use an expensive technique using complex apparatus and individual testing when it gives you similar results to a cheap group test of IQ? It might be useful in testing individuals handicapped in ordinary IQ tests because of language difficulties, poor schooling, or other similar reasons. But from the point of theory they seem conclusive proof against Binet's theory in the form given, and by Ceci in the quote presented a few paragraphs above. If IQ results are determined by the effects of schooling, then IQ has no business to correlate at all with ECTs which by no stretch of the imagination can be considered to have anything to do with school learning! All ECTs by definition are of so simple a kind that even mentally defective children can solve the "problem" faultlessly; the only thing that differentiates bright and dull is the *speed* with which the task is carried out. That was Galton's prediction, and the facts certainly bear out this prediction remarkably well. Furthermore, speed of mental processing so measured correlates equally well with all types of IQ tests, and best with those having the highest loading on g (i.e.,those which are the best measures of g) this would be difficult to explain on any other grounds.

Speed of mental functioning is clearly very relevant to IQ testing, although I shall argue in the next chapter that there is an even more fundamental biological variable that *underlies* such speed measures. But however that may be, ECTs have an important bearing on the Binet-Galton controversy. Apparently abstract ability, reasoning, learning and memory are all dependent on speed of cortical functioning; that is an important lesson to learn.

5

The Biological Basis of Intelligence

Although Galton suggested reaction time and similar tests as biological measures of brain functioning, they are obviously just a halfway house in that direction. What he had in mind did not then exist, namely electronic ways and means of investigating directly what was going on in the brain, such as the electroencephalograph, the positron emission tomography (PET) scan, or the magnetic resonance imaging technique. In turning now to results established with the use of such modern techniques, it may be useful to consider Figure 5.1 which contrasts three different conceptions of intelligence.

This figure shows on the left, the hypothesized biological background of intelligent behaviour. Genetic factors determine neurological structures, physiological mechanisms and biochemical secretions, the interplay of these with each other, and with the information constantly impinging on the cortex through the messages brought to it by the ascending afferent pathways. Those messages are transmitted through the brain, from cell to cell, through the synapses that link the axons of one cell with the dendrites of another (or indeed many others!) We can measure what is going on in the brain by means of the EEG, by recording averaged evoked potentials, the contingent negative variation, the galvanic skin response, and so on. This is what is meant by biological intelligence. (I shall explain some of these concepts presently.)

Differences in this biological intelligence can be measured by means of IQ tests, but only indirectly, and with an admixture of inputs from many environmental sources—socioeconomic status, education, family upbringing, cultural factors, and so on. This is psychometric intelligence or IQ, and we have already discussed this fairly thoroughly. Finally, we have social or practical intelligence, for example, the application of IQ to worldly affairs, like earning a living, engaging in marriage, or interacting with other people. Success in all this is partly due to IQ, but here we also have a whole host of external factors, all of which may influence the

FIGURE 5.1

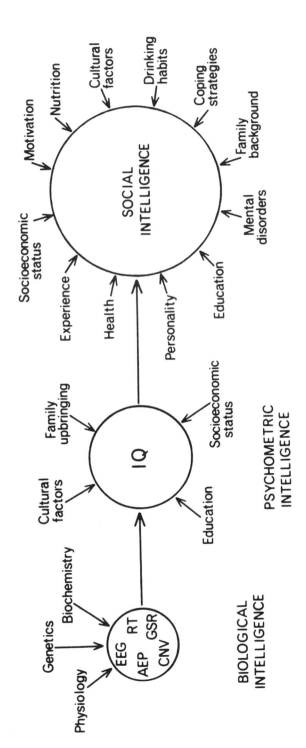

The relation between biological, psychometric and social (or practical) intelligence.

outcome—personality, mental disorder, drinking habits, motivation, nutrition, health, and above all, luck. Clearly, this social or practical intelligence is too complex a concept to be of any scientific value; science relies on the reduction of complex concepts to simpler, more elementary ones. To bring in other completely unconnected factors in this fashion is not useful; we would want to study each separately, and also its interaction with all the others. RT and IT studies straddle the space between biological intelligence and psychometric intelligence; we must now turn to a consideration of biological intelligence itself.

There are some biological correlates of IQ that are fairly obvious, although they have given rise to a great deal of controversy. The most obvious is perhaps brain size; the larger the brain, the higher the IQ. This was as already suggested by Galton who measured the head size of the most successful, and the least successful students at Cambridge, and found a 3.3 percent advantage in the most successful, in spite of the presumably quite small IQ differences. But of course head size is not the same as brain size; there are marked individual differences in skull thickness and shape. Clearly, external head measures are rather an indirect and possibly incorrect index of brain volume. Thus head perimeter and brain volume only correlate 0.23! Nevertheless, external measures of head size have correlated around 0.20 with IQ in numerous investigations, giving what is almost certainly a gross underestimate of the real figure. Corrections for body size make little real difference, the correlation is much the same whether we correct for body size or not. Some investigators have weighed the brain of corpses, or filled the empty brain case with shot, then weighing it, to get a closer approximation, but without much success.

Fortunately recent advances in electronics have put an end to the guessing game. With the use of magnetic resonance imaging it is now possible to measure an individual's actual brain size without having to rely on the external head measurement. The technique is nonintrusive, and has been applied in three instances to date. Correlations average round 0.45, that is to say about 5 times the size of head measurement—IQ correlation ($0.45^2 - 0.20^2$). The existence of a moderately high correlation between brain size and IQ makes sense in that the brain is clearly indicated as the seat of intellect, but the fact that the correlation is far from perfect suggests that other features of the brain are more important than size in determining intelligence.

Readers with an interest in odd and unusual research may like to know that studies have been done to measure intelligence in rats. Using tests of speed or reasoning, accuracy of reasoning, response flexibility, and attention to novelty, researchers found a general factor of intelligence for these rodents. They then measured the brain weight of rats so tested, and found a highly significant correlation! Thus the intraspecies relationship between brain size and IQ holds for rodents as well as for humans.

How does the correlation between brain size and IQ work out in biological terms? Haung found a correlation between brain size of cognitive ability of 0.48 between number of cortical neurons and brain size in humans. A person with a brain size of 1,400 cms^3 has an average 600 million fewer cortical neurons than an individual with a brain size of 1,500 cm^3. The difference between the low end of the normal distribution (1,000 cms^3) and the high end (1,700^3) works out at 4.2 billion neurons. The human brain may contain up to 100 billion (10^{11}) nerve cells, classifiable into 10,000 types resulting in 100,000 billion synapses. Assuming that the brain stores information at the low average rate of one list per synapse (which would require two levels of synaptic activity), the structure as a whole would generate 10^{14} bits of information—compared with 10^9 bits of memory in contemporary supercomputers. It does not seem unlikely that a difference of 4 billion neurons would have a pronounced effect on cognitive ability, although of course other factors in the structure of the brain must also have a pronounced effect. The other physical variable that shows marked correlation with IQ is myopia or short-sightedness. Roughly speaking, myopics have IQs of about 8 points higher than nonmyopias. Myopia is also correlated with scholastic achievement, a correlation mediated by the IQ differences. This relationship is what geneticists call *pleiotropic,* for example, produced by the fact that a single gene has an effect on two (or more) distinct characters. That means that if the gene is segregating at conception, the two characters are affected simultaneously. There is no evidence for a counterhypothesis that seems intuitively appealing, namely that bright youngsters read more and spoil their eyesight. No environmental cause like reading a lot has ever been found to raise IQ by anything like as much as the myopic/nonmyopic difference. The fact that the correlation is found in members of the same family pretty well proves the case for pleiotropy.

Much more interesting have been studies of the physiological events accompanying or underlying cognitive events, particularly electroencephalographic (EEG) investigations. Investigations of brain waves arising spontaneously during periods of rest have been found to show differences between bright and dull, high and low IQ, with correlations of 0.50 obtained in the best and most recent studies. However, these findings have little theoretical basis at the moment, and while they do support the view that there are relations between IQ and physiological events in the brain, they do not tell us very much about the nature of the relationship.

What is interesting is that EEG patterns recorded in 36-hour-old babies have been found to predict later IQ, even Ceci would hardly argue that this correlation was mediated by school learning! Much further work is clearly needed to analyse this early measure of later intelligence in greater detail, but the fact that any correlation is found at all is perhaps surprising.

More important, therefore, have been studies using the so-called averaged-evoked potential (AEP), in which we record the EEG waves following a given stimulus—a sudden noise or a bright flash. Figure 5.2 shows the resting EEG waves on the left; at point A the stimulus is given, (a flash of light; a sudden sound), and the resulting negative (N) and positive (P) waves, dying down after 500 milliseconds, record the AEP we are interested in.

Investigators first looked at the *latencies* and *amplitudes* of the waves. It was expected that the waves would arise more quickly for high IQ children (short latencies), and be larger (great amplitude). The technical problems were horrendous at the beginning, and both positive and negative results were reported. I encouraged one of my Ph.D. students Elaine Hendrickson, to try and see what sort of correlations she could discover with the most modern equipment then available in our department, and found correlations between IQ and latency of between −0.40 and −0.50 for different waves; correlations with amplitude were much smaller (0.20–0.30). Amplitudes have not given good results, and have little theoretical background, but latency fits in well with our RT and IT finding of quicker processing of information. Apparently the information introduced by the signal, whether verbal or aural, is processed more quickly by high IQ brains, giving rise to shorter latencies.

However, Elaine and her husband, Alan Hendrickson, discovered something much more important. It is well known in science that you often only see what you are programmed to see, you are blind to the unexpected. Consider figure 5.3 which shows the AEPs of three children, one bright, one average and one dull (IQs are given in the figure). It is easy to see that the waves (E1, E2, E3 and E4) come much more

FIGURE 5.2

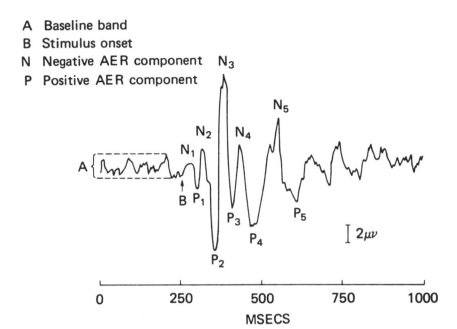

A Baseline band
B Stimulus onset
N Negative AER component
P Positive AER component

Averaged evoked potential responses, following sudden stimulus given at point B.

quickly in the brightest than in the dullest child, and that of course is what anybody familiar with the literature would home in on. But something else distinguishes even more clearly between the children, and that, although always present, had been overlooked before. Clearly the waveform is much more *complex* for the bright child, very *simple* for the dull! For the dull child you have essentially a few simple sinusoidal curves, while for the bright child you have a large number of secondary ups and downs super-imposed on the large curves. It is this *complexity* that is the most distinguishing mark of the AEPs of bright children.

FIGURE 5.3

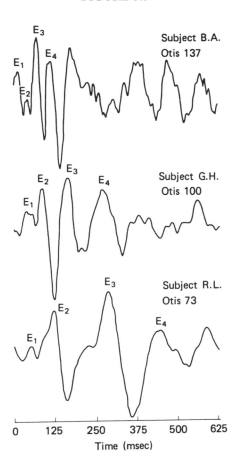

Averaged evoked potential responses of three children of high, average and low IQ, as measured by the Otis test.

The Hendricksons investigated large numbers of children to test the hypothesis that the complexity of the wave form was the most discriminating feature to sort out bright and dull. Figure 5.4 shows the records of a random six bright and six dull children, given a visual stimulus; the difference springs to the eye. In fact it had already been present equally clearly in a similar figure published in 1973 by J. Ertl, the first investigator to take a good look at AEPs; it is difficult to understand why so many investigators (including myself!) had failed to see the obvious!

FIGURE 5.4

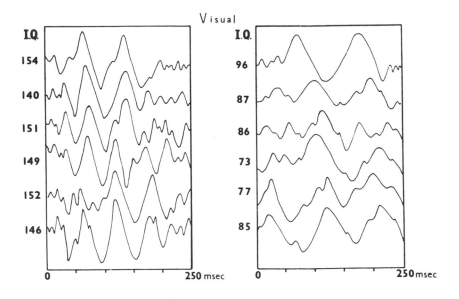

Averaged evoked potential responses of six bright and six dull children.

How do we measure complexity? The Hendricksons used two measures. The first was called the string measure, because at the beginning they used to lay a string along the actual waveform, and then straightened it out to measure its length; the more complex the wave form, the longer the string. (Later, of course, they used more complex statistical analyses, but the name stuck.) The other method was much more important, and theoretically more revealing. It was based on a theory put forward by Alan Hendrickson, namely that people differ in the probability of *errors* arising in the processing of information across the cortex. Many cells are involved, with the electrically coded information, transmitted from the dendrites receiving it, to the axon relaying it across the synapses which turn the message into a chemical code, only for it to be translated again into an electrical one at the other side. Much can go wrong in this. The neuro-transmitters that help the message to cross the synapses may misfire, or the myelin sheet that surrounds the neurons and insulates them may have holes in it—the whole programme is so complex that it seems a miracle that things don't go wrong more often! What would the consequences be of errors occurring?

The AEP, like the RET, is the average of a large number of repetitions; the recording is at the limit of our technical ability, and the signal-to-noise ratio is rather poor, so averaging is essential. But of course you only get the finer details if the messages you are averaging are pretty similar, trough on trough, and peak on peak. If the waves are not identical, you might get trough on peak, which would wipe out the minor waves and leave only the large, sinusoidal ones. Thus the Hendricksons proceeded to measure the *variability* of the many repetitions at every data point (i.e., every two milliseconds); the more errors, the greater the variability. Thus their theory demanded that IQ should be positively correlated with error rate, the string measure would just be another aspect of variability; the more small waves in addition to the few large ones, the longer the string. Their research did in fact give just that result; a very high correlation between IQ, on the one hand, and the string measure and the variability measure on the other.

This theory makes good sense in that abstract thinking would obviously be difficult if the messages passing through the brain were constantly subjected to errors. But we now seem to have two different but equally sensible theories of intelligence: speed of mental processing and error-free mental processing. Fortunately, these two theories can be reduced to one. Messages never pass through just one channel, but through dozens, or even hundreds. Errors therefore are not all that serious; they affect some channels, but not all. However, if incoming messages disagree, due to errors in some of them, the passing-on of the message might be delayed until enough verification is received, and that implies waiting until these further messages arrive. Hence a high degree of error is reflected in slow processing. Thus the *speed* theory is essentially explained in terms of the *error* theory which would be the more fundamental one.

Incoming stimuli, via their axons, are relayed to synapses, and from there to dendrites belonging to different cells. These dendrites end up in a set of synapses making up the *comparator,* which evaluates the incoming messages before passing them on to the effector cells which initiate the response (figure 5.5). If all the different messages are the same, the comparator has to wait until agreement is reached before passing the message on to the effector, and this takes time. Hence *er-*

FIGURE 5.5

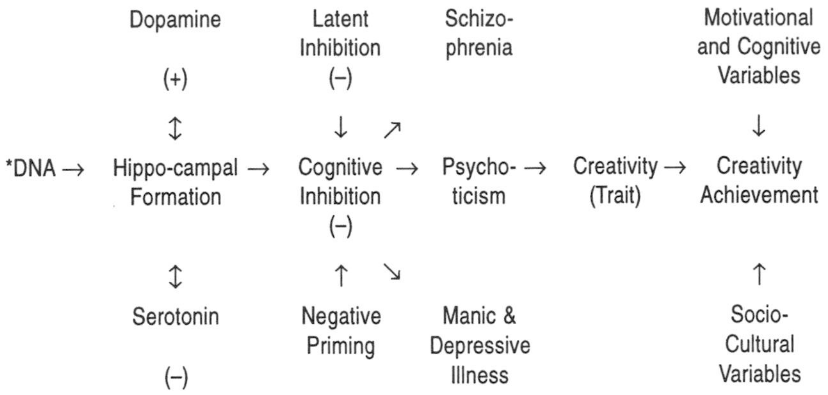

	Dopamine	Latent Inhibition	Schizo-phrenia			Motivational and Cognitive Variables
	(+)	(−)				
	↕	↓ ↗				↓
*DNA →	Hippo-campal → Formation	Cognitive → Inhibition (−)	Psycho- → ticism	Creativity → (Trait)	Creativity Achievement	
	↕	↑ ↘				↑
	Serotonin	Negative Priming	Manic & Depressive Illness			Socio-Cultural Variables
	(−)					

*Genetic Determinants.

Greatly simplified picture of link between incoming stimulus and response effector via synapses and neurons, incorporating a comparator to evaluate incoming stimuli.

rors in transmission result in *slow* transmissions. This is of course a grossly oversimplified picture of what is actually occurring, but it may be helpful in understanding the relation between error and speed. The notion of a comparator has found empirical support in the work of Zobary, Hillman, and Hockstein, and is not just an "ad hoc" invention, dating back to the original work of Y. Sokolov.

The Hendricksons' work has been replicated many times, but there have also been critical studies finding little correlation with the string measure. One important variable seems to be the amount of attention required of the subject when the AEP is being measured. Carrying out the experiment, as the Hendricksons did, in conditions where subjects had nothing to do except sit and listen passively to tones, or look at the flashes of light, gave results as they found. But if subjects had to carry out an attention-demanding task, results changed drastically and might even reverse. This may account for some of the complications observed. There are many other complexities that make the story less simple than this brief record would suggest, but the evidence certainly favours some such theory as that outlined above.

There are other ways of using the AEP. E. Shafer, for instance, argued in favour of what he called a 'neural adaptability" paradigm. This is based on the well-known phenomenon of habituation. A certain stimulus, when presented for the first time, causes cortical arousal, interest, inspection; if presented many times these reactions diminish, and finally cease altogether. We become habituated to this stimulus, or class of stimuli. The baby test I mentioned earlier was based on this principle, and showed that brighter children attend more than duller ones to novel stimuli. Shafer argued that habituation would be shown more strongly by bright than by dull subjects, so that a series of identical stimuli would show *decreasing* amplitudes in the evoked potential, with the decrease more noticeable in the bright than in the dull. Like the Hendricksons, Shafer obtained high correlations with IQ of 0.75 or thereabouts, which is quite remarkable when we bear in mind the lack of complete reliability of the measures involved.

Can we accommodate this paradigm in our general theory? The answer is probably in the affirmative. To recognize a stimulus as being identical with a previous one requires fast and accurate transmission of information across the cortex. If errors occur, transmission will be neither fast nor accurate, so that identification is impaired and hence there will be less habituation.

A line of research that may prove important in spite of its inherent difficulties, has been the study of *dendrite length* in relation to IQ. This work, published by Bob Jacobs, Arnold Scheibel, and Matthew Scholl, essentially suggests that intelligence may be related to the length of a person's *dendrites,* for example, the many appendages of a cell that interact, through synapses, with the *axons* of other cells, pass on any messages received to the cell, and on to the cell's axon, through a synapse, to a dendrite of another cell. Apparently dendrites shorten with age, which may account for the decline of fluid intelligence with age, and dendrite length may be related to IQ—educational history, rather than IQ measures was used, because obviously the measurement of dendrite length cannot be done *in vivo.*

Thus it may be necessary to add length of dendrites to damage of the myelion sheath, synaptic errors, and other possible neuronal malfunction that may affect the degree of error-free transmission that is possible for a given cortex. This is an important if difficult area of research, and it is to be hoped that it will continue to attract research and support.

An interesting recent study has looked at brain biochemistry, particularly intracellular brain p^H, using ^{31}p magnetic resonance spectroscopy, as a possible correlate of IQ. The p^H, of course, is a measure of the acidity or alkalinity of a solution, acid solution having a p^H of less than seven, alkaline solution a p^H greater than seven. It was known that the amplitude of an evoked potential *in vitro* was proportional to p^H, and that increasing intra- and extracellular p^H increases the amplitude of nerve action potentials and decreases conduction time. There are many other studies giving reason to suspect that p^H is associated with the efficacy of conductivity-transmission in the brain and the neuronal level, with alkalinity (higher p^H) being more favourable for brain functioning.

The study was carried out on forty-two school children, and the correlations with Wechsler IQ were 0.52 with the full scale, 0.56 with the verbal scale, and 0.30 with the performance scale. These correlations are in the expected direction, and clearly support the theory linking intracellular brain alkalinity with high IQ. It is also interesting to note that of the twelve subtests of the Wechsler, those that have the highest correlation with g also had the highest correlation with p^H (vocabulary, comprehension, similarities), just as was the case with evoked potentials. This clearly is a direction of research well worth following up. It may also be related to the question of vitamin and mineral uptake; as I shall show in a later chapter, micronutrient supplementation can have a strong effect on raising the IQ and it may do so by increasing the alkalinity of intracellular brain structures.

It should be noted that the "error speed" theory accounts not only for the psychological data, but also for the RT and IT data, particularly for the odd finding that RT variability correlated more highly with IQ than RT itself. Variability is the best available measure of error in the transmission of information, and hence this finding is precisely what a theory postulating the occurrence of errors in the transmission of information through the cortex would predict; no alternative theory seems able to do this. We may characterize this theory as one of cerebral efficiency or integrity; a cortex that performs its function without, or with little error is more efficient than one that commits many errors. This notion of efficiency suggests another mode of investigating the biological basis of intelligence. An engine needs fuel, and the less efficient the engine, the greater its need for fuel. Can we measure the brain's uptake of fuel? The recent advent of positron emission tomography (PET scanning) has made this possible.

The fuel that enables the brain to function is glucose. Although the brain constitutes only about 2 percent of the body's weight, its energy consumption is about 20 percent of total energy requirements. Compared with this high rate of utilization, the energy stores of the brain are almost negligible, and the brain is consequently almost completely dependent on the continuous replenishment of its glucose supplied by the cerebral circulation. It would defy the most fundamental laws of thermodynamics if individual differences in brain power did not find their counterparts in individual differences of brain energy. Positron emission tomography essentially measures the amount of glucose, made radioactive and injected in the subject. There is an uptake period of some thirty minutes for the brain to use the tracer, and during that time the subject typically works on some IQ tests. The subject is then put in the scanner, and his blood flow into the various parts of the brain registered. Cerebral glucose use is monitored. What the scan shows is brain function during the thirty minutes following injection of the isotope tracer, and brain activity while lying in the scanner.

The outcome for normal subjects (mentally defective and Alzheimer patients are not here included) is that the brighter subjects use less glucose than the dull ones, with correlations between –0.50 and –0.80. Correlations are variable because different IQ tests are used, but mainly because usually very few subjects are used. (The procedure is extremely expensive!) But the overall effect is not in doubt, and supports the "efficacy" hypothesis. The studies also throw much light on which parts of the brain are active in different types of mental activity, but this is a complex topic that would take us away from our discussion of the psychophysiology of intelligence.

There is another interesting finding, however, that may be of interest. The density of synapses in the brain increases markedly in the first five years of life, but then decreases dramatically throughout the early teens. This process known as "neural pruning," may result from the development of too many redundant~synaptic connections. Mental retardates, for instance, show higher than normal rates of synaptic density. Thus *brain organization* may be responsible for IQ differences, and it is noteworthy that cerebral glucose use increases with age up to about age five, when the rate is approximately twice that of normal adults. Mirroring the curve of synaptic density, glucose use then falls off dramatically from age five through the early teens. There is thus a possibility that lack of neural pruning produces an inefficient cortex, where the many redundant synapses cause unnecessary uptake of glucose, and are responsible for many errors in transmission.

Oxygen is another requirement for brain functioning, and it is supplied via the red corpuscles that pass the brain-body barrier. It has been found that a trial fibrillation, for example, irregular heartbeat which slows down the circulation, has some effect on producing mental deterioration. Even an occasional loss of heart rhythm produced significant loss of memory and of the ability to concentrate on simple tasks. Research in this field is in its infancy, but anticlogging drugs can reverse the physical pattern, and it would be important to know if they can also reverse the loss of cognitive functioning.

We may end this discussion by presenting in diagrammatic form (figure 5.6) the general theory which seems to summarize most if not all the facts known about the different aspects of intelligence. At the centre lies psychometric intelligence (the IQ), represented most crucially by tests of g_f or fluid intelligence. Its most distal antecedent is DNA, the genetic blueprint of later development. A more proximal antecedent is constituted by the biological intermediaries between DNA and actual behaviour, as manifested in the activities that produce a measurable IQ. The causal chain leads on to the proximal consequences of these differences in the integrity of the cortex and central nervous systems, such as reaction times, inspection times, and variability of both. And finally we have the socially important distal consequences of this complex of biological and environmental causes, namely scholastic achievement, success in selection procedures, and many others which will be discussed in the next section.

This review has covered only a small area of what is an exploding subject matter. New studies appear every week, and so do new theories. I do not wish to give the appearance of saying that the theories here outlined are necessarily the best, or that future research may not change our views about the true underlying brain structure and functions determining differences in IQ. I think research and theory are on the right track, and will soon give us an agreed picture of the biological basis of intelligence. There are too many coalescing streams of evidence to deny that something important is taking place, and that this something is very much in line with Galton's thinking. The theory here outlined may not be correct in any absolute sense, indeed that would be most unlikely at such an early state of research. But it is almost certainly pointing in the right direction, and no theory can be asked to do more than that!

Does all this psychophysiological work help us to develop a realistic conception of intelligence? Critics like Stephen J. Gould often object to the notion that intelligence is a "thing" that is somehow located in the brain; such reification they believe to be unacceptable. In this they are right, of course, but no psychologist I know, or have read, ever suggested such an absurd notion. What we can perhaps say is that intelligence is a function of the *efficient functioning of the brain*. Spearman

FIGURE 5.6

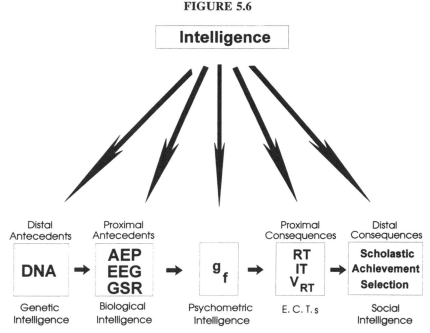

Sequence of variables involved in defining individual differences in intelligence, from DNA to actual-world behavior.

likened intelligence to the functioning of an engine, not an unexpected simile for a man who had been an engineer with the British Army before becoming a psychologist. It is the brain as a whole that enables us to act intelligently; it would be idle to try and locate intelligence in any small part of the brain, as phrenologists once tried to do, and it would certainly be nonsensical to search for a "thing" in the brain that could be identified as "intelligence."

There is evidence that the various special abilities—verbal, spatial, numerical—are associated with special parts of the brain, or even with one or other of the hemispheres. This is similar to increasing the functioning of different parts of an engine, say by special fuel injection (turbo chargers), increasing the number of cylinders, and so on. These chargers may affect special aspects of the engine output (brake horsepower, speed, fuel efficiency), but we are still dealing with an overall effect. This whole line of work is not as advanced as one might have hoped, but positron emission tomography and similar new techniques will soon clarify the situation and enable us to be much more specific than would be possible now. But Spearman's metaphor is a good one, and may help us to better understand just what "intelligence" is.

One further topic may be worthwhile discussing in relation to the biological basis of intelligence, namely sex differences. With respect to IQ, these are relatively small, favouring females up to puberty, males in adulthood. It is rather difficult to come to any rational conclusion on the point because IQ tests are constructed with the express aim of obliterating any sex differences, this puts a constraint on existing tests and makes sex comparison difficult. Quite large differences appear on special abilities, and most work has been directed at these differences. Males are favoured quite strongly on visio-spatial tasks, for example, tasks which involve rotating patterns in one's mind to see what they would look like after rotation, and spatio-temporal tasks like tracking a moving object through space. These differences are quite large, corresponding to the difference between 100 IQ and 112 IQ. Mathematical ability and quantitative tasks generally find males superior after puberty.

On the other hand, some verbal tasks show substantial mean differences favouring females. Verbal fluency is one of these; a typical test would require the subject to name as many words as possible beginning with a given letter. Synonym generation is another such task; given a word, the subject has to give a synonym. Composition, reading, and spelling also show females superior, while dyslexia and other reading disabilities are more frequent in males. In part these gender differences may be social, a consequence of subtle and overt differences between the experiences, expectations, and gender roles of females and males— although of course these in turn may only reflect hormonal influences— testosterone levels in normal males were correlated *positively* with some measures of spatial ability; and *negatively* with some measures of verbal ability. Administration of testosterone increased performance on visio-spatial feats in older males.

But most recent research has concentrated on differences in the sizes and shapes of certain neural structures in the brain. Sex-related differences in some portion of the *corpus callosum,* a bundle of nerves connecting the two hemispheres, have been found correlated with verbal fluency, and recent brain imaging studies have suggested differences between males and females in the lateralization of language. This is a very promising area of research, but published results for the most part await replication and extensions.

A Danish psychologist, Helmuth Nyborg, has put forward a particularly interesting theory about hormonal influences on intelligence, to the effect that too high and too low levels of testosterone lead to low levels of intelligence, with more balanced levels having the highest scores. Figure 5.7 gives the results of his studies, showing levels of intelligence, as measured by three different tests; these are the dependent variables. Hormotype shows high (A6) to low (AO) levels of testosterone with the extremes clearly showing lower intelligence—particularly the A6 hormotype, which has high testosterone levels. Again, there is no independent replication, but the large size of the sample is impressive, and as its basis is a sound theory, results must be taken seriously.

The general outcome of the physiological studies reviewed here marks in many ways a return to Charles Spearman, whose *The Abilities of Man* was the point of departure for the scientific study of intelligence, allowing hypotheticodeductive experiments instead of the largely inductive studies that preceded its publication. Spearman, as befits an experienced engineer, was concerned with the development of *laws,* rather than with the simple manipulation of correlations; he wanted to go into *causal* relations, and discover what lay underneath the phenotypic gallimaufry of psychometric relationships. It is unfortunate that his successors have gone off in a wild pursuit of purely correlational studies, while studiously avoiding any contact with these theoretical ideas which to him were much more important.

In his book he gives his usual soundly academic and historical account of the theory of mental energy, the many different ways in which it has been postulated and pictured, the mental, physical and combined theories that have been constructed around it, and the experimental studies of Lehmann, Wirth, and others into the constancy of the hypothetical energy. It is one of the tragedies of psychology that all the careful experimental work he encountered when a student at Leipzig is no longer accessible to most psychologists because it is written in German, and anything not written in English is *terra incognita* for English-speaking psychologists who seem to have forgotten, or never learned, that science is international.

However that may be, Spearman makes clear the difference between a closed and an open system, with energy remaining *constant* in the former, but depending on levels of input in the latter. He concludes that "the facts of general psychology—quite apart from those of individual differences—strongly support the suggestion of mental energy and engines. Moreover, such an energy would seem to be just what is wanted to explain *g,* whilst the engines might go far towards explaining the *s*'s." (The special abilities or *s*'s which Spearman admitted in addition

FIGURE 5.7

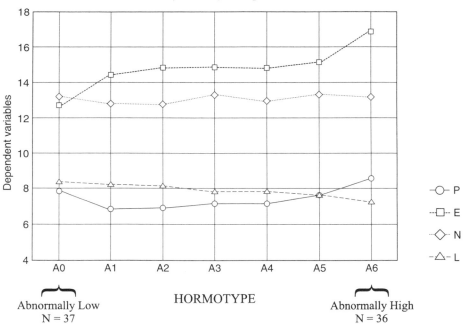

Plot of Means
HORMOTYPE Main Effect
Rao R (42,20350)=2,42;p<.0000

Relation between IQ and hemotype, i.e., the sex hormone ratio shown by different people.

to *g* were abilities specific to any test, and different from those specific to any other test. He later agreed with Thurstone that where tests were similar in content, *s*'s might also be similar and give rise to Thurstone's group factors.)

We may thus regard the brain as an *engine* that does *work* (cognitive processing of information, generation of problem solutions, production of abstract thought and reasoning), and requires *fuel* to produce the *energy* required to drive it (glucose, oxygen), Energy in physics is the capacity of a body or system to do work, and we may thus conceive of *g* as the *energy* of the brain that enables it to do intellectual work. This energy drives all the *engines* (including Thurston's primary abilities, and Spearman's special abilities), some of which may be more efficient than others. Such an engineering view of the brain is certainly in line with modern work, and rescues us from the non-theoretical abyss of mere number-crunching that is modern psychometrics. Factor analysis is a good servant, but a bad master!

This discussion may be of help also in considering again the problem of the one and the many. To succeed in a cognitive problem, we need a number of "faculties." We need to *perceive* the physical aspects of the problem, we need to *remember* (short-term memory) the various aspects after recognising them, we need to *think* about the connections between these aspects, we need to *remember* (long-term memory) relevant aspects previously encountered; messages have to pass through the cortex, correctly addressed and all correctly delivered—how can we say that all these different activities constitute a single entity? But an engine, too, has many parts, that does not mean that these do not work together to produce a common output—energy in some form or another. If any part misfunctions, the output declines. But the misfunctioning part is not identical with the output! The brain acts as a unit, but this unit is made up of 10 billion cells, interacting in complex ways, through numerous structures, hormones, neurotransmitters, neurological structures and physiological mechanisms; supplied with glucose, oxygen and other necessary foods that provide the energy to keep the engine going. The different parts may function more or less effectively, giving small or medium correlations with total IQ; what the IQ really measures is the total effectiveness of the brain.

6

What is the Use of IQ Tests?

It is natural for most people to ask: "What's in it for me?" or "What's the use of it?" Michael Faraday, arguably the most famous physicist of the last century, once exhibited a minute model of the dynamo he had just invented. A tiny old lady approached him and asked timidly, "Please, Mr. Faraday, what is the use of it?" Faraday looked down gravely from his great height, frowned, and said, "Madam, what is the use of a baby?" Now, of course, our whole civilization is built on the use of electricity, the laws of which he more than anyone else discovered and formalized, but at the time few could predict the tremendous consequences that would flow from his discovery. Perhaps appealing more to the mind of modern physicists is Faraday's answer to a similar question by Gladstone, Queen Victoria's chancellor of the exchequer: "One day, Sir, you may tax it." As David Hilbert, one of our greatest mathematicians said,"We must know. We will know." The search for knowledge, regardless of application, is one of man's strongest drives. It may be, as the Bible says, that "he that increaseth knowledge, increaseth sorrow," or, on the other hand, "Knowledge itself is power," as Francis Bacon has it. The pursuit of knowledge needs no excuse or material motivation. To discover the way our brain works is important in itself; like most scientific or mathematical discoveries, work on intelligence is likely to have important practical consequences, but these are not the important sources of our (or at least my!) motivation for exploring these issues.

Yet it would not do to disregard entirely questions regarding the practical consequences of IQ testing. Some of its Marxist critics have accused psychologists of being motivated by a desire to shore up the capitalist enterprise, to try and maintain a conservative dominance, and generally encourage an anti-working-class ethos. I have never understood how IQ testing would do that, even if it tried to do so; the facts of regression to the mean by themselves lead to a social mobility that would outrage any rigid conservative, and encourage any labour supporter. As Robert Burns put it, "Facts are chiels that winna ding, an' downa be disputed"—which, for non-Scottish speakers, means that facts are things that cannot be manipulated or disputed. The facts discovered by psychologists concerning intelligence aid no particular political party, but form a sturdy platform on which to build a better society. As we shall see, the applications of IQ testing have if anything been hostile to conservative policies, using the adjective in the sense of "favouring the preservation of established customs, and opposing innovations." Like any new discovery or invention, it has led inevitably to new and sometimes disturbing developments, all of which have been helpful to the development of greater equality of opportunity.

This development of a true meritocracy is perhaps the most important contribution that IQ testing has made. In the bad old days, and unfortunately to a large extent even now, it was true to say that "it is more important who you know than what you know." This is a well-known saying the truth of which can hardly be gainsaid even though the grammar could be improved. Leadership in politics, in commerce, in industry, and elsewhere often owed more to nepotism, to belonging to a feudal family, to inheriting wealth than to ability, or great creativity. Officers in the army used to buy their appointments, with no nonsense about merit. Captains in the navy often owed their elevation to political connections. Working-class children had no access to a good education, or to university, and few made it into the professions. Psychological testing made great inroads into this corrupt business; perhaps the use of psychological testing for officer selection in the British Army during the Second World War may serve as an example.

As is often the case, the only way in which psychology could gain a foothold in an established organization like the army was through the obvious and catastrophic breakdown of traditional procedures. In the early years of the 1939 war, the army found its officers from among men who had taken a school certificate, or some higher examination, and who had, at the same time, attended one of the schools providing an Officer Training Corps. Selection was carried out by Interview Boards attached to Army Commands, the technique being that of the simple interview lasting for about twenty minutes. In 1941, however, it became clear that this traditional method of officer selection was breaking down. The failure rate at Officer Cadet Training Units (OCTUs.) was rising to quite alarming proportions, a state of affairs which is wasteful and has a very bad effect on the morale of the ranks, who as a consequence did not apply for commissions in anything like the numbers required. In addition, it was found through psychiatric examination of officers who had suffered a breakdown in service that many of these men should never have been commissioned at all. There was growing public concern about this state of affairs, and questions were being asked in Parliament in ever-increasing numbers.

There are many reasons for this failure of traditional methods; one of these, possibly the most important, could be found in the fact that until that time, officers had come almost entirely from one social class. Methods of selection were based on this fact in the sense that they implied the existence of a social background common to selectors and candidates. Reliance on intuitive judgments based on resemblance of candidates to interviewers probably worked reasonably well as long as this fundamental condition was fulfilled, but as the war progressed the reservoir of candidates of this type became exhausted, and very soon selection boards were faced with candidates whose personality and background were quite alien to the officers who had the task of selection. Under those conditions, traditional methods were inadequate and judgments became based on irrelevant factors. Complaints began to be heard that the Board did not take sufficient time and trouble over each candidate, that the qualities which they looked for and the principles on which they worked were not evident, and that consideration of social class and background unduly influenced decisions.

War Officer Selection Boards (WOSBs.) were set up in the summer of 1942 in order to remedy these deficiencies. Most reliance was placed on a variety of standard or "real life" situations, interviews, and paper-and-pencil tests. The Board sifting the evidence consisted of military people (including the president, a regimental officer with the rank of full colonel), a number of officers with regimental experience, referred to as Military Testing Officers, a psychiatrist, and a number of psychologists. WOSBs. thus arose in a crisis situation when traditional methods had broken down, and they were asked to do two things. They were asked to provide the army with a sufficient number of officers of good quality and they were asked to raise the morale of the army regarding applications for commissions by making selection fairer. Their task was an immense one; an impression of its size may be gained from the fact that during these years about 100,000 applications for commissions had to be dealt with. How did the new methods work?

There is very good evidence to show that the new method was definitely superior to the old. For a short while WOSBs and old procedure boards were working side by side, and it was possible to follow up the men whom they had recommended for commission. Of those recommended by WOSBs 35 percent were found to be above average; while of those recommended by old procedures, only 22 percent were above average. The percentage of candidates rated average was almost identical, but those rated below average came from War Office Selection Boards only in 25 percent of the cases, and from old procedure boards in 37 percent of the cases.

The WOSB procedures were not perfect; they tended to rely too much on subjective judgments, rather than objective test results. It was later found that success of OCTU was predicted better by an intelligence test than by the whole WOSB procedure. It was also found that the predictions made by psychiatrists on the basis of their interviews gave the worst predictions of all. But with all their imperfections these methods did serve to right a notorious wrong, and gave access to officer status to many deserving working-class lads who would not have been accepted under the old regime.

Much the same happened, as already mentioned, when IQ tests were introduced into school selection. The immediate effect was to make possible access to better education and university for many able, working-class children who otherwise would have missed out. Thus the effect of IQ testing, both for officer selection and for school selection, was to reduce the influence of class privilege and insist on merit, regardless of class. Marxist interpretation of psychologists acting to support the status quo makes simply no sense at all when we look at the actual facts of the situation.

But the whole principle of selection on the basis of ability has been called into question by critics who insist that it simply means worse education for the less able. This too is not true. Ability grouping, that is, organizing classes in such a way that the pupils in a given class are roughly of similar ability, makes obvious sense as compared with mixed ability classes containing very bright and very dull, as well as average ability children. Of course, common sense is not enough; what does the experimental evidence say? A meta-analysis of fifty-two controlled studies of grouping came to very definite conclusions. In the words of the authors, two independent statisticians:

> Meta-analysis [the procedure used to summarize the results of the fifty-two studies] provides an objective technique for research synthesis. Its emphasis on quantification keeps reviewers from projecting personal needs into the vast ink-blot of educational research. What meta-analysis establishes about grouping seems

clear enough. Meta-analysis showed that students gained somewhat more from grouped classes than they did from ungrouped ones....[The evidence] does not support the view that grouping has unfavourable effects on the achievement of low-aptitude students...

[Some articles] tended to emphasize the negative effects of grouping on the attitudes and self-concepts of low-ability students. Such conclusions, however, were based primarily on anecdotal and uncontrolled studies. The controlled studies that were examined gave a very different picture of the effects of grouping on student attitudes. Students seemed to like their school subjects more when they studied with peers of similar ability, and some students in grouped classes even developed more positive attitudes about themselves and about school.

Thus, common sense and empirical evidence both attest to the superiority of ability grouping where scholastic achievement and subjective well-being are concerned. Why the opposition? There is a myth that the duller pupils get a worse education than the brighter ones, but that is untrue. When properly carried out, ability grouping leads to each child receiving the best education suited to his or her ability. The dull child would not benefit from the type of education suitable for a bright one; he or she would do better, as the research indicates, if education took place in an equal ability class. The same is true of teaching in special classes for retarded children; they would not benefit from being in the same class as nonretarded children. IQ tests do not cause the low ability of some children, they merely quantify the defect and make possible remedial action.

What psychologists are trying to do is of course nothing else but what good educators have always tried to do. As Quintillian put it some 900 years ago, "It is generally and rightly considered a virtue in a teacher to observe accurately the differences in ability among his pupils, and to discover the direction in which the nature of each particular pupil inclines him. There is an incredible amount of variability in talent, and the forms of minds are no less varied than the forms of bodies." IQ testing makes it easier for the teacher to observe these differences among pupils; in a large class, retiring children may not be correctly identified with respect to their intelligence.

But there is of course no suggestion that IQ is the only important variable in this context, as indeed Quintillian already recognized. Personality can be equally important, particularly in interaction with type of teaching. In recent years "discovery learning" has been widely used in preference to "reception learning," that is, the child is not taught facts directly, but is encouraged to find them for himself. Does the new method work any better? The evidence shows that there is little to choose between them on the whole, but it has also been shown that different chil-

FIGURE 6.1

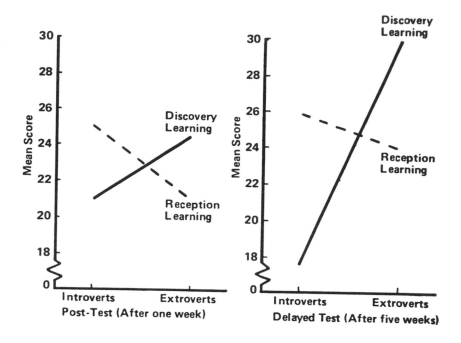

Effects on mastery of discovery and of reception learning in introverted and extraverted children.

dren respond quite differently, with introverted children preferring the reception type of learning, extraverted ones the discovery method of learning. Figure 6.1 shows the results of one such experiment, with children being taught, some by one method, some by the other. Final tests attempted to discover just how much they had learned, one week after the teaching course, and again after 5 weeks. It will be clear how strongly personality interacted with teaching method. Intelligence is not the only important variable in school learning, but it is a very important one.

Selection, of course, has always been necessary in all walks of life, and always will be. Already in the Bible we read that Gideon used a two-stage selection procedure in his war against the Midianites. The first method used was a kind of psychiatric screen based largely on reports of anxiety and depressive features: "Whosoever is fearful and afraid, let him return and depart early from Mount Gilead." The effect appears to have been quite remarkable, because "there returned of the people twenty and two thousand, and there remained ten thousand." Gideon went on to put into effect his second stage, consisting of a psychological performance test. The Bible describes it thus:

> And the Lord said unto Gideon. The people are yet too many; bring them down unto the water, and I will try them for thee there; and it shall be, that of whom I say unto thee, This shall go with thee, the same shall go with thee; and of whomsoever I say unto thee, This shall not go with thee, the same shall not go.
>
> So he brought down the people into the water; and the Lord said unto Gideon, Every one that lappeth of the water with his tongue, as a dog lappeth, him shalt thou set by himself; likewise every one that boweth down upon his knees to drink.
>
> And the number of them that lapped, putting their hand to their mouth, were three hundred men; but all the rest of the people bowed down upon their knees to drink water.
>
> And the Lord said unto Gideon, By the three hundred men that lapped will I save thee, and deliver the Midianites into thine hand; and let all the other people go every man into his place.
>
> Gideon obeyed, and smote the Midianites.

Gideon's test is rather different from that used nowadays, but it is based on the same principle. Looking at those who come forward to the selection process for any particular job, there are always some who can produce two to three times as much as some others, whether the product be coal to be hewn, letters to be typed, or cars to be built. The more complicated the process, the greater the disparity. It is obviously useful to sort out those most likely to produce the most, and psychological tests are very adept at doing just that. Consider some figures showing comparisons between the number of failures in groups selected by means of psychological ability tests and in group selection by other means and trained simultaneously.

As Vernon and Parry point out in their book, *Personnel Selection in the British Forces* from which these figures are taken, "the respective failure rates...showed great improvement attributable to personnel selection." Thus, of drivers selected by the old method, 30 percent were failures, of those selected by the new method, only 14 percent failed. Among clerks, the respective figures are 11 percent and 4 percent. For special operators, the largest of the groups studied, the failure rate under the old method of selection was 60 percent, under the new method it was only 7 percent!

Special interest was shown in the selection of tradesmen and mechanics, where it was possible to compare the failure rates on training courses of some 10,000 army tradesmen, selected by four different procedures during four months of 1942. Those nominated by C.Os. or technical officers had a failure rate of 19.2; those nominated at their own request, one of 19.6; those called up by the Ministry of Labour as semi-qualified tradesmen, one of 19.4. The failure rate of those selected by psychological procedures was 11.1.

Similar figures can be quoted from the other services. The failure rate among naval mechanics and fitters dropped from 14.7 percent to 4.7 percent. What is possibly even more important, the introduction of psychological methods not only reduced the failure rate but also extracted a much larger proportion of trainees from available naval recruits without denuding other mechanical branches which were also making large demands at that time.

It would be pointless to multiply instances, all of which show improvements of between fifty and several hundred percent. Nor can one go through the thousands of published reports dealing with selection work without coming away with the firm conviction that where psychological selection procedures are introduced by competent psychologists, spectacular improvements in performance and considerable reduction in failure rates can be confidently expected.

One example may serve to illustrate the value of ability testing in selection. It has been estimated that the U.S. government saves $16 billion a year by using selection tests for its many employees; that is more than the total budget of many middle-sized nations! And of course it not only saves money but it also improves performance. And the procedure is not only useful for the state, or for industry, by putting a square peg in a square hole, we also do a favour to the person so selected to do what he is best at, rather than being buried in the sort of job for which he is not suited.

Many different tests are of course in use for many different purposes, but it has been found over hundreds of jobs and professions, and equally testing procedures that those tests having the highest g loading, that is, the best measures of general intelligence, turned out to be the best predictors of income and occupational successes. It is not always realized how IQ differences can come into even the most elementary type of skill. Data from the U.S. Army showed that anyone, with a little training, can make a jam sandwich, but to make good scrambled eggs you need a few points more of IQ!

One important point should be stressed, because neglect of its significance may inadvertently suggest quite erroneous conclusions. When we say that a certain test, or battery of tests, is useful in selecting the best among a group of applicants for a given job, how do we know? The answer is that when selected those with the highest scores do better, in the long run, than those with lower scores. But there is an obvious problem—what is one's criterion for assessing how well people actually do on the job? Does psychiatrist A really cure more neurotics than psychiatrist B, or does he cure them more quickly? Does secretary X do the great variety of her jobs better than secretary Y? Perhaps she is better on the telephone, types less fast but more accurately, is good at personal relations but not as reliable as Y—how do we assemble all this, and much more, into a final judgment of respective excellence? And how do we eliminate subjectivity in the judgments—perhaps X is prettier and more nubile than Y? The point is that unless we have a really objective, reliable, and meaningful criterion, we cannot readily evaluate the contributions made by our selection tests!

An example may make this clear. Pilot selection was of the utmost importance for the American Air Force during the Second World War. Pilots accepted for training cost a great deal to train, and, if incompetent, could write off multi-million dollar planes, as well as kill themselves. A large and expensive battery of tests was assembled, and pilots were admitted for training on the basis of results. After training, they were given a passing-out test which consisted of a specified number of manouvres which were rated independently by two experienced instructors. When the test scores were correlated with the instructors' ratings, the results caused consternation—there was no relationship at all! Were the tests utterly useless? Somebody had the good sense to enquire how closely the two instructors agreed in their judgments, which after all formed the criterion. The answer was that the correlation was effectively nil—their judgments didn't agree at all! And with an invalid and meaningless criterion, obviously even a perfect battery of tests could not agree with such a criterion! It became necessary to film all the instruments in flight to get an objective record of how well the prospective pilots had done, and laboriously construct a proper assessment of the excellence of the finished flight; when this was done, there was good agreement between test and criterion. The selection battery worked very well, and is still widely used.

There is another consideration. Consider a situation in which you have 100 applicants for twenty jobs of a given kind. You pick the best twenty on the basis of your tests, and you find that there is a correlation of .30 between test and performance on the job. This is not a high correlation, but as already pointed out it would probably be much higher if you had a perfect criterion, which is unlikely. But also consider that you are running your correlation over the twenty best candidates; if you had admitted all 100, the range of talent would have been much wider, and your correlation much higher! Critics sometimes argue that the figure of .30 is a sort of ceiling beyond which predictive accuracy does not go, and that is too low to be valuable. But the .30 observed does not reflect the true value of the test for reasons given. When you make allowance for the factors mentioned, and correct statistically for lack of validity in the criterion, and using only selected applicants, the apparent value of the selection process becomes clearer, giving correlations in the 60s and 70s. Selection tests work, and work very well indeed. Hence their wide acceptance in industry, commerce, the armed forces, and elsewhere.

The position is very different when we turn from occupational selection to vocational guidance. Here we do not have to select the most promising candidates from a large number of applicants to carry out a specific job; we have to predict for a given person which of many thousand different jobs he might be best suited for. This is very much more difficult, for obvious reasons. Instead of being able to test for the presence of qualities needed for one job, we must now assess the relative presence or absence of abilities involved in a large number of jobs, thus multiplying the amount of testing required a thousandfold. Instead of dealing with a job, about which it is easy to acquire information, we deal with a whole congeries of different jobs masquerading under the same name. A surgeon, a G.P., a consultant in psychiatry, a medical historian, the editor of the *Lancet,* and the head of (the now abolished) LCC medical services, all come under the general heading of "doctor" Nevertheless, their occupations, and therefore, presumably, the abilities needed are as diverse as is conceivable. The term 'secretary' may refer to someone carrying out a highly confidential and qualified job, requiring great intelligence and initiative; it may also refer to a girl whose time is spent almost entirely on gossip and making tea.

Even if all available jobs could be neatly catalogued with specific requirements, nevertheless our knowledge of the abilities and temperamental traits relevant to success in any of these occupations is still so much lacking that, without very large-scale research, predictions would mostly be very difficult. We have information on some twenty or thirty out of the many thousands of jobs between which a choice has to be made, and there is no reasonable prospect of adding to this number to any considerable extent in the near future.

Perhaps one of the main reasons for this comparatively undeveloped study of vocational guidance as compared with industrial selection is the fact that while occupational selection more than pays for itself—in all the examples given, the immediate financial return to the company initiating the investigation more than paid for the whole inquiry in less than one year—there is little immediate financial gain for anyone in vocational guidance. It pays for itself in terms of individual happiness and productivity, and therefore, presumably, in greater social usefulness of the person successfully advised, but such long-range considerations seldom play a role in our social and political thinking, and such work as has been done in this field has been undertaken almost exclusively by private organizations like the National Institute of Industrial Psychology (now, alas, defunct), which are not subsidized by the government.

In spite of the difficulties attending vocational guidance, there is good evidence that, even in its very early stage of development and in the absence of much desirable knowledge, it does have potentialities far beyond what one would have imagined. I will only quote one example, the Birmingham Vocational Experiment, in which 1,639 children were followed up over a period of two years, and 603 of them over four years. Half of these, the experimental group, had been given vocational guidance along psychological lines, the other half, the control group, had only received advice from teachers used as advisers, in the usual way. Various criteria were used to judge the efficacy of the advice, such as employers' ratings and the length of time during which positions were held. We may divide both the experimental, psychologically guided group, and the control group into two parts—those who took jobs in accordance with advice, and those who took jobs not in accordance with advice. Taking the psychologically guided group first, we find that at the end of two years, 90 percent of those in "accordance" jobs were satisfied with their jobs, whereas only 26 percent of those in "non-accordance" jobs were. At the end of four years, the percentages were, respectively, 93 and 33. Thus, of those who followed the psychological advice, about three times as many were satisfied as of those who did not follow the psychological advice.

The position is quite different in the control group, where of those who followed the advice, 64 percent were satisfied with their jobs after two and after four years, whereas of those who did not follow the advice, 76 percent and 78 percent were satisfied. Thus, if anything, the children who followed the employment officer's advice were less satisfied than those who did not!

Findings relating to the retention of jobs were similar. In the experimental group, those in "accordance" jobs retained their first job for over two years in 60 percent of the cases, and over four in 46 percent of the cases; percentages in the "non-accordance" jobs were 11 and 11 respectively. In the control group, the figures for "accordance" jobs were 37 percent and 27 percent for two and four years respectively; for "non-accordance" jobs they were 33 percent and 26 percent respectively. Thus, there is practically no difference in retention of jobs in the control group between "accordance" and "non-accordance" boys and girls; there is a very large difference in the psychologically guided group. This experiment carried out under the auspices of the National Institute of Industrial Psychology, was done many years ago. Its findings had been largely neglected by society until the Second World War, when vocational guidance and occupational selection came together in the Forces Personnel Selection work.

These are just some of the practical uses of ability testing. Greater, more widespread use of these procedures would quite certainly lead to greater equality of opportunity, and less "old school tie" nepotism. It would open up society to those with the greatest ability, rather than to the scions of feudal families or the progeny of wealthy parents. It would ensure an appropriate education for all grades of ability, without punishing the outstandingly bright, as we now do, by refusing them the specially advanced instruction they need, or the very dull by forcing them into absurd competition with others congenitally much brighter. Ability testing would not make this into a perfect world, but it would do a little to make it more just, more compassionate, more fair. That, I feel, is a worthwhile aim for us to pursue. That critics should have suggested that IQ testing impedes the search for equality, and is hostile to its achievements, is part of the paradox I mentioned at the beginning of this chapter; it is an absurdity, a tragicomedy in the history of science.

Critics like Stephen J. Gould, disregarding the evidence, would have none of this. "Intelligence," he says, "is a breakthrough concept." Triumphantly, he goes on: "The tests are nearly useless as tools, as confirmed by the well-documented fact that such tests do not predict anything except success at school. Earnings, occupation, productivity—all the important measures of success—are unrelated to test scores." Wow! Clearly Gould is quite unacquainted with the thousands of studies that have proved the opposite, only a few typical ones of which have been cited here. Let me here just give one example of Gould's foolishness, relating to the notion that IQ is unrelated to earnings. Helmuth Nyborg has analysed data provided by the United States Army about 4,376 middle-aged veterans, giving their IQ scores and their earnings. The results are shown in figure 6.2. The IQ scores are given in deciles, that is, the highest percent, the next 10 percent, and so on down to the lowest 10 percent.

What do we find? There is a straight downward trend in earnings from the highest IQ group to the lowest. The group of veterans did not include anyone of really low intelligence; they would have been rejected at intake. They did not include many of the highest intelligence; they would have been selected out and prevented from army duty by

FIGURE 6.2

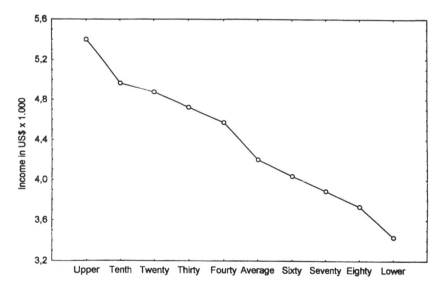

Total household income by general intelligence in 4.376 middle-aged men

Relation between IQ and average earnings in middle-aged adults.

virtue of their professional status. Had the group been included, the line would have been even steeper. Many similar studies exist to show how wrong Gould is, here as elsewhere. How can one trust a person so prejudiced as to neglect overwhelming evidence?

There is another point. There are studies showing little difference in earnings between high and low IQ groups, but they deal with people of thirty or under. Now, working-class people achieve maximum earnings by that age, or before; middle-class people have only just finished professional training, and are at the lowest point of their earning curve; ten or twenty years later they would earn many times more than at that early point of their careers. To make a comparison at that age is farcical and meaningless; to be realistic one would have to compare high- and low-IQ groups with regard to their highest earnings, or total lifetime earnings. If that were done, the data might produce an even higher correlation between earnings and IQ. Look again at table 2.1; is there any doubt that high IQ goes with high earnings?

It is of course true also that sporting ability, as in boxing, tennis, golf, soccer, or American football, even in conjunction with moderate IQ, can lead to great riches. So for talent in music, dancing, acting, and other types of entertainment. The numbers involved are tiny, but the people concerned are very visible, and their earnings often quite prodigious. But overall they produce only a tiny anomaly in the comparisons based on millions. And of course earnings are not the only reward for work; a successful scientist receives satisfaction from the work he is doing, even though he could earn much more if he used his intelligence in a more readily saleable way. It is not suggested that there is anything like a perfect relation between earnings and IQ; to say anything like this would be foolish. Many factors in addition to IQ come into consideration. But that IQ does strongly predict earning power is not in any doubt.

There is one important use of IQ testing that is seldom mentioned in the textbooks, and that was emphasized in Herrnstein and Murray's famous (or infamous?) book, *The Bell Curve*. The authors argued, and applied evidence for their argument, that as meritocracy extends its influence, ability and job requirements will come closer and closer together, compared to feudal times, when a man's job was defined by the social status of his family. There was little social mobility, and hence there were high IQ people in all social groups—almost like a caste system, in fact. Now the bright rise, the dull sink on the whole, and social-class lines become much more clearly drawn in terms of intellectual ability. Family influence, nepotism, and similar factors still play a role, of course, but it is much less influential than it used to be.

These developments, aided by IQ testing, are also assisted by the increasing requirements for high intelligence. The large number of jobs requiring brawn rather than brains is being reduced drastically by the introduction of robots, and other devices allocating heavy muscular work to machines. This makes a large, low IQ slice of the population redundant, increases unemployment of a permanent kind, and leads to the creation of an "underclass," unable to cope with an increasingly complex world. What once required many typists to do is now done by a computer and photocopier outfit, supervised by a high IQ operative. Work that used to be done by thousands of bank clerks is now done centrally by computer. Luddite trade unions still force management to "carry" thousands of employees whose true usefulness is zero, and whose replacement by machines would improve services and lower costs, but as the demise of the communist empire showed, overmanning and visions of permanent and universal employment are unrealistic responses to real changes.

The acceptance of this factual argument was hindered by irrelevant disputes about racial differences in IQ—the argument would remain valid in a society exclusively inhabited by white, blue-eyed, flaxen-haired Vikings! It was also rendered less acceptable because the authors advocated methods of counteracting this general trend which to most people seemed unlikely to produce any great reliefs. Strip these irrelevances away, and we are truly faced with a very real problem. Already stress levels in all strata of society have risen dramatically, at least in part because of these changes, and progress along these lines seems inexorable. If in a feudal society your father is a smith, then there is a very high probability that you will be a smith; there is no threat to your employment, or your position in society. Now the whole function of the smithy may suddenly be taken over by an automated assembly, and you have no certainty of employment. If you are bright, you may study computer technology and rise in the social scale, as you would never have been able to do in feudal times. If you are not—Heaven help you! Unemployment and sinking into the underclass awaits you.

I will not follow Herrnstein and Murray into suggesting a way out of this situation. The function of the scientist is to report facts, and theories based on these facts; society must ponder the problems thrown up by these facts, and decide what to do. The problem is much wider than the competence of the individual scientist. Knowing about intelligence, and observing social trends may suffice to highlight the problems, but to answer it much further knowledge (economics, sociology, politics, international trade, industrial production) is needed. The scientist's contribution is limited but important. Problems do not usually go away; they require serious consideration and some form of a solution. It is time society addressed this problem, and tried to find a solution. In this process the expert in IQ testing may play a small but not unimportant role; no more is claimed here.

7

Can We Improve IQ?

Seeing how important IQ is in education and real life, it is not surprising that many efforts have been made over the years to take underprivileged children, usually blacks, and attempt to raise their IQ, and also their scholastic achievements, by means of special educational help, assistance with living conditions, and in many other ways. Given that 20 percent to 30 percent of the determining factors for IQ differences are environmental, it should in theory be possible to do quite a lot for such youngsters, and many claims have in fact been made for specific methodologies. In this section I shall examine some of these claims. I will not dwell too long on some early studies that were obviously open to severe criticism. Thus the so-called Iowa studies, carried out in the early thirties, showed for instance that six children, placed in an orphanage ward with older retarded females for an average of six months, went from a mean IQ of 63 to one of 93! But the initial tests were given when the kids were less than seventeen months of age, when IQ simply could not be measured reliably. Many other studies allegedly producing similar increases were reported, but all have been criticized and few if any experts would nowadays place any reliance to these claims.

In 1946, a great deal of interest was shown in the reports of Bernardine Schmidt who studied the educational, social and vocational development of mentally retarded children. Her subjects were 254 retarded boys and girls between twelve and fourteen years of age, with IQs ranging from 27 to 69. Some of the children were used as a control for others who received treatment. The study continued for eight years. During years one to three, the children participated in either experimental or nonexperimental schools, while years four to eight consisted of a follow-up of the students after they had left the schools. The special training programme used consisted of several different types of teaching: (a) The children were taught personal hygiene and grooming, and given job responsibilities; (b) they were given academic training in reading, writing, spelling and arithmetic; (c) they were given training to develop their "hard skills," such as sewing, carpentry, cooking, etc.; (d) they were provided with better work and study habits and experiences, along with the provision of occupational and vocational information and guidance. For 254 in the experimental group, the mean IQ rose after eighteen months from 52 to 65, and after another eighteen months to 72. On the final school testing, mean IQs of 83 were reported, which rose to 89 during the after-school period. This is a gain of 37 points! By the end of the school period, only 7 percent were reported as still retarded. The controls if anything went down in IQ, so that a comparison gave the experimental group a gain of some 40 points of IQ.

Critics soon discovered many areas of doubt! First, Schmidt had reported the initial IQ of her children to be about 50, but the schools assigned to these classes only children between 50 and 75 IQs. In fact at the time of Schmidt's study the average IQ of children in relevant classes was 69. How can we explain this 30-point discrepancy? Second, no-one in the Chicago system knew of her having been a "head teacher," as she claimed, or that she had been supervising a number of classes. The teachers in the schools in question were surprised to hear that Schmidt had planned and supervised their work! Third, many other discrepancies were found, and there was a plethora of arithmetical errors and discrepancies in her tables. Schmidt in her reply made no attempt to explain why the initial IQs of the children in her experiment were so much lower than the average for similar classes, nor why she claimed to be a "head teacher" who planned and supervised other teachers. Herman Spitz, who has summarized Schmidt's work, the criticisms and her replies, concluded that, "the best estimate of the Bernardine study is that it was largely, if not entirely, fraudulent and that in fact there was no miracle in Chicago." Note that others who tried her methods (which in any case were not in any sense original) failed to produce any similar miraculous improvement.

Bernardine Schmidt was followed thirty-five years later by another Chicago teacher, Marva Collins, who made even more remarkable claims. She had opened a private school for children who came from public schools (in the American sense, i.e., inner-city comprehensives) labelled retarded, troublesome, and disturbed. According to full-page advertisements in the *Wall Street Journal*, at ages five to ten her pupils read and discussed the classics, rather than the banal Dick and Jane books. According to the advertisement, it is humbling to see "retarded" youngsters expound on Thoreau, Dante, Aristotle and Chaucer. There was a "docudrama" on television, and she was invited to lecture all over the country at $10,000 a lecture. No reports on her work were ever published in a professional journal, and one investigator found that half of her students failed the California Achievement Test—not a difficult test at those ages. As Spitz, after detailing her story, remarks, this sadly familiar affair "demonstrated once again how the wish to believe can cloud our critical faculties."

There are many other projects of a similar kind, but perhaps the most famous has been the "Milwaukee Miracle." This was initiated by Dr. Rick Heber, who claimed that the IQs of twenty deprived children had been raised by some 30 points. The project was very expensive, costing some $14 million—something like $700,000 per child! The alleged results were never published in technical journals but given to the credulous press which eagerly accepted these claims. Heber actually went to prison for misuse of research grant money, which he apparently spent on racehorses and the like. Finally, a colleague of Heber published a serious account of the major results of all this work. Much more modest findings suggested a true increase in IQ which however did not last very long; as usual results are only temporary. Furthermore, there have been many justified criticisms of this final report, drawing attention to serious weaknesses in methodology.

It is interesting to consider the treatment this project received *before* any serious journal publication of results. Heber had been appointed chief adviser on mental retardation to a U.S. president, and serious papers suggested that the project had "settled once and for all" the questions of heredity versus environment for the intelligence of slum children (*Washington Post*), and that Heber "has proved" that IQ could be raised more than 30 points (*New York Times*). The *Times* did not print one word about the Heber scandal, neither did the news weeklies, *Science* magazine, or the national television networks. (They all reported in great detail the alleged fraudulence of Sir Cyril Burt, whose data supported the genetic position, although they had not previously reported his positive results.)

One further protagonist of the teachability of IQ notions deserves mention, namely Reuben Feuerstein and his theory of mediated learning experience. He pioneered an intervention programme called "Environmental Enrichment" (IE), implemented by the processes of mediated learning. This mediator is defined in terms of "arousing in the child vigilance, curiosity, and sensitivity to the mediated stimulus, and creating for, and with, the child temporal, spatial, and causal relationships among stimuli." According to Feuerstein, "individual differences in cognitive functioning, stemming from environmental influences, are mainly dependent on the quality and quantity of mediated learning experience (MLE) that the individual received. The more properly mediated the learning experience, the more effective will be the learner's cognitive modifiability." This system has been widely used, particularly in Israel with immigrant children. Does it work?

Much of the literature is propagandist rather than evaluative, hortatory rather than critical. We are told much about what *can* be done with the method, but little about what *has* been done. The studies that have been reported are weak in methodology and statistics, and where actual IQ measures are concerned, give little evidence of unusual achievement. In one study, not atypical of many others, Feuerstein compared the effects of an IE programme with a regular school curriculum, referred to as GE (general enrichment). Over a two-year-period some tests showed a slight improvement of the IE group over the GE group. Thus on the Primary Mental Abilities test of Thurstone, the final total score (*not* IQ!) was 172 for the IE group, as compared with 164 for the GE group. On many tests there was no significant improvement. The whole movement is an example of the triumph of hope over experience; Feuerstein's methods do not seem to perform better than many less ambitious ones.

Finally, a few words may be said about Project Head Start, inaugurated May 18, 1965, by President Lyndon B. Johnson as part of his war on poverty. More than 1,600 federal grants were awarded, and 9,508 graded centers were established so that hundreds of thousands of underprivileged children could be given a "head start" during the summer months before entering kindergarten or first grade. The project was later extended to reach some 530,000 children in 11,000 centres, and four-year programmes were instituted. By 1984, the programme, which is still functioning, had received a billion dollars (1,000 million), the latest appropriation planned by President Clinton for 1998 is 8 billion dollars! The programme does not only provide early intellectual and educational stimulation, but also nutritional and medical assistance, and it involves parents in the education of their children, and attempts to foster social competence and improved motivation. Thousands of studies have been done to evaluate the effects of the project which of course go well beyond increasing IQ levels. As far as IQ is concerned an evaluation by the Westinghouse Learning Corporation is perhaps the best technically, and not atypical in its outcome. Choosing four centres for their assessment, they compared similar groups of Head Start and non-Head Start children but produced no reliable differences between experimental and comparison groups. The children who had participated in full year programmes also failed to show any significant effects overall. When a "Follow Through" project was started to extend into primary grades the special training given to Head Start children, in the hope that a more sustained effect would produce a more permanent effect, it became clear again that no improvements in IQ were forthcoming.

These and countless other programmes have led to certain conclusions which are now quite firmly established. You can, by assiduous efforts, increase IQ a little, but it will soon revert to its previous level. Much of the effect, if any, is probably one of "teaching the test," that is, teaching the children something related to the context or working of the test. Typical IQ tests used in such studies use vocabulary items where the meaning of words is examined; these words can be part of the specialized training, and often are. Similarly, letter and number sequence tests benefit from additional learning of the letters of the alphabet, or of number properties, and number manipulation. Improvements in IQ due to such cases are clearly not real improvements in intelligence, and vanish once the special teaching is discontinued. To say this is not to say that you cannot improve children's scholastic achievement by added and improved teaching, increased motivation, and more interesting presentation; obviously all this can be done, and when you add greater maintenance of discipline, tremendous improvements can be achieved. In fact, by reversing the changes in teaching introduced by "progressive" thinkers in the educational field, you can bring the educational achievements of children up to the standard of fifty years ago. But what you cannot do is to improve in any lasting manner the IQs of these children.

To say this is not to play down the very real achievements of the Head Start program. Concentration on IQ changes obscures the many real advantages enjoyed by the children affected, and the general educational achievements often reported. The early stress on IQ improvement was undoubtedly misplaced. Critics should not dwell exclusively on this relative failure; the programme was much broader in its aims, and should be evaluated in these terms.

Is there nothing in the environment that can raise the IQ? If 30 percent of the observed differences in IQ are due to environmental causes, surely it should be possible to discover some of these environmental agents. One of the reasons for the failure of the Head Start and all the other programmes to make much difference is the simple fact that little if any research has been directed at finding such evanescent causes. This may sound unlikely, but what seems to have happened is this. Psychologists who believe in the behaviourist chimera of environmental determination of IQ have simply listed possible (and plausible) environmental causes, but have refused to develop appropriate methods of demonstrating that these beliefs were in fact justified. They imagined that you could prove that parents who had large numbers of books in their home, bought prestigious newspapers and magazines, and sent their children to good schools *produced* the children's high IQ by means of such environmental factors. But clearly that is a naive way of looking at things; the high IQ of the child might simply be a consequence of direct inheritance, regardless of the books, magazines, and schools. The fact that adopted children do not seem to benefit much in the long run would seem to disprove the environmentalist argument. As already mentioned, unrelated children in the same adoptive homes show no IQ connection; this is impossible to reconcile with the hypothetical influence on IQ of the family environment.

Thus the task of scientifically *proving* the importance of a given environmental factor for raising the IQ level is not an easy one; you have to demonstrate that heredity is not the proper cause, and that can only be shown by actual genetic or intervention studies. And as we have seen, when such intervention has been tried, it has only had slight and quickly dissipating results. However, there is one exception to this rule, and interestingly enough the environmental agent involved is not psychological or educational, but itself biological. I am referring to vitamin and mineral supplementation of a child's diet that is deficient as far as these micro-nutrients are concerned. The Germans have a saying: "Man ist was man isst" (one is what one eats), and perhaps the brain can only function when certain vitamins and minerals are included in the diet. This, as I shall document, is apparently the case, and considerable increases in IQ can be produced in children deficient in micro-nutrients.

Before turning to the data, I will set down the detailed theory involved, and what we may expect: (1) Improvement in IQ due to dietary supplementation will only occur in a minority of ordinary, well-fed children, because most will have an adequate diet so far as vitamins and minerals are concerned. (2) Improvement will only occur in tests of fluid ability (nonverbal tests), and not in tests of crystallized ability (verbal tests). Taking supplementation pills may improve your ability to take in information, reason abstractly and solve problems, but it is not likely to give you knowledge you didn't have before. (3) The effect is likely to be greatest in the very young, less in the secondary school child, and least in the late teens. (4) Large groups are needed to establish the result. This is due to the assumption that only a proportion (say 25 percent) of the children tested are likely to be deficient in micronutrients. If the whole group tested improves by 3.5 IQ points, as compared with a placebo group, then the 25 percent who are deficient would improve by 14 points, the remainder by 0 points. (This is of course just an illustration. Vitamin deficiency is not an all-or-none effect, but rises gradually from none to severe, hence there would be a gradation in IQ improvement.) But while an improvement by 14 points is quite remarkable, to pin down an overall improvement of 3.5 points needs a large sample.

There are ten recent studies all of which have found differences between experimental and placebo groups in the right direction. Not all the differences were statistically significant, probably because in some the samples were too small, duration of supplementation too short, badly chosen tests of IQ used, and for various other reasons. But the fact remains that out of ten studies not a single one failed to show that micronutrient supplementation *increased* the level of fluid intelligence, and *failed* to increase the level of crystallized ability. Furthermore, the greatest increases occurred in the younger children, as expected. The average improvement over all the groups was 3.5 points of IQ, as compared with placebo groups.

Only one study investigated the question of whether it was only the children deficient in micro-nutrients who benefitted. Thus, the largest of all by a long chalk, used four hundred children in all, and took blood samples of the children at the beginning of the experiment, and at the end three months later. Analysis of these blood samples showed that it was indeed the children with low vitamin and mineral (mainly vitamin) levels who improved, with little or no improvement for the children with an adequate balance.

It should perhaps be said that on re-testing, a child's IQ increases simply because of the practice he has had in doing IQ tests (test sophistication). Thus it is always necessary to have a control group that receives placebo pills similar to the genuine supplementation pills. Improvement thus means the advantage of the therapy group over the control group, rather than raw improvement scores.

FIGURE 7.1

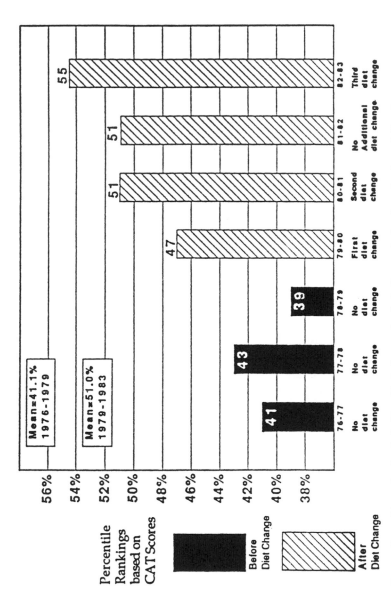

Percentile ranking of schools in New York State schools before and after introduction of diet change.

These ten studies are all relatively recent, but there had of course been encouraging signs before that IQ would respond to supplementation. R.F. Harrell had already in 1955 published the results of an experiment showing that giving pregnant women in deprived areas vitamin supplementation increased the IQ of their offspring by 8 points later in life. Even more impressive, and indicative of the possible social importance of the effects of dietary improvement, were the results of a large-scale study concerned with educational achievement. Around 1980, the New York schools made revision in the type of food supplied to the children, eliminating preservatives, synthetic colours, and synthetic flavours. They also diminished progressively high use of sucrose foods. Such changes for the better were made during 1979–1980, 1980–1981, and 1982–1983, and during these years a scholastic achievement test, given throughout the country, was routinely administered. This test decides the scholastic status of the schools involved. Figure 7.1 shows the results. New York schools were at the 19th percentile, that is, well below the average, in 1978–1979. They rose to the 47th percentile, or just below the mean, in 1979–1980, and to the 51st percentile (just above the mean) in 1980–1981. No change in the diet during the next year produced no change in the standing of the schools. But 1982–1983 again increased the school standing to the 55th percentile, that is, well above the mean. There is thus a considerable improvement in the scholastic achievement of hundreds of thousands of children due to slight improvements in nutrition! Clearly we are dealing with an important issue here.

You may feel that I am not being honest here. I have said that micronutrient supplementation improves *fluid* (nonverbal) intelligence but not *crystallized* (verbal) ability. Yet here we have a powerful effect on academic achievement, that is, on crystallized ability! The answer is quite simple. The influence of supplementation is on fluid ability; this enables the children to learn better *after* receiving the supplementation (or the better diet in the case of the New York schools). This better learning results in the better achievement scores of the children *a year after* the improvements were introduced. But in the IQ testing carried out in the experiments mentioned, the tests of crystallized ability in fact deal with knowledge acquired *before* the supplementation took effect! Only teaching that took place after the beginning of supplementation could have an effect, and we did find such an effect when looking at school performance of the children in our experiment that measured achievements in subjects taught *subsequent* to the beginnings of supplementation.

These studies only hint at what might be accomplished. All the experiments dealt with ordinary, healthy, well-fed children mostly of middle-class origin. If it is in such a group we find one-in-four to be seriously deficient in vitamins and minerals, and likely to respond with the significant rise in IQ after supplementation, what might we not find in a study of deprived inner-city children, or children in an African famine area? The refusal of government agencies to finance or undertake such studies is an indication of how seriously they take the problem, and how much importance they attribute to it. President Clinton is happy to promise 8 billion dollars for a Head Start programme that is widely acknowledged to produce no increase in IQ, but refuses to spend 1 percent of that amount which would revolutionize the whole of American education. Quem deus vult perdere...(Whom the gods would destroy...).

8

Many Intelligences?

I have already mentioned the major difference between Galton and Binet. Galton thought in terms of one intelligence, Binet in terms of many intelligences. Spearman put Galton's notion into a testable statistical form; Thurstone did the same for Binet's. The final outcome of their empirical studies was, as I have pointed out, a compromise; a general factor of intelligence (g) was much the most powerful, but in addition there were a number of special abilities each of which contributed only a small amount to the total picture, but this small amount could be very important in special cases. If you want to be an outstanding physicist or astronomer, writer or historian, engineer or architect, you would need, in addition to a high IQ, special numerical, verbal, or visuo-spatial abilities, respectively. It is this combination that is important; IQ without special abilities is not enough!

How many of these special abilities are there? So far something like two dozen have been uncovered, measured, and made into tests; probably a few have been missed, but I doubt if many more of any importance will be found. John Carroll has published an 800-page book, *Human Cognitive Abilities*, which surveys all the published work, and that roughly is the estimate he ends up with. He divides his factors up into domains; domains of language, of reasoning, of memory and learning, visual perception, auditory perception, idea production, cognitive speed, and psychomotor abilities; clearly many of these are rather peripheral to what we mean by "intelligence." But they all correlate positively with IQ, as well as measuring something over and above in their special fields.

This hierarchical model—lowest level, individual tests or test items, next level special abilities identified by observed correlations between tests or test items, highest level identified by correlations between special abilities—contains an obvious problem. Looking at tests of special abilities, each contains essentially three separate abilities. First of all, it measures *g* or general intelligence. Second, it measures the special ability it was designed to measure. Third, it measures something specific to that test—something no other test measures. Thus you can never measure special abilities in isolation; you must use statistical methods to separate *g* from special ability from specific context. To do the latter you must use several special ability tests and average them. To do the former you must obtain a measure of *g* and subtract it from your special ability test score. This can be done, but it means a lot of testing!

This general hierarchical model is what we might call the "orthodox" model. But there are still psychologists who believe in "many intelligences," and continue to argue in favour of such a Binetian notion. The most famous was probably J.P. Guilford, whose *A Structure of Intellect Theory* maintains that there are at least 120 separate "intelligences" (later to grow to 150!), which are defined in terms of the combination of five operations of evaluation, convergent production, divergent production, memory, and cognition, six products (units, classes, relations, systems, train formations, and implications). and four types of content (figural, symbolic, semantic, and behavioural). He attempted to develop tests corresponding to every possible one of these 120 combinations, but his system failed the crucial test—the various tests he constructed were not independent of each other, but quite highly correlated. This of course was to be expected from the law of the "positive manifold" we have encountered before, but it completely destroyed Guilford's structural model. (The model did enable him to construct a large number of novel tests; this was one good outcome of this otherwise fruitless endeavour.)

More recently Howard Gardner has taken up the Binet mantle. He has asserted that there are *multiple intelligences,* of which he recognizes seven. These are verbal and mathematico-logical, spatial, musical, personal intelligence (interpersonal skills), intrapsychic capacity, and kinesthetic ability, as shown by outstanding athletes and dancers. It is a curious list; to call physical grace an "intelligence" seems somewhat odd. It remains to be seen if "intrapsychic capacity" can be measured, and means anything other than absence of neuroticism. But of course the main question is: Are there seven intelligences actually separate and independent? Oddly enough, Gardner avoids any answer to this question. He nowhere indicates how you could measure some of these "intelligences" (such as the intrapsychic ability), and he nowhere tries to discover the actual correlations between these "intelligences." But of course we do know that verbal ability, mathematico-logical ability, and spatial ability are quite highly correlated; to pretend that they are quite separate and independent is simply untrue.

Gardner relies on anecdotal evidence entirely. Thus he reports on five children with IQs from 125 to 133; none of them were good at the kinesthetic "movement" type of activity, and they excelled at different things—four in music, two in the visual arts, one in logic, two in language, and so on. It is difficult to understand what Gardner is saying that is not covered by the orthodox hierarchical model. He is attacking an imaginary foe, namely complete dependence on just one general intelligence, but that notion died many years ago, and has not had a single proponent over the last fifty years! You can always slay imaginary dragons with equally imaginary swords. Gardner never acknowledges the true orthodoxy, and never provides any empirical evidence for his esoteric and quite unrealistic notions. No wonder he gained high academic acclaim and a strongly partisan following—you only have to attack the IQ to become famous and popular; however nonsensical the attack, and however weak the alleged evidence for your own systems!

An offspring of the Gardner tradition is of particular interest because he exemplifies more clearly than most the fundamental absurdity of the tendency to class almost any type of behaviour as an "intelligence." David Goleman published his book on *Emotional Intelligence* with the rather ambitious claim that it was "the ground-breaking book that redefines intelligence and success." He also claimed that his EQ (emotional quotient) could "matter more than IQ"—although having no actual way of measuring this EQ. What he was saying, in principle, was simply that IQ is not everything, that high IQ people are not always the most successful in everyday life, and that emotional factors could be important. What then constitutes this "emotional intelligence"? There are five main "abilities" involved. The first is *knowing one's emotions:*"self-awareness is the keystone of emotional intelligence." Managing emotions is the second: "handling feelings so that they are appropriate is an ability that builds on self-awareness." The third is motivating oneself: "marshalling emotions in the service of a goal." Next comes recognizing emotions in others: "empathy is the fundamental "people skill." And finally we have *handling relationships*: skill in managing emotions in others. If these five "abilities" define "emotional intelligence," we would expect some evidence that they are highly correlated; Goleman admits that they might be quite uncorrelated, and in any case if we cannot measure them, how do we know how they are related? So the whole theory is built on quicksand; there is no sound scientific basis.

But there are even more serious objections that go to the root of the matter. As I have shown in figure 5.1, social and practical intelligence is a descriptive term that refers to our success at meeting the practical challenges of everyday life. IQ plays a part, but has never been suggested, as Goleman maintains, to act as the *only* actor in this play. Twelve others are suggested in my figure 5.1, which dates back many years, and expresses a general consensus among psychologists working in this field; there probably are many more. Those relevant to Goleman's misconceived "emotional intelligence" are personality, mental disorders and coping strategies; in particular, what is usually referred to as "neuroticism" in personality description almost exactly coincides with Goleman's concept. But neuroticism is not a *cognitive* ability, or lack of ability; it refers to quite another side of personality, namely the *emotional*. There are hundreds of investigations demonstrating the fact that emotional instability can interfere in practical matters with the proper application of our cognitive abilities, although Goleman seems unaware of this large literature. But to call this "emotional intelligence" makes the term "intelligence" scientifically meaningless; it brings together two unrelated things—neuroticism and intelligence in one ugly hybrid.

To illustrate the scientific absurdity of "emotional intelligence," consider a physicist who argued that "length" didn't tell you everything about the universe. Consequently, he argues, I introduced the concept of "hot lengths," this is much more useful because it explains many things that length cannot explain, such as boiling a kettle, or burning the toast. In presenting his case, the self-same physicist would conveniently forget to mention all the work that has been done on heat, and present his contribution as "ground-breaking." Can you imagine physicists taking such a contribution seriously? Psychology, alas, is still very far from being a science, and all this talk of "multiple intelligence" illustrates this only too well.

Is it true neuroticism lies at the heart of "social" or "practical" intelligence? Epstein and Meier, like Goleman dissatisfied with IQ measures, constructed a Constructive Thinking Inventory, correlated to IQ, which they argued would predict "success in living" better than IQ tests. It did, but correlations were derisorily small (from .19 to .39), and the Inventory correlated .59 with a measure of neuroticism. We are clearly dealing with an index of emotional reactivity, not of cognitive ability.

Perhaps the most academically acceptable exponent of intelligence as to what makes us successful in real life is Robert Sternberg. His "triarchic theory" is too complex to present here; it is "contextualist" in nature, and seeks to view intelligence in terms of the context in which it occurs. This implies, as the author acknowledges in his book *Beyond IQ*, a good deal of overinclusiveness. The contextualist view presented here is certainly highly inclusive in the sense that it includes within the realm of intelligence characteristics that typically might be placed in the realm of personality or motivation: "For example, motivational phenomena relevant to purposive adaptive behaviour—such as motivation to perform well in one's career—would be considered part of intelligence, broadly defined."

This, surely is a contradiction in terms. Science seeks to analyse *complex* phenomena, such as "success in life," into simpler, better defined, independent concepts, like intelligence, personality, motivation, and so on. Following Sternberg we would have to define height as part of intelligence; it has been shown that tall people are more successful, earn more, do better in the general business of competitive life. Does that make any sense? Surely the scientific method is to classify the various components (IQ, personality, motivation, physique, etc.) all of which contribute to worldly success, study them separately, look at their interaction, specify their relation with life success, and attempt to formulate theories *for each one separately* why they have the success they have in mediating worldly success.

Nor is it clear what "worldly success" means. I have become a successful psychologist earning less than an averagely competent shopkeeper. I could have become a multimillionaire had I concentrated on writing popular books on psychology—several of those I wrote in the interstices of my career were best-sellers selling in the millions. Would that have indicated greater worldly success? Money is not everything, and the satisfaction of doing scientific research was far more important to me than earning lots of money. Did I make the wrong choice? How *do* we define worldly success? There are problems here Sternberg does not begin to consider. Motivation to succeed does not define our private definitions of success. Is a very rich hooker successful? A dead hero? A fraudulent banker not found out by the police? A martyr? A genius like Lobachevsky, who discovered n-dimensional geometry and was considered insane and sent to the outer confines of Russia? The term "success" has no obvious scientific meaning, and requires far more research than it has received.

But what is the alternative to "multiple intelligences," and the challenge of delving into the real world? IQ is real enough in this context;

figure 6.2 shows this relation between IQ and income for a sample of veterans in the U.S. Army that covers the middle ground of intelligence. There is a direct, linear relationship—higher IQ measures higher income. This takes us from the academic field right into ordinary life, the life lived by largely nonacademic people. The same group shows that it does not pay to be high on neuroticism; when income is plotted against neuroticism, the slant shows high income to go with low neuroticism. Obviously IQ and neuroticism *together* predict income better than either alone—but that does not justify us in talking about "emotional intelligence."

The final verdict on recent works on "multiple intelligences" must be that they are premature crystallization of spurious orthodoxy. They are premature in that the necessary empirical work has not been done to show that, say, Gardner's seven "intelligences" are truly independent; they are spurious because what we already know is in contradiction to any such claim. The Spearman-Thurstone agreement on a *hierarchical* model, with a number of special abilities correlating together to give rise to a factor of general intelligence, is widely accepted and represents the fact adequately. There is no real alternative with anything like the same weight of evidence behind it.

I have tried, in the remainder of this book, to indicate how I consider research into what happens in the real world should be pursued. As my example I have purposely taken the most difficult topics I could find—genius and creativity, intuition and originality. Critics often hold out these topics as being outside the possibility of scientific research; IQ is all right, they say, but these concepts are of much greater importance and interest, and your measurement and science cannot begin to cope with them! Perhaps so, but hope springs eternal, and perhaps science can make some inroads into this forbidden field. One great advantage is that creativity *in real life* combines IQ and personality, motivation and special abilities in a fascinating combination that transcends the undefined "practical intelligence" and the "emotional intelligence" of the Gardners and Golemans. The discussion is necessarily rather lengthy, because the quest is complicated, but I have found that one worked-out example is worth a lot of purely theoretical writing.

Conforming to Sternberg's notion of "contextualism," I have also tried to fit creativity and genius into a contextual and historical background. This is interesting and helpful, but does not alter the main conclusion, as we shall see. But it does suggest an important division of the concept of "creativity." On the one hand, it is defined as a *trait*, normally distributed and measurable by tests of different kinds and varieties. Creativity can also be defined in terms of the successful production of original work (artistic, scientific, technological, whatever) which fills a social need and receives peer approbation. The relationship between the former, psychodynamic concept, and the latter, life work concept, illustrates much of what I have been saying at an abstract level in this chapter.

9

Creativity in History—What is Genius?

Hitherto, I have dealt almost entirely with *g*, or general intelligence. On occasion I have mentioned the existence of special abilities, like numerical, visuo-spatial, or verbal ability, but without dealing at any length with these important aspects of intelligence. One reason is of course that much less is known about special abilities; another that they have much less overall importance than general intelligence. But they do have some importance, and they do determine to some extent the social and practical application of our cognitive abilities. A physicist without exceptional numerical ability is unlikely to be outstanding in his field, but lack of verbal ability is quite common, and no hindrance. In a historian the opposite is true. It is particularly in relation to outstanding individuals that special abilities emerge as essential complements to general ability. This suggested to me that it might be interesting to discuss at some length one special ability, namely "creativity," and its exultant culmination, genius.

There is another reason for this choice. When talking to "hard" scientists, philosophers, or just high-IQ people who take an interest in psychology, about intelligence, they almost invariably tell me that IQ is not the measure of man, and that they would be far more interested in problems such as those presented by creativity and "genius"—the obvious implication being that science is incapable of dealing with such arcane matters. Now of course it is easy to reply that no psychologist ever suggested that IQ was the measure of man, and that Stephen J. Gould was just as wrong in entitling his book *The Mismeasure of Man*. IQ testing deals with one aspect of human behaviour, namely cognitive functioning; there are many other aspects of personality that are equally or more important. There is no *one* measure of man, and to suggest that there is is completely unrealistic. Newton studied the laws according to which bodies attract each other, but he never suggested that his formula was a measure of nature; there are many other laws.

Ever since I published my first article on intelligence in an academic journal in 1939, I have been intrigued by the notion of "creativity." Indeed, even before I ever knew there was such a thing as psychology, I read several books on "genius" by psychiatrists, philosophers, and historians. Being intrigued by the subject is not unusual; ever since the days of Aristotle and Plato, people have admired and wondered about the ways in which poets, painters, sculptors, scientists, dramatists, mathematicians, and musicians seemed almost effortlessly to transcend the bounds of ordinary existence, and soar on upwards into immortality. Admittedly, in the Dark Ages before the Renaissance, sanctity rather than genius was admired and sought after, but ever since then creativity has been lauded to the skies, and regarded with awe, admiration, and astonished delight.

Historians and philosophers of science have been rather more churlish. They have discriminated between the "context of discovery" *(ars inveniendi)* which is of course where creativity makes its appearance, and the "context of justification" *(ars demonstrandi)* where you have to justify and prove the correctness of your creative ideas. These two notions make the distinction between the way a scientific or mathematical result is discovered, and the way in which it is presented, justified, and defended to the scientific or mathematical community. Most philosophers have claimed that epistemology is concerned only with the context of justification; the context of discovery is properly the concern of psychology and history, not philosophy. You can almost hear the "And good riddance!" with which philosophers part company with the burdensome notion of creativity, and hand over the task of dealing with it to psychology—with the obvious belief that psychology will not be able to do much with the foundling.

But of couse the context of justification is much less interesting to most people than the context of discovery; it is also much more relevant to music and painting, poetry and drama. Who would want to "justify" *Hamlet*, or Beethoven's 9th, or Titian's paintings? But until recently psychologists have been rather reluctant to take up the burden, for every article on creativity there are hundreds on intelligence, which of course enters into creative achievement, but is not identical with it. Historians have been less reluctant, but does their work really throw much light on the process of creativity?

Many of my readers will be familiar with Arthur Koestler's book, *The Act of Creation*, which, in a very readable form, gives an excellent account of what historians have discovered about genius and creativity.

I remember him sending me a copy, and our discussing it. I told him how much I admired the way he had with words, and the interesting manner in which he had strung together his chapters. "But, Arthur, why haven't you even mentioned all the experiments psychologists have done with tests of creativity? Or the studies by Catherine Cox on intelligence and personality of geniuses? Or the experimental work of Westcott on intuition? You quote Freud twenty times, although he never did an experiment on creativity (or anything else!) in his life, but never a mention of Guilford, who inspired a large number of experimental studies on creativity, and taught us how to measure it. Where is all the work of the famous Institute of Personality Assessment and Research, pioneering countless studies of originality and creativity? You have a hundred pages of pontificating about specific humans, but not one mention of the hundreds of experiments in the field. Why?" He looked genuinely contrite, and said: "I didn't know all this work existed!" In this he did not differ from other historians of genius and creativity; they thrive on telling anecdotes unlikely to be true and authentic, but shy away from factual research.

One possible argument that Koestler was able to employ was the following: "Genius," he would say, "is a unique flowering of human intelligence; his recognitions may be delayed a hundred years or more, and by that time he is beyond the reach of all your testing and investigating. Even if he is recognized during his lifetime, he will be old and beyond his creative phase. And in addition, how many geniuses are there in a given year? Centuries may pass before another genius is born; can the psychologist wait that long?" "Well," I said, "you cannot see or approach a black hole, but Newton predicted the existence of such phenomena, and science now accepts their existence, and has much to say about their properties. Given the laws of gravitation, we can make fairly confident predictions about objects we cannot study directly. Newton predicted that the earth would be oblate, although there was no way of measuring this; for two hundred years scientists mounted expeditions to measure the length of the equator and the distance from pole to pole; some results favoured Newton, some contradicted his prediction. Now of course we know he was right, and few sensible people ever doubted it. Science is not purely inductive; there are ways of going beyond simple observation and developing hypothetico-deductive frameworks which can generate important predictions."

Can we find such predictions in the volumes of historians and philosophers? Do they put forward important new ideas that might serve to explain the act of creation? Let us consider Koestler's book, if only because he is often claimed to have put his finger on the cause of creativity. This he finds in the act of "bisociation," a term he coined "in order to make a distinction between the routine skills of thinking on a single 'plane,' as it were, and the creative act, which always operates on more than one plane." In other words, bisociation means the bringing together of the ideas, or sets of ideas, which have previously not been brought together, and which in association solve a problem or produce a joke, or create a work of art. True, but merely a description of what is occurring, not an explanation—and hardly an original description; it is in the tradition of associative thinking that goes back to Aristotle.

Do historians have any other contribution to make? There is a good deal of agreement on one other point, namely the psychopathology of genius. Aristotle was one of the first to declare that "no great genius has ever been without some madness," and this notion has persisted throughout the centuries. Many books have been written on the topic, most writers giving long lists of "mad" geniuses, others declaring that genius is as far above ordinary humanity as psychotics are below it, thus denying any possibility of psychopathology being associated with genius. There are many problems in getting at the truth. Psychiatric diagnoses are so unreliable and inaccurate even when applied to living persons studied in great detail over a long period of time, that the notion of applying it at second hand to people long dead is not appealing. Also it is difficult to know if psychopathology occurs more frequently in geniuses than in the common man, unless we can say with some certainty how frequently it occurred in the common man *at the time the genius lived*—which we do not really know!

The best evidence available, using an agreed system of classification (the Diagnostic and Statistical Manual of Mental Disorders—DSM-III), has been provided recently by Felix Post, who carefully read through the biographies written about 291 famous men of science, politics, music, art, writing, and thinking, and diagnosed them in terms of factual accounts of their behaviour. He found the least amount of marked or severe psychopathology in scientists (44 percent); composers showed 50 percent, politicians 59 percent, artists 56 percent, thinkers 62 percent and writers 88 percent. Whatever ordinary men might have shown of psychopathology during the last century (when most of the geniuses lived), it is unlikely to have been quite that much! So Post agrees with the best qualified psychiatrists who have done similar studies that there is a close relation between genius and psychopathology, but he also found strong evidence of what psychologists call ego-strength—a high degree of motivation, marked ability to work hard, intense concentration. Normally ego-strength and psychopathology are negatively correlated (around −0.60), thus the combination of the two make the genius quite unusual.

One other finding by Post and his predecessors is important—actual functional psychosis like schizophrenia, was almost entirely absent in his group. The dead hand of schizophrenia kills creativity; it is milder forms of psychopathology that allow it to flourish. But in the *Erbkreis* of the genius, that is, in his relatives, there is much psychopathology, and also much schizophrenia. There are many studies to support this view. Heston studied offspring of schizophrenic mothers raised by foster parents, and found that although about half showed psychosocial disability, the remaining half were notably successful adults, possessing artistic talents and demonstrating imaginative adaptations to life to a degree not found in the control groups. Karlsson found that among relatives of schizophrenics there was a high incidence of individuals of great creative achievement. McNeil studied the occurrence of mental illness in highly creative adopted children and their biological parents, discovering that the mental illness rates in the adoptees and in their biological parents were positively and significantly related to the creativity level of the adoptees.

Several studies have looked at psychopathology among creative artists well below the genius level, but nevertheless acknowledged among other artists and critics as being creative at a high level. An unusually large number of these artists was found to be troubled by psychopathology, usually severe bouts of depression. They tended to reject lithium therapy, which tends to at least ameliorate these bouts of depression, on the grounds that they were afraid the treatment would kill their creativity along with the depression. They were willing to suffer the depressive episodes in order to be creative when the depression lifted!

Like it or not, there is a close connection between psychopathology and creativity, although of course among the millions suffering from psychopathology, only a few are likely to be creative. The link seems to be causal, and not just correlational. How does it work? I shall return to that question later on. First of all we will have to look at what psychologists have done in order to measure creativity and intuition, and determine whether this work with groups of perfectly ordinary men and women is in line with the testimony of history, so briefly distilled in this section. It bears out Dryden's famous saying:

Great wits are sure to madness near alli'd—
And thin partitions do their bounds divide.

But note that they are "near alli'd," not identical, and that there are "thin partitions" between them. Dryden drew attention to a close relationship; he did not suggest that actual madness was the trademark of genius.

Knowing this much about genius can help us to decide whether the "creativity" we measure in more ordinary people is in essence similar to that shown by the genius. If it is, we would expect the creativity in less exalted people would also be linked with psychopathology; in this way we might be able to support the theory that the creativity we measure bears some relation to the creativity shown by the genius. Later on we shall come across other such links, until we finally find a causal nexus that ties together all these arguments. And of course above all we must be able to *define* genius so that we may recognize it, and pin it down.

While the notion of the "mad genius" was popular since the days of Plato and Aristotle, the scientific study of genius may be said to have started with the publication of Sir Francis Galton's *Hereditary Genius* in 1869. He defined genius in terms of social recognition or "eminence"; genius was an extreme point on a graded scale of eminence. Having argued that 250 men in a million became "eminent," and that there are 400 idiots and imbeciles in a million, he goes on to describe his system of "grading":

> The number of grades into which we may divide ability is purely a matter of option. We may consult our convenience by sorting Englishmen into a few large classes or into many small ones. I will select a system of classification that shall be easily comparable with the numbers of eminent men. We have seen that 250 men per million become eminent; accordingly, I have so contrived the classes in the following table that the two highest, F and G, together with X (which includes all cases beyond G, and which are unclassed), shall amount to about that number—namely, to 248 per million.

Galton's table is really very similar to ours. Figure 9.1, with classes F, G & X being at the extreme right-hand end. His classes A and a refer to the IQ 100–110 and the IQ 90–100 group, and so on. This is how he describes them, capital letters referring to the above 100 IQ, small letters the below 100 IQ group:

> It will, I trust, be clearly understood that the numbers of men in the several classes in my table depend on no uncertain hypothesis. They are determined by the assured law of deviations from an average. It is an absolute fact that if we pick out of each million the one man who is naturally the ablest, and also the one who is the most stupid, and divide the remaining 999,998 men into fourteen

classes, the average ability in each being separated from that of its neighbours by *equal grades,* then the number in each of those classes will, on the average of many millions, be as is stated in the table. The table may be applied to special, just as truly as to general ability. It would be true for every examination that brought out natural gifts, whether held in painting, in music, or in statesmanship. The proportion between the different classes would be identical in all these cases, although the classes would be made up of different individuals, according as the examination differed in its purport.

It will be seen that more than half of each million is contained in the two mediocre classes a and A; the four mediocre classes a, b, A, B, contain more than four-fifths, and the six mediocre classes more than nineteen-twentieths of the entire population. Thus, the rarity of commanding ability, and the vast abundance of mediocrity, is no accident, but follows of necessity, from the very nature of these things.

The meaning of the word "mediocrity" admits of little doubt. It defines the standard of intellectual power found in most provincial gatherings, because the attractions of a more stirring life in the metropolis and elsewhere, are apt to draw away the abler classes of man, and the silly and imbecile do not take a part in the gatherings. Hence, the residuum that forms the bulk of the general society of small provincial places, is commonly very pure in its mediocrity.

The class C possesses abilities a trifle higher than those commonly possessed by the foreman of an ordinary jury. D includes the mass of men who obtain the ordinary prizes of life. E is a stage higher. Then we reach F, the lowest of those yet superior classes of intellect.

On descending the scale, we find by the time we have reached f, that we are already among the idiots and imbeciles. We have seen that there are 400 idiots and imbeciles, to every million of persons living in this country, but that 30 per cent of their number, appear to be light cases, to whom the name of idiot is inappropriate. There will remain 280 true idiots and imbeciles, to every million of our population. This ratio coincides very closely with the requirements of class f. No doubt a certain proportion of them are idiotic owing to some fortuitous cause, which may interfere with the working of a naturally good brain, such as a bit of dirt may cause a first-rate chronometer to keep worse time than an ordinary watch. But, I presume, from the usual smallness of head and absence of disease among these persons, that the proportion of accidental idiots cannot be very large.

Hence we arrive at the undeniable, but unexpected conclusion, that eminently gifted men are raised as much above mediocrity as idiots are depressed below it; a fact that is calculated to considerably enlarge our ideas of the enormous differences of intellectual gifts between man and man.

In other words, Galton grades eminence (genius) in terms of a normal Gaussian curve, with capital letters denoting groups above the mean, and small letters denoting groups below the mean, the highest (X) denoting the most eminent or genius group. He believes, as we shall see shortly, that personal qualities like zeal and hard work are also needed, but he does not specify creativity as separate from intelligence; his curve seems to identify intelligence rather than creativity, assuming the two to be identical. Galton nowhere discusses this problem.

Galton's view of genius is defined by two key notions which recur again and again in later discussions. Essentially genius is defined in terms of a person's posthumous reputation, making it a social and interpersonal construct. Reputation for Galton means "the opinions of contemporaries, revised by posterity…the reputation of a leader of opinion, of an originator, of a man to whom the world deliberately acknowledges itself largely indebted." But Galton also recognized and indeed emphasized natural ability as the major source of genius, and hence of reputation. By "natural ability" he meant

> those qualities of intellect and disposition, which urge and qualify a man to perform acts that lead to reputation. I do not mean capacity without zeal, nor zeal without capacity, not even a combination of both of them, without an adequate power of doing a great deal of very laborious work. But I mean a nature which, when left to itself, will, urged by an interest stimulus, climb the path that leads to eminence, and has strength to reach the summit—one which, if hindered or thwarted, will fret and strive until the hindrance is overcome.

We may incorporate Galton's view in a diagram.

Capacity (intelligence, special abilities) ⟶
Zeal (persistence, hard work) ⟶ Reputation ⟶ Genius
Striving (motivation, fighting spirit) ⟶

This combination of qualities, which Galton apparently regarded as synergistic, i.e. multiplicative rather than additive, almost infallably leads to eminence: "It is almost a contradiction in terms, to doubt that such men will generally become eminent," for "the men who achieve eminence, and those who are naturally capable are, to a large extent, identical."

Galton's theory stands or falls by one simple fact; reliability of grading. Is there enough agreement between competent judges on the relative standing of scientists, writers, artists, poets, and composers on this continuum of eminence? If there is not, Galton's idea breaks down completely. And appearances suggest that he may not be right. *De gustibus non est disputandum*, we say, or *chacun a son gout*; there is no arguing about taste. There may be more agreement in science, but art must be the real battleground, for here subjectivity seems to rule supreme. But appearance may be playing us false, what does experiment have to say? Is there, or is there not, marked agreement on artistic excellence? Are those right who believe in complete relativism—all have won, and all must have prizes? The answer is that such studies strongly support Galton, and the option of an objective grading system.

Consider figure 9.1. This is a graph I constructed from the results of a study by E. Folgmann, who used the members of the New York Philharmonic, and the Boston, Minneapolis and Philadelphia Symphony Orchestras to rank seventeen of the best-known classical composers; he added two popular turn-of-the-century composers, Victor Herbert and Edward MacDowell, to define a bottom line. There was very clear agreement, with Beethoven, Brahms, Mozart, Wagner and Bach at the top; Chopin, Verdi, Stravinsky, and Grieg at the bottom, and MacDowell and Herbert nowhere. You may not agree with every detail, but overall I have met very few people who felt that this rank order was incorrect.

Of course there are certain problems. People who prefer opera to lieder may put Verdi higher and Schubert lower. The Boston Symphony Orchestra had the higher percentage of French musicians, and they placed Berlioz, Debussy, and Franck unusually high. The Minneapolis Symphony Orchestra has an unusually high number of musicians of Scandinavian extraction, and this may account for the unusually high position given to Grieg by them. The views of the conductors also play a part. Stokowski's high regard for Bach, and Toscanini's low opinion of Tchaikowsky, played a part in the respective rating given these two composers by members of the Philadelphia and New York orchestras respectively. There are minor factors of this kind to influence individual judgments, but if sufficient and varied samples are used, these sources of error should cancel out.

Many other studies of composers have given similar support to Galton's position, as have similar ratings of philosophers, painters, psychologists, and scientists; even for presidents of the United States (hardly geniuses!) expert historians have provided a chorus of agreement. Furthermore, there is agreement over time—ratings do not change suddenly, but remain at a certain level. Nor is this a follow-my-leader effect. Dean Simonton has summarized and carried out many historiometric studies which clearly support Galton. We may provisionally accept the notion of genius or "eminence" as being defined by the social consensus of experts in a given field, not necessarily immediate, but arrived at over the centuries. Some might have ranked Salieri over Mozart in their time, but no musicians would doubt the verdict of history now. Genius declares himself by the production of highly creative work, acknowledged as such by posterity, and usually even by contemporary opinion, even if such recognition is not immediate. What about Gray's "mute inglorious Milton, or Cromwell guiltless of his country's blood"? By definition they do not qualify; their achievement was not such as to produce the necessary acclaim, either in their lifetime or thereafter.

FIGURE 9.1

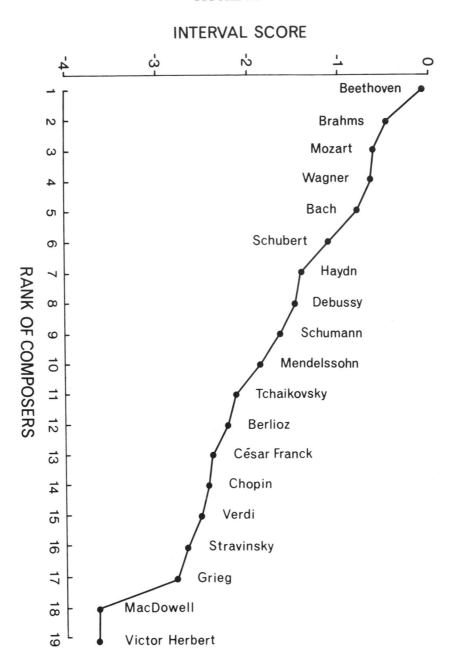

Ranking of famous composers by members of four famous symphony orchestras.

10

Creativity and Intelligence

When one tries to characterize the creative person, or the genius, the first term that comes into one's mind is undoubtedly "intelligence." It is very difficult to think of a "stupid" genius, this seems to be a contradiction in terms. But just what is the intelligence of the typical genius? And does it depend on what he is a genius in—science, mathematics, music, painting, or what? Clearly this is not an easy question to answer—there aren't that many geniuses around, and if you tried to give them an IQ test they would probably send you away with a flea in your ear! But high IQ is shown in quite young children in the things they can do, and that may give us a clue when we look at the early history of geniuses. Let us take as an example Sir Francis Galton, an authentic genius about whose childhood a lot is known. At the age of twelve months he knew his capital letters, and his alphabet by eighteen months; he could read a little book when two and a half years old, and he could sign his name before 3 years. Before his fifth birthday, he wrote the following letter to his sister:

My dear Adele,

I am 4 years old and I can read any English book. I can say the Latin Substantives and Adjectives and active verbs besides 52 lines of Latin poetry. I can cast up any sum in addition and can multiply by 2, 3, 4, 5, 6, 7, 8, (9), 10, (11).

I can also say the pence table. I read French a little and I know the clock.

Francis Galton

(The numbers 9 and 11 are put in brackets, because little Francis, evidently feeling he had claimed too much, had scratched out one of the numbers with a knife and pasted some paper over the other.) His reading at the age of five years was intelligent and not the mechanical kind, as demonstrated by his ability at that age to offer quotations which would fit a given situation. By six, the boy had become thoroughly conversant with the *Iliad* and the *Odyssey*; he also read

125

Scott, Cowper, Pope, and Shakespeare for pleasure, and, reading a page twice over, could repeat it by heart.

The account of Francis' accomplishments goes on forever, but this will be enough to show that he was advanced well beyond his years. It is possible to estimate his mental age from these performances, and by dividing by his chronological age to arrive at an estimate of his IQ, which would have been around 180. Catherine Cox carried out this task on 301 historical geniuses, estimating their mental ages from what was known about their different accomplishments, and dividing by their chronological ages. She did this twice for each genius—once for his childhood, once for his early adulthood. These IQs were all well above 100, and she averaged them according to type of genius. Thus artists averaged 122 (135), writers of poetry and drama 141 (149), musicians 130 (140), writers of essays of histories, 139 (148), soldiers 115 (125), scientists 135 (152), philosophers 147 (156), revolutionary statesmen 140 (144), religious leaders 132 (145), and statesmen 135 (147). (Figures in brackets refer to IQ estimates in early adulthood, figures not in brackets to IQ estimates in childhood.)

Cox found that the more was known about a person's youthful accomplishments, that is, what he had done *before* he was engaged in doing the things that made him known as a genius, the higher was his IQ. This makes sense; if very little is known of what the genius had done as a child, then you couldn't rate his mental age much or anything above the average, which is 100. So she proceeded to make a statistical correction in each case for lack of knowledge; this bumped up the figure considerably for the geniuses about whom little was in fact known. The corrected figures are as follows: artists 135 (160), writers of poetry and drama 149 (165), musicians 140 (160), writers of essays and history 148 (170), soldiers 125 (140), scientists 152 (175), philosophers 154 (180), revolutionary statesmen 144 (165). If the correction is permissible, we end up with IQ averaging around 160, soldiers being the lowest, scientists and philosophers the highest.

I am rather doubtful about the justification for making the correction. To do so assumes that the geniuses about whom least is known were precocious but their previous activities were not recorded. This may be true, but it is also possible to argue that perhaps there was nothing much to record! I feel uneasy about making such assumptions; doing so may be very misleading. But there is another criticism, even more central to the whole argument. Galton had read the *Iliad* and the *Odyssey* at an incredibly young age, but then his sister had been teaching him, at least giving him these books. Perhaps many other children might have been familiar with Homer if an older sister had bullied them into reading them! In other words, some at least of these geniuses were force-fed in a way that few children are—Galton by his sister; John Stuart Mill by his father, and so on. I am not saying that that is all. You wouldn't get many children to write and calculate as early as Galton did, whatever you tried to make them do. But to calculate actual IQs is going over the top; we are justified in saying that all these kids were pretty bright, but I don't believe that we can pin this down to actual IQ values.

What is obvious is that geniuses have a high degree of intelligence, but not outrageously high—there are many accounts of people in the population with IQs as high who have not achieved anything like the status of genius. Indeed, they may have achieved very little; there are large numbers of Mensa members who are elected on the basis of an IQ test, but whose creative achievements are nil. High intelligence seems to be a *necessary* qualification for high creativity, but it does not seem a *sufficient* one.

This is borne out by another study carried out in the early twenties by the same group of Californian psychologists Cox belonged to. This is a very famous follow-up study of high IQ children (135 and above) who were followed into adulthood to see what became of them as compared with children of ordinary intelligence. Terman, who originated those "Genetic Studies of Genius," as he called them, selected 857 male and 671 female children on the basis of their high IQs; the mean was 151 for both sexes. Seventy-seven who were tested with the newly translated and standardized Binet test had IQs of 170 or higher—well at or above the level of Cox's geniuses. What happened to these potential geniuses—did they revolutionize society? Did they monopolize the Nobel Prize? Did they prove outstanding in the arts? The answer in brief is that they did very well in terms of achievement, but none reached the Nobel Prize level, let alone that of genius. They did very well at University, many were cited in *American Men of Science* (including seven of the women!), the *Directory of American Scholars*, or *Who's Who in America*. They published novels, volumes of poetry, technical, professional or scholarly books, plays, essays, and scientific papers. They took out many patents, made substantial contributions to the physical, biological and social sciences, and became leaders in university faculties. All this by the time the children had reached the age of 40; they continued to do even better as they grew older, but never to the genius level, or anything approaching it. It seems clear that these data powerfully confirm the suspicion that intelligence is not a sufficient trait for truly creative achievement of the highest grade.

Both Cox and Terman suggest from their studies that personality may be an important ingredient. Terman looked at the personalities of the most and least successful of his subjects; they did not differ in IQ. The successful ones were less moody, impulsive, or conformist; they showed more self-confidence, sociability, perseverance, integration towards goals, absence of inferiority feelings, and common sense as compared to the less successful. When rated by the investigators, the successful ones were superior in appearance, attractiveness, poise, speech, alertness, friendliness, attentiveness, curiosity, and originality. Note the stress on *originality* and *lack of conformity*; these are also essential qualities of genius, and are part and parcel of *creativity*. Clearly greater creativity is involved in success, even at this below-genius level.

Cox also looked at personality traits shown by her geniuses, and found that particularly high came a trait she called *persistence,* that is, a tendency to invest effort in one's endeavours, to be highly motivated to succeed, and to continue working on one's ideas in spite of criticism, ridicule and apparent failure. It also specifies sheer hard work! Edison considered genius "one percent inspiration—ninety-nine per cent perspiration"; for Buffon genius was "but a great aptitude for patience"; Frederick the Great thought it was a "transcendent capacity for taking trouble." Cox concluded her statistical comparison by saying that persistence was possibly even more important than intelligence, although obviously both were needed.

Modern students have given IQ and personality tests to outstanding scientists and artists, with results not dissimilar to those of Cox and Terman. High-flyers have high IQs, are strongly motivated, and work extremely hard. These are not unexpected results; the notion of genius mysteriously pouring out treasure without effort has been shown to be quite wrong, even for the likes of Mozart who is often portrayed as working miracles without effort! There is no achievement without hard work, and no genius without an iron will to succeed.

Intelligence is clearly not the same as creativity, even though a high degree of intelligence may be needed for creative achievement. Is there any way we can measure creativity? First of course we must agree on the meaning of the concept and try to define it in descriptive terms. Creativity clearly implies *originality* of thinking, and agreed *usefulness* of the result of such thinking. It is the bringing together of two or more ideas that have not previously been brought together in the present context, but the result has to be judged successful before we can talk about *creativity*-social approbation, as in the case of genius, is essential, even though it may be delayed. An example may make this definition clear.

Consider U.S. Patent 5,163,44. It concerns the musical condom, officially described as the "force-sensitive, sound-playing condom." It combines in one package two of our most pressing requirements, safe sex and continuous entertainment. The inventor, Paul Lyons, assembled a piece of electric sound transducer, microchip, power supply, and miniature circuitry in the rim of a condom, so that when pressure was applied, it emitted "a pre-determined melody or a voice message." For Lyons, it fulfilled all the demands of a money-making product of the nineties—inexpensive novelty appeal, built-in obsolescence, and a combination of two demands never previously put together—musical entertainment and safe sex. This, surely, is an example of creativity par excellence!

We may analyse the notion of "biosociation," as Koestler calls it, a little further. We may start with another invention of Galton's, the word association test. We call out a word, and the subject of the experiment has to reply immediately with the first thing that comes into his mind. If you call out: "Table," he is very likely to reply: "Chair," because that association has been well established over the years. We might say that this association is typical of a steep association gradient, with the reply close to the stimulus. A reply of "cutlery" would be a little less usual, and indicative of a gradient slightly less steep. "Lip" would be somewhat more unusual, and "concertina" almost unique, suggesting a very shallow associative gradient. "Steep," in this connection, means simply that the associated word is close to the stimulus word in meaning, or is associated with it through usage. "Shallow" means that there is only a very loose and unusual association between the two. If creativity is defined by the making of unusual associations, then perhaps the word association test could be used as a measure? We could give a set of a hundred words as stimuli to a thousand people, and record their responses. These would then be tabulated, for each stimulus word separately, and we would note how frequently each response word was given. Some, like "chair" would be very frequent responses to "table"; others, like "cutlery" would be much less frequent, and some, like "concertina" would be unique, that is, given only by one person.

We would then look at each person's 100 responses and average the response frequencies of all these words, so that someone who had many unusual responses would have a high average, someone with few unique responses a very low average. Would a high score mean that the person in question was really creative? This of course is an empirical question, but it immediately brings up the problem of how to define creativity, seeing that our subjects are unlikely to include many geniuses! The most acceptable answer has been given by the member of IPAR, the Institute of Personality Assessment and Research, whose work at Berkeley I was privileged to witness when I was visiting professor at that august university.

In fact IPAR used two criteria. The first was the consensus of experts in a given field. Thus they would study architects, say, and ask experienced architects to nominate the most creative architects they knew. These would then be invited to spend a few days at the Institute, to be interviewed, studied, observed, subjected to many different tests, and discussed by the staff. These creative people would be complemented by a number of equally well-known architects who had no particular claim to being creative, according to the judges. There was also a third group, made up of architects who had studied with the creative ones, but who had not been rated as being highly creative; they were judged to be intermediate in creativity. We may call this the "nominative" procedure. It differed from the "judgment" procedure, in which various groups would be invited to come to the Institute, when the psychologists would interact with them over several days and then rate them for creativity—independently of the tests, of course, which would later be correlated with the averaged creativity ratings of the psychologists.

Before IPAR started this work, M.T. Bingham had given a word association test to Amy Lowell, the poetess; he found that "she gave a higher proportion of unique responses than those of anyone outside a mental institution." With the architects, too, there was a highly significant correlation between creativity and unusualness of responses. The nominated creative group had a mean score of 204; the noncreative scored 114, with the middle group scoring 128. The correlation of 0.50 may not seem remarkable, but remember that this is just one brief test to explore one of the most complex and little understood of human behaviours. Also the criterion was almost certainly far from perfect—some of the unselected probably were more creative than some of those chosen as being creative. In such unexplored fields, criteria are seldom perfect, or anything near it, and that inevitably depresses correlations. This is only an illustration; other studies have also given positive results, with groups other than architects.

Word association tests are not only, and far from the most widely used, measures of creativity. Most research has concentrated on divergent tests of intelligence, as opposed to the convergent type of test usually used in IQ testing. Consider such a typical test item:

A   C   E   G   I   ?

The next letter is obviously K, because the series progresses by jumping one letter. It thus converges upon the solution; there can only be one correct answer. But now consider some problems that do not have a single correct answer. Here are a few examples. We might ask subjects to list six uses to which a brick or some other common object could be put (Unusual Uses). The score would be the infrequency and originality of answers in the sample studied. Or we might ask subjects to write down what would happen if certain changes could suddenly take place, for example, if the water level rose twelve feet all over the world. The least obvious answers would receive the highest scores (Consequences). In another test, two story plots would be presented, and subjects would have to write as many titles as they could think of for each plot. Titles would be rated for cleverness (Plot titles.) In another test, subjects would be required to make up as many words as possible from the letters in the word "generation," and infrequent words would be rewarded (Anagrams). Or the subject would be given fifty words which he would be asked to use in making up a story, which would then be rated for originality (Word Arrangement Test). These are typical divergent type tests; do they measure creativity? In one study from IPAR, it was found that such tests correlate together quite well, indicating that they measure pretty much the same thing, and that this total score correlated 0.55 with a rating of creativity made by staff members independently of the tests themselves. This suggests validation for divergent tests. Such divergent tests do not correlate highly with convergent-type IQ tests.

Some of the most impressive studies on divergent thinking tests have been carried out by E.P. Torrance, who tried to answer the question of whether such tests given to young children could predict creativity in later life. Torrance used the following criteria:

1. Quantity of publicly recognized and acknowledged creative achievements (patents and inventions); novels, plays that were publicly produced; musical compositions that were publicly performed; awards for artworks in a juried exhibition, founding a business; founding a journal or professional organiza-

tion; developing an innovative technique in medicine, surgery, science, business, teaching, etc.

2. Quality of creative achievements. Subjects were asked to identify what they considered their three most creative achievements; these data, plus responses to the check-list of achievements, were judged by three judges.

3. Quality of creative achievement implied by future career image. Three judges assessed this primarily by responses to the following two questions in the follow-up: (1) What are your career ambitions? For example, what position, responsibility, or reward do you wish to attain? What do you hope to accomplish? (2) If you could do or be whatever you choose in the next 10 years, what would it be?

We thus have three major criteria, namely quality, quantity and aspirations, to correlate with the various scores obtained many years earlier on the Torrance Test of Creative Thinking.

It is impossible to discuss all the many studies carried out by Torrance, using children of various ages, and following them up over different periods, but the results are very clear. There are highly significant positive correlations between the children's divergent thinking scores, and later creative achievement; a correlation of 0.60 is perhaps typical of the results achieved. Twelve years is probably a minimum follow-up period, less than that does not give the children sufficient time to demonstrate their creativity (or lack of it!) in any convincing manner. Convergent intelligence was also measured, but did not correlate at all with creative achievement.

We have so far looked at two major types of creative measures: Word Association Unusual Responses and Divergent Thinking Unusual Responses. There are many more tests of creativity (such as the wisdom boards, shown in figure 1.1), but they have been used less frequently, and with less success. For our purposes, just one further test will be mentioned, namely the Figure Preference Test. Essentially this consisted of 62 single-line drawings, some of which are simple, balanced, symmetrical, while others are complex, unbalanced, asymmetrical. The score, essentially, is the subject's preference for the complex over the simple; he is asked for each design whether he likes it or dislikes it? The test is very simple, but it is reliable, and independent of convergent intelligence. The authors of this Barron-Welsh Art Scale, to give it its proper title, administered it together with an ordinary IQ test, and divided their population into four groups, depending on whether they showed high or low *origence* on the complexity test, and high or low *intellectence* on the IQ test. (Origence and intellectence are the terms coined by George Welsh).

Origence was found to be correlated with ratings of creativity, impulsiveness, psychopathology, flexibility and nonconformity. It was also correlated with independence of judgment, as tested by means of the Asch (1956) test. This consists of an experimental social situation in which the subject is put under pressure to conform to a group opinion which is false. There are from eight to sixteen ostensible subjects, only one of whom, however, is naive; the rest are employed by the experimenter. The task is to judge which of three lines of variable lengths meets a standard line. The subjects, one by one, announce their judgments publicly. The naive subject is so placed as to be one of the last to announce his judgment. On the critical trials, the hired majority gives a prearranged false answer. The experimental variable is called Yielding, which is defined as agreeing with group opinion when it is in error. Complexity was significantly and negatively correlated with Yielding in two separate samples.

The origence conception was also tried out on the IPAB sample of architects we have already encountered in connection with the Word Association Test. The correlation between creativity and origence was .47, almost identical with the association found between creativity and unusual word association. Many other studies could be mentioned, and other tests of complexity have been constructed and used, but the major result has always been positive; there does appear to be a genuine connection between creativity and preference for complex as opposed to simple visual stimuli.

The IPAR work produced one further result that should be mentioned because it will be fundamental for our future arguments. They found quite regularly that the more creative people were characterized by a certain degree of psychopathology—not to the extent of actual psychosis, but as indicated by being considerably above the average in their scores on the psychopathological scales of the Minnesota Multiphasic Personality Inventory. At the same time they scored highly on the ego-strength scale, a result very much in line with the Post study of geniuses referred to in an earlier section. This association is thus not confined to genius; it is also notable in the lower ranks of creative people. This suggests that there may be a causal, not just a correlational link between psychopathology and creativity, prevented from spilling over into actual psychosis by a high degree of ego-strength. This association will give us the clue to the construction of a *causal model* of creativity and genius to be considered in a later chapter.

Does measurement of creativity throw some light on the rather nebulous concept of intuition? Can we measure intuition? Professor M. Westcott has shown that even elusive traits like intuition can be measured. He argued that what we mean by intuition is essentially the ability to jump to conclusions on the basis of insufficient evidence; we literally take an intellectual leap instead of plodding along lines of logic to a predestined conclusion. This brief argument led to his experimental design. Set your subject a problem that is insoluble as it stands. It can be solved logically if you are given a number of cues. But these are hidden, and you can ask for the first one to be disclosed, making solution a little easier. You can then ask for the second one, then the third, and so on until you feel you can guess the answer. Some people (the plodders) require to look at all or most of the cues; your intuitive person takes a leap at the solution after only receiving a few cues. This tendency can be measured reliably; in other words, a given person behaves in the same fashion time after time. And it has nothing much to do with intelligence; dull people can be intuitive, bright ones can be plodders.

But of course you can arrive at the wrong solution, whether you are intuitive or a plodder. Hence Westcott finished up with four groups: Intuitive-correct, Plodder-correct, Intuitive-wrong; Plodder-wrong. The personality characteristics showed that the intuitives were similar to *creative* people, the plodder to noncreative ones. Thus, this test of intuition could also be used to identify creativity. When we look at geniuses, do we find a similar distinction between those who get the answer right, and those who get it wrong? Newton and Einstein were hugely intuitive, and mostly right; Marx and Freud were hugely intuitive, and mostly wrong. Intuition is well worth a lot of further investigation; its study can throw a great deal of light on the nature of creativity. But even now we can say quite categorically that we can measure creativity and intuitive ability as special abilities within general intelligence; if we combine results from divergent thinking tests, word association tests, and preference for complex figures with the results of tests of intuition, we would get a score that mirrored pretty accurately a person's creativity. This, to my mind, is a remarkable achievement.

11

Conditions for Excellence and Achievement

Genius as a Male Characteristic

Much research has gone into looking at the correlates of genius, in the hope of finding out the conditions favouring the emergence of creative excellence. The most obvious characteristic of the genius, of course, is *maleness*. For whatever reason—and I emphasize the point that there is much argument about the *causes* of the obvious discrepancy—genius and creativity of the highest level are found almost only in males. In the list of geniuses studied by Cox there were no women. There are none in lists of leading mathematicians. None would be found among the 100 best-known sculptors, painters, dramatists, or composers, and hardly any among the greatest scientists. Only among poets and novelists do we find a small proportion of women near the top class. The facts are so obvious, and so well known, that documentation is hardly necessary, but the facts do not speak directly to the reasons why men are so predominant among this elite of creativity.

Feminists often argue that male suppression may have been responsible for this failure of women to shine in the arts and sciences, and it is difficult to disagree. When women are not admitted to universities, their chances of shining in academic and scientific subjects must be low. Yet in the Middle Ages, convents were repositories of knowledge, and nuns had an education not necessarily inferior to that of monks. Having to look after children is another reason frequently given, but it has been found that women in academe published less than men, but marriage and family obligations do not generally account for the gender difference observed—women with children published as much as their single female colleagues. But of course women now average 1.8 children in Great Britain; things might have been very different when they used to have 8 or more!

Another possible reason lies in the apparent preference of women to have broad rather than narrow interests. Research on highly gifted boys

135

and girls equal in mathematical ability showed that boys tended to concentrate all their efforts on mathematics, and achieved greater success than girls who spread their efforts more widely. It is not known whether this is a universal tendency, but it may account for much of the difference in creativity; absolute concentration is essential for great achievement. Why boys and girls should differ in this respect is not known.

My own view is that the most important cause of the difference in creative achievement is rooted in personality, and the psychophysiological and neuro-hormonal bases of these personality differences. Males and females differ profoundly in a personality variable essentially concerned with psychopathology; I have called this personality dimension "psychoticism," and I will describe it in detail in a later section. Now I will only draw attention to the fact that males are much higher on this dimension than females, and that psychoticism is highly correlated with creativity. Why this is so I shall try to explain in due course. Psychoticism is not only correlated with creativity, but also with the fighting spirit that is needed to help the creative person, or the genius, to overcome the difficulties envious mediocrity creates to prevent orthodoxy from being overthrown. This is the combination required for genius to prove itself, and both form part of psychoticism.

The Influence of Religion

Religion seems at first sight an unlikely candidate for genius status, but while many scientists have been agnostics or atheists, the religion practised by their parents has frequently been correlated with their achievements. Jews have always been the most successful, and continue to be so to this day. Protestants come next, and Catholics are the least successful. Looking at American Nobel Prize winners, we find 4 percent of Americans are Catholics, but only 1 percent of Nobel Laureates have been. Jews constitute 3 percent of the American population, but 27 percent of American Nobel Prize winners. This is a remarkable disproportion, even without considering the anti-Semitism so prevalent in America during the first decades of this century, when most of the laureates did their work. A similar disproportion exists when we compare Protestant countries like England, Northern Germany, and Scandinavia, with Catholic countries like Italy, Spain and France.

Differences between European countries can hardly be due to differences in IQ; those named are for all practical purposes on the same level. Jews, however, have always scored higher than any other group, whether national or religious. But here again causation is uncertain; the great stress Jews lay on education might, in whole or in part, be responsible for their high showing. Protestants tend to emphasize the importance of *work* and Catholics of *faith*, that may have something to do with the absence of achievement differential. The truth is that we do not know the reasons for these differences, and in the absence of knowledge we have to guess. Such guesses may make for reasonable theories, but the theories certainly require proof before they can be accepted.

The Japanese are certainly doing exceptionally well in science and mathematics, perhaps due to superior intelligence—(they outscore Caucasians on IQ tests), but their patterns of achievement differs profoundly from that of the Jews. Japanese excel in practical, down-to-earth sciences, Jews in the highest flights of theoretical physics. The possible lack of creativity in Japanese scientists has often been remarked, but it is unclear whether this is due to their highly regimented school system, or whether their school system is just a reflection of a genetic preference for regimentation, possibly produced by the pressure of a hostile environment requiring co-ordinated group action.

The Importance of the Middle Class

There is much evidence, for all historical epochs of which we have some knowledge, that creative people, regardless of discipline, have in the main come from the so-called middle- or upper classes, more particularly from professional homes. The fathers of Cox's geniuses were noblemen or professional men in over half the cases; skilled workmen, lower business men, semiskilled and unskilled fathers made up only 13 percent of the total. A sample of eminent writers and scientists in the eighteenth century showed a very similar picture. In our own time a similar condition prevails; of Nobel laureates, fathers were professional men in 54 percent of all cases; this should be compared with a figure of 3.5 percent among all employed males, and 29 percent among science doctorates.

Again, we have to guess at the causes. Financial status of parents may of course be a contributing factor, but this does not explain why the fathers of people with science doctorates are so much less frequently of professional status. And 75 percent of Jewish Nobel laureates came from lower socioeconomic backgrounds, suggesting that it was the motivational properties of the family, rather than their financial status, that produced the drive to eminence of the Nobel Prize winners.

Professional men usually score very high on IQ tests, so perhaps it is inherited intelligence that is in part responsible for the achievements of the progeny of such men. Motivation is certainly a vital factor in creative achievement (or indeed any form of achievement!), but it is doubtful to what extent motivation can be externally imposed. Existing evidence does not really tell us about real-life motivation; experimental studies deal with weak and short-term motivational situations that cannot be generalized to life-long drives and accomplishments. George Washington Carver, whose life history I shall present in chapter 12, serves as an ever-present warning not to over-estimate the importance of external factors in explaining creative achievements.

Intellectual Stimulation

The influence of the home environment is curiously contradictory. On the one hand we find that a large number of geniuses have been educated by their parents and siblings, who often devoted much of their time to this task—Galton, J.S. Mill, Pascal, Mozart, and many others are often cited in this connection. Parents may appear as role models, even if they do not participate directly in the child's education. But there are far more instances where parents failed to provide a good environment, and even showed hostility to the budding genius. The parents of Berlioz actively opposed his choice of music as a profession, and he grew up in a small village that provided no musical inspiration. The great mathematicians cited earlier found little in the way of role models as an encouragement in the home circle. Mozart was coached from an early age by his father, but Wagner did not even develop an interest in music till he was fifteen—and then only as an addition to his dramatic writings! On the whole intellectual stimulation in the home seems of doubtful importance; it may simply be irrelevant in most cases.

What has been firmly established, however, is what may appear as contradictory to the belief in helpful, harmonious homes as a good background to the growth of genius. A disproportionate number of creative achievers lost one or both parents in childhood. In a study of 699 famous historical figures, it was found that one in four had lost at least one parent before the age of ten. By the age of fifteen the loss exceeded 14 percent, and 45 percent below the age of twenty. In more recent years, we find that around the beginning of this century, death of one or both parents was *three times* more frequent among eminent people than in the general population. Remember that these eminent people came largely from the professional strata, where parents would normally live much longer than would be true of the general population, and the disproportion becomes even more astounding.

Even more recently, Roe found a three times greater loss of parents in the eminent scientists she studied; 26 percent as compared with 8 percent in the general American population. The only other group with similar childhood bereavements are delinquents and severe depressives—both groups with high scores on the personality continuum of psychoticism, which is also characteristic of creative achievers.

In the IPAR studies already mentioned, it was found that loving supportive parents, a happy home environment, and parental stimulation were far more frequently found in their bright, well-adjusted, low-creative subjects. Their most creative subjects had suffered many traumatic experiences, brutality, deprivation and frustration in childhood. In a study of 400 eminent historical figures, it was found that 75 percent had suffered broken homes, rejection by their parents, many of whom were over-possessive, estranged, or dominating. More than one in four had a physical handicap! In the present century, 85 percent of 400 eminent people had come from highly troubled homes. Others have found lack of attachment, affection, warmth, and closeness between children who grew up to be famous scientists, and their parents. The picture is pretty grim—perhaps being a genius is not as attractive a proposition as it might appear at first!

Age of Creativity

Many people have commented on the fact that creativity seemed to be a prerogative of youth. The problem was attacked first by a British author, G. Beard, who studied more than a thousand biographies of eminent persons and carefully noted the age at which they produced their major contributions. His book was published in 1874; he found that achievement increased fairly rapidly from twenty to forty, with a peak just short of forty, and then declined very slowly over the years. H.C. Lehman eighty years later carried out similar studies in a more systematic, objective and quantitative manner, but his conclusions were in fact very similar. The decline after the age of forty was in *quality* rather than *quantity;* in other words, the genius produces almost as much later in life as he did earlier, but the work is less original.

The general curve of creative production is somewhat different for different disciplines, but only with respect to the peak of the curve.

Poets and mathematicians achieve success earliest, physical scientists later, biological scientists later still, and scholars last. Even within a given field variations occur. If we look at classical music, the peak for composing instrumental works occurred between twenty-five and twenty-nine, for symphonies between thirty and thirty-four, for chamber music between thirty-five and thirty-nine, and for opera between forty and forty-four. But in all cases achievement increased up to a point, then declined; the general shape of the curve remained unaltered. Beard tried to explain it by postulating two factors in creative achievement, enthusiasm and experience. Both are needed to produce high-quality creative work. Experience, he thought, keeps growing constantly, but enthusiasm declines after a while. The product of the two would give us a peak around forty; the genius has enough experience, and has not yet lost his enthusiasm. Beard does not explain *why* enthusiasm should decline so conveniently, just when the genius is most successful, is getting widely recognized, and receives adulation and support.

However, the point about experience is well taken. You need more experience to produce original work in biology than in physics; in psychology than in mathematics; in writing tragedies than in writing poetry. We can discern some meaningful relations here but a final understanding is still far from our grasp. The same is true of another aspect of the age factor—life span. It has been found that dying early (at age thirty or forty years of age) or very late (eighty to ninety) is much more advisable than dying at sixty, if you want recognition. At sixty you are too old to be regarded as the traditional youthful genius, and not old enough to have become a living legend of artistic or scholastic greatness. Military and political leaders show the "youth" effect even more strongly. I suppose they are found out if they live long enough!

Seasons of Birth

There are some very curious facts concerning the season of the year when eminent people are born, the major one being that it coincides with the season when schizophrenics and manic-depressive psychotics are born! Eminent people, defined as being listed in the *Encyclopaedia Britannica*, showed a strong tendency to be born in the months between the winter solstice and the spring equinox; at the peak, in February, thirty-six eminent persons were born per day as compared with twenty-seven at the trough! As over 11,000 people were involved, there is no question about the statistical significance of the outcome. Nor can it be said to be related to IQ; there the effect is in the opposite direction, although much weaker.

It is not at all clear why eminent people should be conceived in May-June, as opposed to other people. Nor is it clear why the same should be true of functional psychotics! They also are born with disconcerting frequency in the early months of the year, around February, and no obvious explanation has been offered to explain this very odd behaviour. In the absence of such an explanation it is difficult to see whether the coincidence can be interpreted as support of the genius—psychopathology interaction we have encountered before; it is somewhat uncanny to see it emerging in this connection! Pointing out the problem may lead someone to investigate it further; at the moment the facts are not in dispute, but the causes for their existence remain shrouded in fog.

Periodic Variations

As if this were not enough spooky oddities, Professor Suitbert Ertel has recently added another. Already some two-thousand years ago the Roman historian Velleius Pateraulus has noted that geniuses appear in clusters, and now the recognition of "golden ages" and "dark ages" is commonplace. Ertel took up a suggestion made by the Russian historian, A.L. Chizhevsky, that high sun-spot activity might be related to cyclic events in world history like revolutions, epidemics, mass migration, and other disasters. The evidence was not convincing, although intriguing, and Chizhevsky was sent to Siberia for his troubles by Stalin, apparently for suggesting that it was the sun rather than the doctrines of dialectical materialism which lay behind the great upheavals of history.

Ertel was intrigued and devoted a good deal of time and energy to demonstrating that the theory was correct; over long historical periods, and even in recent times, high sun spot activity was indeed correlated with civic unrest, revolutions and the like. But Ertel extended that line of argument to suggest that if civic unrest and other disasters were connected with *high* sun spot activity, perhaps *low* sun spot activity *was* connected with outbursts of cultural activity—production of high-level artistic, scientific, and philosophical works. How the strong magnetic fields inside sun-spots and the energy dissipated when magnetic fields are annihilated to produce huge discharges (solar flares), which in turn generate highly energetic X-rays, shooting vast numbers of high-speed particles from the sun, can influence aggressive impulses on earth, cannot at present be explained. These certainly are quite remarkable physical effects; the high-speed particles from the sun impinge on the earth's outer magnetic field to produce the so-called magnetic storms which are immensely powerful, and produce in turn physical and biological phenomena on the earth that are well recognized, from the disruption of telephone and radar communications to weather changes and chemical reactions. So there is a clear *possibility* of solar flares influencing human behaviour through a chain of physical events, but just how is unknown.

What Ertel did, in brief, was to go to the library and consult various text books, encyclopaedias, and other reference works to determine the exact years when outstanding scientific, artistic, and philosophical works had been produced. He did this not only for Europe but also for Chinese, Arabic, Greek, Indian, and various other cultures, going back over centuries. In all these countries he found that *periods of great cultural activity were characterized by periods of low solar activity!* This was true, not only for all the cultures studied, but also for all the different cultural activities studied—poetry, painting, science, philosophy, and so on. He noted that the Maunder Minimum, a period of minimum solar activity from 1621 to 1710, was characterized by an extended period of cultural activity, so were other solar minima (Schwabe, Gort, Wolf, and Sporer). The appearance of the Renaissance to coincide with the Maunder Minimum is not unexpected on the basis of Ertel's theory.

However difficult to explain, the facts do not admit of any doubt; there is a close coincidence of solar activity and human behaviour. When the sun is active, cultural events take second place to revolutions and civic disturbances; when the sun is inactive, cultural phenomena flourish all over the earth. Presumably the latter state is the natural one, to be disturbed by solar activity, an *inactive* sun can hardly produce great cultural achievements! It must be the active sun, shooting off masses of powerful particles, that disrupts the even patterns of our lives.

I have reviewed some of the many external factors that may determine and influence creative achievement. They are contrasted with the internal factors that predispose an individual genetically to produce great art, or great science. Obviously such external factors are important; it is impossible to conceive of an Einstein born in a Kraal, a Mozart born in an igloo, a Titian born in a tepee. Great art and great science both need cultural and social prerequisites; in their absence even the genius has little chance to produce the great works that are within him.

In a similar vein, dictatorships make great art and great science unlikely, if not impossible; the crazy interference of a Stalin or a Hitler made artists and scientists largely sterile. The total configuration of elements that need to fit together to produce creative achievements, whether in the arts or in the sciences, clearly needs to incorporate external as well as internal factors.

I have so far not made a distinction between two different meanings of the word "creativity," a distinction that is absolutely vital. By the term, creativity, we may mean a general mental trait, probably fairly normally distributed (i.e., with most people around the average, few very much above or below the average), that predisposes people to produce original ideas. The resulting products, like the solutions to divergent tests, or associations to a word association test, are quite mundane, and of no social value. On the other hand, we may call a person "creative" because he has accomplished something that is both original *and* of great social value. The mature products of great scientists, painters, composers, mathematicians, and poets are of this kind. Here we do not have any sort of "normal" distribution; there are a handful of creative artists, and a whole lot of also-rans. A proper model of creativity has to make clear the relation between these two different conceptions of the term.

In essence, I have already suggested the nature of such a model. Genius, or the production of truly creative works of art or science, requires a number of qualities of which trait creativity is only one. I have already suggested several psychological components, such as high intelligence, persistence, ego-strength, and psychopathological trait creativity. There are also social conditions such as living in a country which is at peace, coming from a middle-class home, growing up among people who *value* art and science. The inhabitants of Athens and Sparta probably had very similar heredity, but the former valued culture, the latter despised it. Hence the great disparity in the production of worthwhile sculpture, drama, or painting, between the two, to say nothing of philosophy, science, and mathematics.

Looking at only the psychological qualities listed above, they are pretty well found to be normally distributed; why is creative achievement so different? The answer is probably that these qualities do not *add* together, in which case they would produce a fairly normal distribution. I am suggesting that they *multiply* and such multiplication produces a very obviously J-shaped distribution. An example will make this clear. Let us consider two correlated factors determining creative achievement, namely *intelligence* and *creativity*. Imagine that each is distributed into five classes, from low to high, allotted marks of 0, 1, 2, 3 and 4 respectively, with frequencies 1, 4, 6, 4, 1, as fits the normal distribution. Thus out of sixteen people, one has a zero score, or one of 4; ten have a score of 1, or of 3; six have a score of 2. If we now combine the marks of our subjects by multiplication, rather than addition, 50 percent will have a score between 0 and 1; 36 percent between 1 and 2, 11 percent between 2 and 3; 3 percent between 3 and 4; and 0.4 percent between 4 and 5. (I am redistributing marks in 5 classes, as before). Thus now out of 200 people, less than one will have the highest score, but 100 will have the lowest! Extend this method to five or six different attributes, and you will find only 1 in a million getting the really high score!

This tendency to J-shaped distribution has actually been found in many instances of persons producing creative works, and formulae have been suggested (those of Lotka and Price) to give an exact estimate of the effect. Before looking at these, let us look at some well-known facts. Concentrating on scientific achievement, where judgments are perhaps more objective than in art, it is well-known that a small proportion of active scientists is responsible for the major number of creative works. Thus Dennis found that the top 10 percent most productive contributors in a variety of scientific disciplines were responsible for about half of the total works published whereas the bottom 50 percent were less productive and contributed only about 15 percent of the total output. In psychology, for instance, the most prolific author can claim more contributions than can eighty colleagues in the lower half of the distribution. These data in fact under-estimate the difference because they only include those who have made at least one contribution, thus leaving out of consideration all those never making any contribution at all!

These laws do not only apply to scientific productions, but have far wider applicability. Dennis found similar distributions in the publication of secular music and in the books represented in the Library of Congress. Simonton demonstrated its applicability to classical music. As he points out, about 256 composers account for all the music heard in the modern repertoire, but a mere sixteen are responsible for creating half of the pieces heard.

Price's Law which is rather simpler than Lotka's states that if $x\sqrt{k}$ represents the total number of contributors to a given field, thus $\sqrt{k}$ will be the predicted number of contributors who will generate half of all contributions. The larger the discipline, the more elitist the outcome! To take an actual example, I have already quoted Simonton who showed that of $\sqrt{256}$ classical composers whose works are still heard, 16 are responsible for creating 50 percent of the pieces heard. But $\sqrt{256} = 16$. QED!

The law does not always fit so precisely, but wherever it has been tried, it seems to work reasonably well. Thus creative achievement can best be viewed as the product of (1) cognitive abilities, like intelligence, acquired knowledge, technical skills, and special talents (e.g., musical, verbal, numerical); (2) personality traits, like originality, persistence, nonconformity, psychopathology and motivation; and (3) external, environmental variables, like politico-religious factors, socioeconomic conditions, and educational provisions. The actual factors involved will vary from case to case, as will their relative importance, but they are likely to act multiplicatively not simply in an additive manner.

Certain important consequences follow from this model. Where there are a number of determinants of a given outcome (here creative achievement), none by itself will correlate highly with the outcome. The square of the correlation is an indication of the contribution that factor makes to the total; if we look at ten independent factors, then on average each cannot make a greater contribution than 10 percent, otherwise the total would exceed 100 percent, which is impossible. But 10 percent corresponds to a correlation of 0.31. That is not a high correlation, but it is roughly what we might expect from actually finding the correlation between creativity (as a trait) and creative achievement! The importance of trait creativity to achievement is not measured by its possibly low correlation; without trait creativity, all the other factors, however highly developed, would come to nothing—however impressive, multiplied by zero they would still amount to zero! Hence the many superbly gifted nonentities who inhabit our universities—the vital spark of creativity is missing!

Synergistic interaction leads us back to the question of *configuration.* Were it simply a question of adding together all the qualities needed for the genius, we would have thousands of them running about, and creative achievement would abound. Furthermore, Galton's notion of genius running in the family would be found to be true. But configuration means the absence of even one element produces a fatal flaw which cannot be corrected by increasing the excellence of the other elements. Hence the odd genetic propensities of geniuses often, indeed usually, coming from very ordinary stock; the accidental configuration produced by the segregation of genes cannot be predicted, and may strike anywhere! Producing a genius is like dicing ten sixes in a row—highly unlikely, but it does happen very, very occasionally!

12

Genius and Heredity

Is genius due to heredity, or is it the result of education and other environmental determinants? Galton argued that there was great *familial aggregation*, in other words, that eminence ran in families; this he regarded as evidence of genetic determination. Galton was wrong, both in matters of fact and in matters of *interpretation*. Let us take the latter first. If you find that within one family there are a number of eminent judges, this could certainly be due to heredity. However, it could equally certainly be due to environment. If you are born the son of an eminent judge, you are likely to go to a public school (English for private school), to go on to Oxford or Cambridge, take a degree in law, thus following the family tradition. Finally, with a gentle push from your father, and granted that it is more important whom you know than what you know, you are likely to find your path up the judicial ladder eased considerably—as contrasted, say, with the son of a mine worker! (Remember that Galton wrote in the middle of the last century, when England was even more feudal than it is now!

It should be pretty obvious to anyone looking at the matter in an unprejudiced manner that a simple correlation between parental and filial behaviour cannot possibly throw any light on the vexed question of nature and nurture. Either or both, in various combinations, could be responsible; we definitely need much clearer experimental designs to come to any reasonable conclusion. For the past fifty years or more, psychologists have argued that if you can show that if a father beats the everlasting daylights out of his son, and the son becomes a vicious psychopath, then it follows that the beatings the son received caused him to become a psychopath. Perhaps, but it is equally likely that the bad genes that caused the father's aggressive behaviour were inherited by his son and caused his aggressive behaviour. Or perhaps the son behaved in a psychopathic fashion when young, and this caused the father to see a savage beating as his only recourse. The data are inca-

147

pable of deciding between these (and other?) possibilities, and Galton's interpretation of his findings in genetic terms is as unacceptable as the interpretation by modern psychologists of their findings in environmental terms.

But naturally Galton's data have been reexamined by modern workers, and it has been found that only judges seemed to congregate within families; no such aggregation was found in other professions. More recent studies have failed to support Galton's view, using new material; Bullough and his co-workers found that "creative achievement was rarely carried on in the same family beyond one generation," and contrary to the assumption of Galton, creative achievers did not usually have children who also achieved. It has been argued that consequently heredity factors play a minor role at best in the determination of creativity. Clearly this conclusion follows as little from the new facts as Galton's did from the old facts; both are irrelevant to the nature-nurture debate.

In an earlier chapter I have discussed the phenomenon of *regression to the mean*; however creative the father, the children would on average be much lower in creativity, having regressed to the mean. Furthermore, half their genes are likely to have come from their mother, who is not likely to have been a genius (there is no known marriage between two geniuses!) This could itself rule out the likelihood of the child being a genius. Most important, however, is a third argument. Genius is the outcome of the synergistic (multiplicative) combination of *several* traits and abilities; as I shall argue later you do not inherit such *patterns* from your parents; so your inheriting just some of the constituents, such as high IQ, would not be able to reconstitute the pattern of creative achievement. This introduces the concept of *emergenesis*, closely related to the genetic fact of epistasis, that is, the interaction between different gene loci. In other words, human traits are likely to be governed by assemblies or combinations of genes whose interaction may not be additive but synergistic. Let me explain.

We start with the *genome*, that is, the entire collection of genes arranged in their forty-six chromosomes. These can be thought of as a blueprint or, better still, a very large book of instructions, each of whose 100,000 or so pages representing a different gene. Of these, about three-quarters are identical for all normal human individuals (*monomorphic genes,* determining that we have two legs and two arms, one nose, etc.) Some of these we share with other animals, many of them with the higher apes; only some are quite specifically human. Other genes are *polymorphic*, and responsible for genetically based individual differences within a given species. Genes have different *alleles*, that is, different variations or forms of expression, varying from two to twenty or so.

Genetic effects tend to be *additive*. We inherit "tall" genes from father or mother, on a random basis, and our height is determined by the *sum* of these genes (and some small environmental input via nutritional differences). Phenotypic height correlates about .95 for MZ twins, and .50 for DZ twins who only inherit half the same genes as their siblings. Height aggregates within a family because parents share 50 percent genetic variance with their children. And there is of course some regression to the mean. This is the model that is normally applied to intelligence, but it is not the only one, and it does not fit differences in creativity.

Many bodily features, like the eyes, are not constructed on this additive model, but rather on a *configural* model, in which all the component genes are essential, and the absence of, or change in any one, can produce a large and possibly disastrous change in the result. Polymorphic genes, as well as monomorphic genes, can behave in this configural manner. Traits and abilities that depend on *configuration* and polymorphic genes segregating independently would be shared (to the extent of genetic contribution) by MZ twins, who share all their genes and hence all gene configurations, but would not be likely to be shared by DZ twins, siblings, or parents and offspring. Such traits, while genetic, would not tend to run in families. As an example, consider facial beauty. This depends on the *configuration* of many different components (nose, forehead, ears, chin, lips, hair, etc.); any of these is inherited independently of the others, and hence their *configuration* will be identical for MZ twins (who inherit all the components in an identical manner), but not for DZ twins. The heritability of *individual elements* will be half that of the MZ twins, but the inheritance of the *configuration* will be practically nil for the DZ twins.

Remember Blaise Pascal's well-known words: "Le nez de Cleopatre: s'il eût eté plus court, toute la face de la terre aurait change." (Had Cleopatra's nose been shorter, the whole history of the world would have been different.) It is the whole facial configuration that made Cleopatra beautiful; sisters and DZ twins would have inherited length of nose separately from their inheritance of other facial features, but only MZ twins would have inherited the whole configuration, and hence her beauty!

If great creativity is the product of such a configuration, it clearly will not be inherited from a father (who has it) and a mother (who has not). Fathers and sons are genetically as close as DZ twins, hence the configuration is very unlikely to be inherited from father to son in any simple fashion. Does this mean that heredity plays no part? Quite the contrary. We can argue for the importance of heredity on precisely opposite lines to those adopted by Galton. The random segregation of genes that produces the genome of the child will very occasionally, and extremely rarely, produce a configuration necessary to give rise to a *genius*, and this may happen to any couple who are not themselves in the genius or even the high eminence class. Indeed, because over 99.9999 percent of the human race does not belong to this class, the genius is much more likely to come from relatively undistinguished parents who constitute the vast majority! Is this in fact true?

I have made a very thorough bibliographic study of the parents of children who grew up to be universally recognized as geniuses. Of the two dozen mathematicians who achieved immortal fame, only one or two came from families with any distinction in mathematics whatsoever. Gauss, perhaps the most famous, came from a completely undistinguished peasant family, as did Newton. The only possible exceptions are the Bernouilli family, which contained one genius and several high-ranking mathematicians. The same applies to scientists, painters, poets, dramatists, and composers. There is no case of a genius having a genius for a father—the best we can do is Mozart, whose father was a reasonably good musician, and Bach, who had several musically gifted relatives in his family, none of genius rank. For the great majority, father and mother were very ordinary folk, without any special gifts or achievements of their famous children!

In the vast majority of cases these very ordinary parents did not provide any particularly promising environment for their children. Michael Faraday, arguably the greatest physicist of the nineteenth century, grew up in great poverty, and with little education, as already mentioned. Most genomes come from middle-class families admittedly, but there was nothing to distinguish their upbringing or schooling from that received by millions of perfectly ordinary dullards who never achieved anything in the least creative. Occasionally of course the parents provided a hothouse atmosphere for the budding genius. John Stuart Mill was coached by his father, but Immanuel Kant, a much greater philosopher, was not. Galton was coached by his sister Adele, but Darwin was not so coached. Mozart was coached by his father, but Brahms was not. For every case where there was some favourable environmental factor, there are dozens where there was not. Let me give one example that may serve to give environmentalists sleepless nights, namely that of George Washington Carver, born into slavery. His heroic struggles to create an institute out of literally nothing are part of Negro history. He changed the agricultural and the eating habits of the South; he created, singlehanded, a pattern of growing food, harvesting, and cooking it which was to lift Negroes (and whites too!) out of the abject state of poverty and hunger to which they had been condemned by their own ignorance. And in addition to all his practical and teaching work, administration and speechmaking, he had time to do creative and indeed fundamental research; he was one of the first scientists to work in the field of synthetics, and is credited with creating the science of chemurgy—"agricultural chemistry." The American peanut industry is based on his work; today this is America's sixth most important agricultural product, with many hundreds of byproducts. He became more and more obsessed with the vision that out of agriculture and industrial waste useful materials could be created, and this entirely original idea is widely believed to have been Carver's most important contribution.

The number of his discoveries and inventions is legion; in his field, he was as productive as Edison. He could have become a millionaire many times over but he never accepted money for his discoveries. Nor would he accept an increase in his salary, which remained at the 125 dollars a month (£100 per year) which Washington had originally offered him. (He once declined an offer by Edison to work for him for a minimum salary of 100,000 dollars.) He finally died, over eighty, in 1943. His death was mourned all over the United States. The *New York Herald Tribune* wrote: "Dr. Carver was, as everyone knows, a Negro. But he triumphed over every obstacle. Perhaps there is no one in this century whose example has done more to promote a better understanding between the races. Such greatness partakes of the eternal." He himself was never bitter, in spite of all the persecutions he and his fellow-blacks had to endure: "No man can drag me down so low as to make me hate him." This was the epitaph on his grave: "He could have added fortune to fame, but caring for neither, he found happiness and honour in being helpful to the world."

What about his background? He was born the son of slaves; his mother, a widow, and her two children were abducted by raiders, and he was rescued by the farmer who owned him. He was brought up by the farmer and his wife, but was not allowed by the authorities to attend school as he wished. He suffered endless illnesses, and being a weakling, no good for hard work, he helped around the house. He became interested in nature, learned to tend flowers, and became an expert gardener. He also learned to make drawings and pictures, using paint self-made from the juice of berries, drawing on stones. His only teaching was by the wife of the farmer who set him free at the end of the Civil War. He applied to a college for admission, but was rejected when they discovered that he was black. Finally, he did gain acceptance elsewhere, and the rest, as they say, is history.

This brief story of a great scientist and a fine human being raises some very fundamental problems. Every year colleges and universities in the U.S. produce tens of thousands of agriculturalists, biologists, biochemists, and other experts in the fields in which George Carver worked. Every one of these has a family background, an education, and a degree of support compared with which Carver's would simply have been nonexistent. His father dead before he was born; his mother abducted while he was a baby; born a black slave in the deep South, weak and ailing, growing up in a poverty-stricken house with hardly any books, with the white people who brought him up not far from illiterate, denied schooling because of his colour, having to piece together the rudiments of an education while constantly hungry, and having to earn every penny he spent by performing the most menial jobs imaginable; exposed all the time to recurring traumas assumed to have been brought on by his early abduction under extremely unfavourable weather conditions (to say nothing of his emotional reactions); having only the most elementary and poorest kind of teaching; rejected because of his colour by institutes of higher learning; always having to work his way through secondary school and college; this kind of handicap is practically unknown now—however poor the education given to black children in the U.S. today. And compared with the education of black children, that of the favoured white boys and girls who present themselves with shining faces at the commencement ceremonies at American colleges and universities, has been exemplary—incorporating all the advances that modern educational science has been able to think up. And all these educational advantages are linked with, in most cases, happy, peaceful childhood experiences under the wise guidance and care of loving parents.

On the basis of an environmentalistic hypothesis, what wonders would we not expect these prodigies to perform! Surely soon the world will be completely changed by their discoveries—each one of them many times as productive, as inventive, as sagacious as the poor, ignorant black boy with his botched education and his nonexistent family life!

But reality teaches us that out of all these tens of thousands of molly-coddled youngsters, with all their highly favoured upbringing, their high standard of education, their impeccable family background, not one is likely to achieve even a tithe of what the untutored, self-taught George Washington Carver managed to do. Something, one cannot but feel, has gone seriously wrong; if environment is so all-powerful, then how can the worst type of environment imaginable produce such a wonderful human being, so outstanding a scientist, and how can the best type of environment that oceans of money can buy and the top brains in education conceive, produce so vast a number of nonentities, with perhaps a few reasonable scientists sprinkled among them?

It is difficult to know how persuasive these facts are in relation to the postulation of strong genetic involvement in creativity. One interesting study on this question, by Niels Waller and his associates, used the Creative Personality Scale on MZ (identical) and DZ (fraternal) twins. This is a scale that has successfully discriminated between creative and noncreative people, and possesses at least some degree of validity. The correlations found were 0.54 for MZ twins and –0.06 for DZ twins. These correlations are very interesting. As expected, MZ twins are much more alike than DZ twins; that is not the most interesting point. Normally DZ twins show a correlation *half* that of MZ twins; twice the difference then gives you an estimate of heritability. But twice 0.60 is 1.20—we can hardly have a heritability of 120 percent! Clearly the DZ correlation is far too low (essentially zero), and that strongly suggests emergenesis, or the inheritance of a *configuration* of traits which may show ordinary inheritance *singly,* but where the configural combination is only inherited as such by MZ twins. I shall come back to this configuration theory, after examining some of the elements (other than intelligence and creativity) that may go into creative achievement.

Twin studies actually using tests of creative thinking and ideational fluency have always reported higher correlations for MZ than for DZ twins, with heredity accounting for something like 25 percent of the total phenotypic variation. But these studies were mostly on a small scale, and the heritabilities therefore are not too reliably assessed. Also we would be happier if the means of several different tests had been used to measure creativity (e.g., divergent thinking, word association, picture complexity); no one test can tease out more than a small part of the concept of creativity. No doubt larger and better investigations will be forthcoming in the future. (Heritability estimates need large numbers of subjects to give reliable results; in recent studies of personality samples of 15,000 twins have been used! This also enables the investigator to go beyond simple estimates of heritability, and describe the detailed architecture of inheritance.) Overall we may conclude that genetic factors do play a part in creativity, but that the precise details are yet to be ascertained.

An intriguing question here is whether genius and creativity are identical in science and the arts, or whether they are quite different. It is certainly often said that creativity in science and in the arts is very different. If Newton had not lived, someone else would have produced the theory of gravitation, but if Beethoven had not lived, we would never have had the Ninth Symphony. Superficially this is true, but in actual fact the argument is very doubtful. It is true that we would not have had the *particular* set of notes that constitutes the Ninth Symphony, but without Newton we would not have had his *Opticks*, his *Principia*, or his infinitesimal calculus in the form he presented them. It is true that Leibnitz also produced his version of the infinitesimal calculus, but the two are certainly not the same—for one thing the notation originated by Leibnitz is greatly superior, and English mathematics suffered for a long time by adhering to Newton's notations. Newton's *Principia* is far more than a formula for calculating physical attraction; it incorporates philosophical assumptions about time and space, and prescriptions about scientific methodology. It also includes, as does the *Opticks*, insights and intuitions that seem uncanny, and led research into directions that might otherwise not have been followed. The work of a genius has a certain wholeness, a unique combination of elements, that makes it a work of art.

This aesthetic quality of scientific achievement is commented on by many outstanding scientists, and on tests creative scientists came out very high on aesthetic values. Max Born wrote that the advent of relativity made the universe of science not only grander but also more beautiful. Einstein insisted that scientific theories should be judged in terms of beauty, and Max Planck suggested that the new ideas of science are not generated by deduction but by "artistically creative imagination." We have already seen that "intuition" is an essential aspect of creativity, as much as science in the arts. Paul Dirac, on receiving the Nobel Prize for physics, remarked, "It seems that if one is working from the point of view of getting beauty in one's equations and if one has really sound insight, one is on a sure line of progress." Hardy, a famous British mathematician, argued that there was no permanent place in the world for ugly mathematics, and another mathematician, Jacques

Hadamard, suggested that mathematical invention is choice guided by aesthetic sense, and that the decisions of mathematicians are influenced by their sense of beauty.

Thomas Kuhn, the philosopher of science, argued that application of aesthetic sensitivity was essential to the progress of science:

> Something must make at least a few scientists feel that they are on the right track, and sometimes it is only personal and inarticulate aesthetic considerations that can do that. Men have been converted by them at times when most of the articulate technical arguments pointed the other way...even today Einstein's general theory attracts men principally on aesthetic grounds, an appeal that few people outside mathematics have been able to feel.

It is always wrong to look at some specific feature of a genuine creative scientific mathematical achievement and say: "This could and would have been found by someone else." It is the whole configuration of the scientist's creation that is unique and *in that form* would not have been produced by someone else. And the fundamental principle of great art, unity in variety, is also basic to scientific theories aspiring to beauty.

But it will be objected, scientific advancement is predictable, artistic advancement is not. Does that not tell them apart? This is a frequent misapprehension; in fact scientific progress is *not* predictable, even in broad outline, but artistic change is predictable. The Chinese invented many of the things we pride ourselves on, long before we did: the printing press, the suspension bridge, the parachute, the seismograph, mustard gas, the blast furnace, the stirrup, gunpowder—there is no end to the number of these "one-off" discoveries. Robert Temple's *The Genius of China* gives an unending list of creative achievements. But one thing is missing—they failed to develop *science* in the Western sense! This unique achievement eluded them; there was all the variety, but no unity. They never had a Galileo, or a Newton, to show them the right way to the creation of scientific systems, all-embracing theories, co-ordinated discoveries as part of a larger plan. Nobody could have predicted this failure. All the elements seemed to be there a thousand years before they came together in Europe, yet—nothing happened. All we have are one-off discoveries, showing individual genius of the highest order. But no systematic science!

And who would have predicted the emergence of relativity theory, or quantum mechanics! Physicists used to say that all the fundamental discoveries had been made, and it only remained to dot the i's and cross the t's of Newton's theories. The revolution that occurred at the turn of the century shook the world of science to its very foundations. There was no way of predicting the outcome of the revolution, and nobody actually did predict what happened. So this illusion of scientific predictability is just that—an illusion.

But surely at least some scientific developments are predictable, whereas nothing in art obeys any laws or rules of any kind? The recent book by Colin Martindale, *The Clockwork Muse*, will soon show the hollowness of that argument. Martindale in his book argues that there are two forces that shape artistic production. The first is *originality*; what has been done once cannot be done again. So there is a drive among artists to be original, to do what has not been done before. This accounts for periodic revolutions. The rise of the impressionist school of painting is such a revolution. But between revolutions—you can't have these all the time, of course—there is a shift from what he calls *conceptual* to *primordial* expression. Conceptual thinking is abstract, logical, and reality-oriented. Primordial thinking is free-associative, concrete, irrational and autistic. It is the thought of dreams and reveries. Martindale's theory is essentially this. We demand from art that it should produce *arousal*. Emily Dickinson, the American poet, once defined *arousal potential* in poetry as follows: "If I read a book and it makes my whole body so cold a fire can never warm me, I know *that* is poetry. These are the only ways I know it. Is there any other way?" Well, other people get goose-pimples when confronted with great art, but the point will be clear. Great art is not boring; it is arousing cognitively, emotionally, physically.

Now it is well-documented that if a *novel* stimulus produces arousal, repetition of identical or similar stimuli leads to a lowering of arousal. Hence the demand for *novelty*; we are tired of repetitions, however excellent technically, of what we have seen or heard before. So the artist searches for novelty, for ways of increasing arousal. The best way of doing this, is by increasing *primordial content* of the poem, or the painting. Another is to change style, as the impressionists did. The two interact; when a new style is introduced, this is enough to produce arousal, and conceptual thinking takes over. But after a while the new style becomes well known and sufficiently explored, and we need an increase in primordial thinking to maintain arousal. This increase cannot be maintained indefinitely, and finally leads to a new style, and a reduction in primordial thinking.

Martindale used a quantitative method of measuring the variables in his equation, using *verse* as his medium. (He also applied his theory to painting and other types of art). Using material from 170 British poets born in thirty-three consecutive twenty-year periods from 1290 through 1949, he found as predicted that primordial content increased across time, with superimposed quasiperiodic oscillations due to stylistic changes. Chaucerian, Skeltonic, Tudor, Jacobean, neoclassic, preromantic, romantic, postromantic, and modern. The introduction of a new style is followed by a *decline* in primordial content, and then by a rise to a higher level. Figure 12.1 shows the actual process, quantitatively determined by Martindale's analysis. It bears out his theory in great detail, and demonstrates that poetry is highly predictable as indeed is painting and other types of artistic product. Of course there are many qualifications, but in essence Martindale has proved his point.

Martindale's theory is typical of scientific creativity—bringing together a number of ideas rumbling in their separate containers. And who can say whether this particular theory would ever have been put forward if Martindale had not been there to present it? In the form he has given it, it will undoubtedly lead to much research that will certainly modify the theory, until in the end we will understand much better our emotional and cognitive reactions to artistic productions. His work is unique in the same way an artist's work is unique. Once the idea has been put forward, many others can jump in and develop it. In the same way many painters can now paint *in the style* of Van Gogh, or Cezanne, or Monet, often indistinguishable from the original even to expert eyes. Expert forgers have got away with it time and again; once the door is opened by the genius, others far from being geniuses can imitate, improve, change. But that does not alter the fact that without the genius there could be nothing to imitate, improve, or change.

It has been argued by sociologists that the existence of multiples (doubles, triples, or quadruples) show that genius is not needed for creative achievement in science, because if two or three, or four people can invent or discover the same thing around the same time, the invention or discovery is a function of the time, of circumstances, of society, and not of the creative genius. This is not an acceptable argument. In the first place, the actual *nature* of the alleged doubles has often been very different; I have made the point already in connection with the invention of the calculus. Two discoveries or inventions may seem vaguely similar, but differ in very profound ways. Second, alleged doubles often occur sufficiently distant in point of time, so that one discoverer or inventor might have heard of the other person's findings. These would then not be genuine doubles. And finally, Dean Simonton

FIGURE 12.1

THE CLOCKWORK MUSE

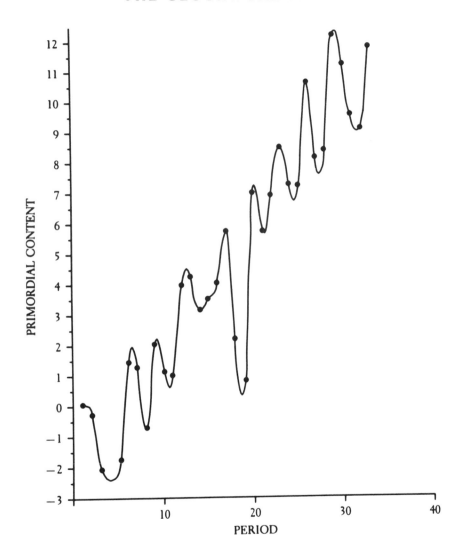

Premordial control, in press, in successive period, falling after style changes, and rising again prior to the next style change.

has made a statistical analysis of doubles, triples, and higher multiples, and shown that they obey a general law, usually called the Poisson distribution. This is a formula describing the frequencies with which rare events occur; when I was teaching statistics I used to illustrate it by counting the number of female visitors to a burlesque show, but orthodox statisticians prefer the number of men in Prussian-mounted regiments killed by being kicked to death by their horses. The formula fits the actual distribution of multiples perfectly.

Given that the formula fits doublets, triplets, and all higher multiples, we can use it to estimate the very much larger number of singletons (only one person made the discovery or invention), and nulltons (nobody made the discovery or invention, although it was there to be made). The statistical argument is too involved to state here, but I will quote Simonton's conclusion: "Rather than endorsing the Zeitgeist or social deterministic interpretation, multiples lend strong support to the notion that chance plays a predominant role in scientific discovery and technological inventions." In other words, a given genius has a certain chance of solving a given problem; there is a much lower probability that two geniuses will solve it around the same time, and a very low probability indeed that three will do so. But there is a strong probability that no-one will come up with the right answers!

Of course there are differences between creativity in the arts and the sciences, but these are probably less profound and less far-spreading than is usually assumed. Success in either demands high creativity and intuitive ability, as well as specific abilities. But all have in common the need for creativity.

13

Psychopathology and Creativity

So far I have been concerned with some of the facts relevant to a *description* of the creative mind, quantified as far as possible but still purely descriptive. But of course what we are really looking for scientifically is a *causal* account, a theory or a model that can explain *why* and *how* creative people are able to do what they do so well. Such a theory has to be based, of course, on the facts I have discussed in previous sections, but it has to go well beyond them before we can claim to have a proper account of creativity. Such an account must begin, I believe, with the paradox that psychopathology seems closely linked with genius and creativity generally, but that actual psychosis is detrimental to genuine creativity. This paradox may find its solution in a theory I put forward some forty years ago, and I will discuss this theory in this section before going on to use it for a causal account of creativity.

Psychiatrists, being medically trained, have always tried to impose a medical model on the plethora of mental disorders, attempting to sort them out into disease categories. Thus Emil Kraepelin recognized two major functional psychoses: manic depressive insanity and dementia praecox, renamed schizophrenia by Eugen Bleuler. But such a diagnostic scheme, although convenient, immediately ran into difficulties. Kraepelin himself recognized some of these when he said: "No experienced psychologist will deny that there is an alarmingly large number of cases in which it seems impossible, in spite of the most careful observation, to make a firm diagnosis…it is becoming increasingly clear that we cannot distinguish satisfactorily between these two illnesses, and this raises the suspicion that our formulation of the problems may be incorrect." The well-known difficulty of obtaining acceptable reliabilities in the diagnosis of psychotic disorders bears ample testimony to the difficulty of this problem—different psychiatrists come up with different diagnoses of the same patients.

I have suggested, on the basis of a large body of experimental data, that the fault lies in the medical model. We are dealing with a continuum, as in the case of blood pressure, where normality blends slowly into disease. Figure 13.1 shows roughly what this continuum is meant to be; it ranges from altruistic, socialized, conformist behaviour to subclinical, schizoid, and finally psychotic behaviour. Psychotic manifestations are graded in terms of severity, with "schizophrenic" the most severe, and unipolar depression the least, manic depressive and schizo-affective manifestations in between. This personality dimension, underlying the continuum, I called *psychoticism,* and the normal curve indicates that it is distributed roughly normally. The line P_A indicates that the further to the right a person's score on psychoticism is, the more likely is he to succumb to a psychotic type of disorder under stress.

This dimension of personality is additional to, and independent of, the other major dimensions of personality, extraversion-introversion (E) and neuroticism-stability (N). The personality traits that have been found characteristic of psychoticism (P) are shown in figure 13.2, thus the high-P scorer is cold, aggressive, impersonal, egocentric, impulsive, antisocial, tough-minded, unempathic—and creative! This personality picture is not very different from that of the *schizoid personality* as pointed out by Eugen Bleuler, the son of Manfred. He regarded schizoid people as being near psychotic, but not quite certifiable, such people

FIGURE 13.1

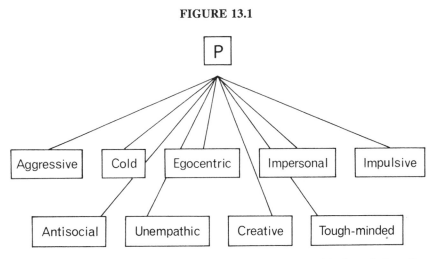

Diagrammatic representation of traits intercorrelating to provide formulations for the concept of psychoticism.

FIGURE 13.2

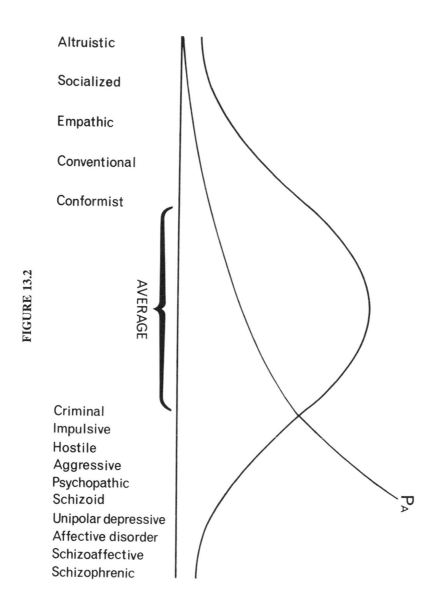

FIGURE 13.2

The psychoticism continuum, PA, indicates the probability of developing psychosis under stress, for different parts of the continuum.

are often found in the schizophrenic *Erbkreis,* that is, among close relatives of schizophrenics.

This is how Bleuler described the schizoid personality:

> He is taciturn or has little regard for the effects on others of what he says. Sometimes he appears tense and becomes irritated by senseless provocation. He appears as insincere and indirect in communication. His behaviour is aloof and devoid of human warmth; yet he does have a rich inner-life. In this sense he is introverted. Ambivalent moods are more pronounced in the schizoid than in others, just as he distorts the meanings of, and introduces excessive doubts into, his own concepts. But on the other hand, the schizoid is also capable of pursuing his own thoughts and of following his own interests and drives, without giving enough consideration to other people and to the actual realities of life. He is autistic. The better side of this autism reveals a sturdiness of character, and inflexibility of purpose, an independence and a *predisposition to creativity.* The worse side of it becomes manifest in a lack of consideration for others, unsociability, a world-alien attitude, stubbornness, ego-centricity, and occasionally even cruelty.

This agrees well with my conception of P. Note the phrase I have put in italics: "predisposition to creativity." This is in essence the hypothesis I wish to present, namely that high P is closely and causally related to creativity. This notion would explain our paradox—creativity is linked indissolubly with psychoticism, but actual psychosis destroys this link. But before presenting the large body of evidence supporting this view, I shall discuss the differences between Bleuler's hypothesis and mine, the ways schizoid behaviour and P differ from one another.

Bleuler regarded schizoid behaviour as closely linked with schizophrenia; he did not extend the connection to manic-depressive behaviour, or extend it as a continuum to normal behaviour. Such an extension is crucial to my model, and also essential for any theory of creativity; severe depression has been linked time and again with creative performance in poetry writing, and other artistic pursuits. Several studies of poets and writers found well over half to be suffering from such depressions. Thus a theory that fails to link schizoid behaviour to depression cannot explain why depression, too, is so closely linked with creativity. The hypothesis that an underlying and predisposing personality structure is basic to all types of functional psychoses is unique to the conception of P.

In view of the continuing insistence of psychiatry to regard schizophrenia and manic-depressive illness as separate disorders, what is the evidence supporting the P concept? I have reviewed the very extensive evidence in my book on genius; here I will only point out a few particularly relevant studies. Professor R.E. Kendell selected a group of patients diagnosed repeatedly as suffering from schizophrenia, and another group diagnosed as suffering from affective disorder, thus creating two groups that should have nothing in common on the Kraepelin-Bleuler hypothesis. He then created a scale, made up of the symptoms that best differentiated the two groups. Diagnostic items favouring affective illness (early morning waking, delusions of guilt) were counted on one side, items favouring a diagnosis for schizophrenia (affective flattening, lack of insight) on the other. Plotting the distribution of points should have given a clear bipolar distribution, with affective disorders on the one side, schizophrenics on the other. Nothing of the kind happened, most people were in the middle! A repetition of the study produced a normal curve, again with most patients in the middle. When you remember that these were as clear cases of schizophrenia and affective disorders as you are likely to get, it is clear that there is no such absolute difference between the groups as Kraepelin supposed.

Figure 13.3 shows the actual incidence of the most discriminating symptoms. What is most surprising is that both groups show the great majority of symptoms to much the same extent, none are found truly typical of either group. And these were picked out as the most diagnostic! Of course, there are some differences in the symptomatology of these two groups, but none are absolute, and *similarities* are much more striking than differences. Clearly we are dealing with a continuum, not different disease entities.

If Kraepelin was right, there should be a clear relation between diagnosis and outcome variables; such as occupational record, time in hospital, or social outcome. No such differences were found. What is found is that the likelihood of schizo-affective patients (cry-for-help label stuck on the large number of patients nobody can diagnose as either schizophrenic or affective) getting better, is intermediate between that of schizophrenic (worst diagnosis) and manic-depressive (better diagnosis). Thus on our continuum I have put schizophrenia at the end, and the others at lower levels of P, as shown in figure 13.1.

The response to medication might mark out a clear-cut difference, but does not in fact do so; both diagnostic groups may respond to similar drugs. Even ECT is not a specific treatment for manic-depressives; many schizophrenics also respond to it. It is also found that frequently the biological abnormalities reported in schizophrenia and assumed to be of aetiological significance are subsequently found in affective disorders also. And epidemiological findings relating to sex ratio, age-incidence, risk of suicide, and seasonal variation on onset of birth are

FIGURE 13.3

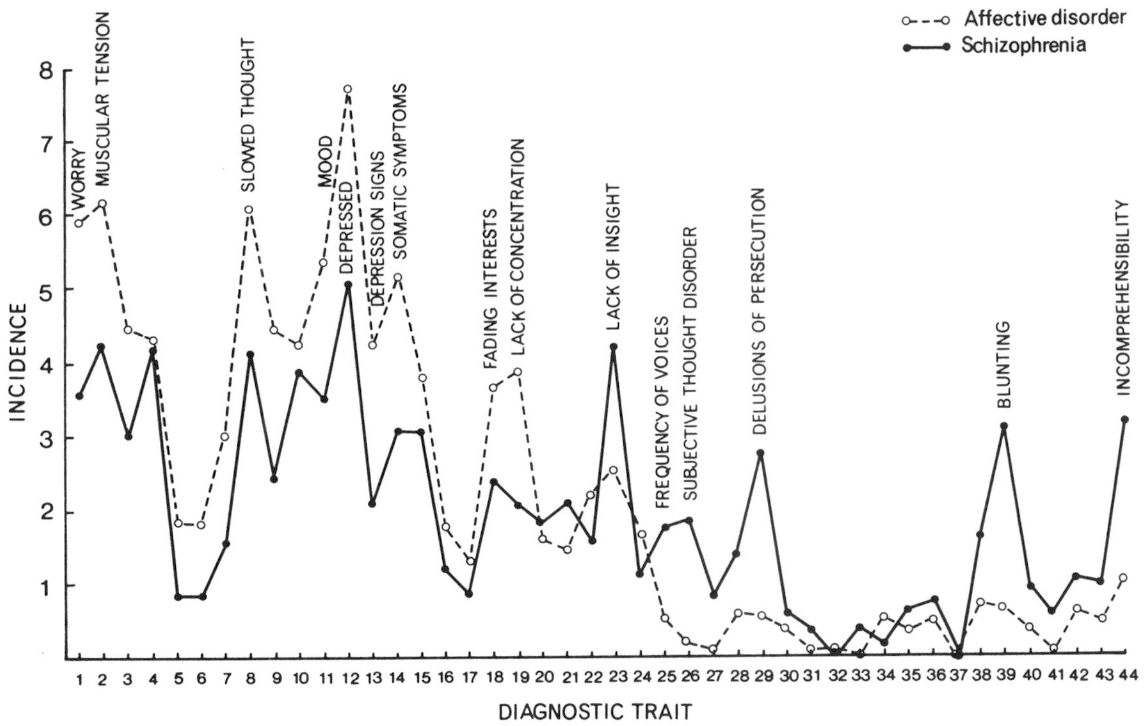

Incidence of various symptoms in representative patients suffering from schizophrenia and affective disorder.

similar for both diagnostic categories, although there are differences in age of onset by sex.

Finally, a large number of studies have shown that schizotypal personality disorder (schizoid) is also genetically linked to affective disorder, including affective disorder with psychotic features. There are many findings showing that there are no absolute differences between schizophrenia and manic depressive psychosis, as Kraepelin's hypothesis requires, and it is difficult not to postulate a *continuum* as representing the facts.

But does this continuum coincide with P, as measured by the Eysenck Personality Questionnaire? Again there are too many studies to review here, but I shall pick out the most important. There are obvious methodological problems in answering such a question, and I have constructed a special type of analysis that can satisfactorily answer the problem. Let us assume the existence of a continuum, such as that shown in figure 13.1. Let us subdivide it into two parts, one to the extreme left, containing normal subjects (defined as not having been diagnosed as suffering a psychotic disorder), the other to the extreme right, containing patients suffering from functional psychoses. On Kraepelin's hypothesis, and general psychiatric practice of regarding schizophrenia and manic-depressive illness as two separate diseases, both quite different from normality, there does not exist such a continuum. To decide between the two theories, continuum or not, we have to find an experimental *paradigm* that would give clearly different answers according to which theory was correct. I have suggested the proportionality criterion.

Let us take a test that clearly discriminates between normals and psychotics; let us call this test T. On the continuum hypothesis, and assuming that P represents this continuum, we would expect that in the normal part of the continuum, T would also distinguish between high scorers on P (P+) and low scorers on P (P–) in the sense that P+ scorers, as compared with P– scorers, should react to the test, T, as psychotics do compared to normals. None of these predictions would apply to the Kraepelin hypothesis, nor would they apply if P was not a good measure of the hypothetical continuum. How does the test work out?

As an example, consider HLA B27, a subsystem of the human leucocyte antigen system which is found more frequently in schizophrenics than in normal, nonpsychotic subjects. It has been found that both in a normal, and also in a psychotic group of subjects, those with HLA B27 had higher P scores than those without, exactly as demanded by the continuity hypothesis, and the theory that P measures the continuum involved. This is only one of many tests that have been used, and these tests encompass a wide variety of types. One class deals with *biological* variables; HLA B27 is one example, others are mono-amine oxydase, serotonin, and dopamine. A second class deals with laboratory behaviour, such as eye-tracking, dichotic shadowing, and sensitivity levels. A third is concerned with learning and conditioning variables, such as latent inhibition and negative priming. These are important for our causal theory, and I will come back to them later. Yet a fourth is concerned with psychological variables (word association, hallucinatory activities.) And finally we have physiological variables such as electro-myography and autonomic-perceptual inversion to give us a fifth set of variables. It is the variety of variables which makes the results impressive; for all of these variables the test resulted in a *positive* outcome. To obtain successful results over a wide array of variables, suggests that the underlying hypothesis is likely to be on the right lines.

The theoretical prediction that emerges from the preceding arguments is of course that P, representing the psychopathological personality trait that has been associated so frequently with creativity and creative achievement, would be correlated with measures of trait creativity, and with actual creative achievement. The evidence clearly supports such a conclusion, and will be briefly reviewed here. Let us look first of all at creativity tests of the divergent type, because these have been more widely used than any others to measure creativity. Early studies, using a variety of subjects and tests, came up with convincing positive correlations between P and divergent thinking creativity. They also showed *negative* correlations between P and an acceptance of the existing culture, and found high P scorers to have unusual associative processes.

The most impressive study, authored by Erik Woody and Gordon Claridge, used 100 university students, all of high intelligence, and administered the Wallach-Kogan Creativity tests to them. There are five divergent thinking tests included in this well-known and widely used measure; the titles will suffice to give an indication of what the subject has to do. The correlation of the unusual responses scores on this test with P were very high indeed; 0.61 with Instances, 0.64 with Patterns Meanings; 0.66 with Uses, 0.68 with Similarities, 0.65 with Line Meanings. When all tests and scores were combined, the correlation with P amounted to 0.84; considering that neither P nor divergent thinking is measured with anything like perfect reliability; this is a truly astonishing figure for a correlation between a personality trait (P) and an ability measure.

Nor does it stand alone; quite recently Antonia Stavridon and Adrian Furnham carried out a replication and attained correlations only slightly lower—0.49, 0.49, 0.51, 0.44 and 0.33. Other authors have also found positive correlations between P and divergent thinking scores, and we must add the large number who found positive correlations with other similar measures of psychopathology. We may consider that this measure of creativity certainly correlates positively with psychoticism.

In an experiment of my own, I used the word association test, the Barron-Welsh Art Scale, personality scales measuring P, E, N, and L (a measure of conformity), impulsiveness, venturesomeness, and empathy, as well as verbal and nonverbal IQ tests. The results were analysed by a multidimensional scaling technique, which puts together in two-dimensional space, tests that belong together because of their intercorrelations. The IQ tests come out on a separate group, not related to creativity at all. There was also a creativity complex, made up of the Barron-Welsh complexity score, the P+ score, as well as impulsiveness, venturesomeness, and extraversion scores—all personality traits that had often been found in creative individuals. And finally there was a group of measures indicative of low creativity, conformity, common word association responses, empathy and neuroticism, that is, lack of ego-strengths. These results are just what theory would predict, and they lend support to the existence of a strong bond between personality and creativity.

Similar results to those outlined above have been found when psychopathology was measured using various schizotypy scales; I will not go into detail here. These studies, and those already discussed, have just one weakness; they do not deal with actual creative achievement of a high order. Does our theory work there as well?

The answer seems to be in the affirmative. There are obvious problems here, not so much in identifying the most creative artists, but rather in persuading them to take part in a psychological experiment! Artists, and artistic people in general, tend to regard science with a frown, and psychologists in particular tend to be viewed as enemies of art and culture! I had been working on the construction of a measure of visual aesthetic sensitivity together with K.O. Goetz, perhaps the best-known German nonrepresentational painter and Karen Goetz, his wife and also a well-known painter. They managed to succeed where I had failed, in persuading 147 male and 110 female leading German painters and sculptors to fill in my personality questionnaire. The outcome was very clear. Male artists had much higher P scores than male nonartists, and female artists had much higher P scores than female nonartists. Goetz, knowing these artists personally, was able to supplement the questionnaire results with detailed stories about their behaviour that left little doubt about the validity of the high-P scores!

The work of Goetz thus offers important support for the results of Woody and Claridge, and the other authors cited above, in that their work uses actual artistic achievement as a criterion for the measurement of creativity and originality. In doing so they give credibility to the validity of divergent thinking tests as measures of creativity and originality, and the fact that both in the artistic and in the nonartistic population studied by other investigators, significant correlations found between psychoticism and creativity and originality very much strengthens the hypothetical link between the personality trait and the behavioural pattern. We may thus be justified in concluding that originality and creativity are the outcome of certain traits, rather than (or as well as) aspects of cognitive ability.

Does the fact that creative people have high P scores serve to explain anything? In the next chapter I will try and disentangle the complexity of creative cognitive processes characteristic of creative thinking; here I will end up by looking at the behaviour of creative people. The main clue to an understanding here of the fact, apparent in every study so far done, that males have much higher P scores than females. High P scorers also tend to have higher concentrations of testosterone, the male hormone. Why should this be so?

Men have always shown high P type behaviour—aggressiveness, hostility, egocentricity, impulsiveness, lack of conformity, and antisocial traits, while women have tended to show typical low P behaviour. No doubt evolution accounts for these differences, just as it no doubt accounts for the much higher neuroticism scores of women. Differences in physical strength, employment as warriors and hunters, defence of their families—all these and other factors as well have given rise over the millenia to typical masculine and feminine behaviours observed not only in humans but also in apes and most other mammals. And of course it is precisely this type of behaviour that is needed by the budding genius to combat the onslaught of his less-gifted, mediocre colleagues, envious of his superior gifts, determined to defend endangered orthodoxy, and certain of their rectitude! His creed must be that of the poet who wrote:

When defiance fierce is thrown
At the Gods to whom you bow,
Rest the lips of the unknown
Tenderest upon my brow!

Intellectual and other mental gifts are the essential basis on which genius and creativity are built, but unless the creative person can defend his creation against all the evils I have described in an earlier chapter, and defend it vigorously, there is little chance of it surviving. Hence the need for the masculine, P+ behaviours in the creative person. And possibly it is the comparative absence of these (not always attractive) qualities that make it difficult for women to reach the highest levels of creativity, and aspire to the name of genius. Not every creative artist or scientist has such a difficult time as those mentioned earlier, but most do, and genetically this need of creativity to fight for recognition may have led to the firm connection between them in the Personality dimension P.

14

Cognition and Creativity

There is considerable agreement that the essential nature of creativity and intuition lies in the bringing together of ideas, facts, theories, concepts, hypotheses, impressions, perceptions, thoughts, views, or notions that had not previously been associated, but that in combination produce a result judged useful by those acquainted with the field in question. Note that there are two equally important requirements. The first relates to the steepness of the associative gradient I have referred to earlier; most associations are close to the idea with which they are associated, giving a steep gradient. Associations characteristic of a shallow gradient are unusual, and far from being close to the idea with which they are associated. The "word salad," the unconnected ideas often produced by the schizophrenic would fit this part of the description of creativity, but not the second part—the result has no social value at all, it is essentially meaningless, at least to the listener.

Yet the mechanisms underlying the word salad of the schizophrenic and the remote associations of the creative person may be similar cognitively, and it seemed worthwhile to pursue this idea, particularly in view of the association between the two furnished by their relation to the personality trait of psychoticism. There is a long history of study of psychotic cognitions, and this may be of interest to the student of creativity. Let us begin with the concept of "overinclusiveness" originated by N. Cameron some fifty years ago. It is a term to characterize the inability of schizophrenics to maintain the normal conceptual boundaries, and their liability to incorporate into their concepts elements, some of them personal, which are merely associated with the concept, without being an essential part of it. Experimentally this can be tested by such measures as object-sorting tests. You present the subject with a number of objects and ask him to sort these into groups. The principles of grouping may be colour, use, size, material, or anything else relevant. Indeed, you can sort words or ideas in a similar manner. The main point is that psychotics use more categories to sort things into, but these are often meaningless. High P scorers also use more categories than low P scorers, but these are meaningful and often original.

It has been suggested that it is possible to reformulate Cameron's theory of overinclusion in a slightly more general way so that a number of predictions follow from it. Concept formation can be regarded as largely the result of discrimination learning. When a child first hears a word in a certain context, the word is associated with the entire situation (stimulus compound). As the word is heard again and again, only certain aspects of the stimulus compound are reinforced. Gradually the extraneous aspects cease to evoke the response (the word), having become "inhibited" through lack of "reinforcement." The "inhibition" is in some sense an active process, as it suppresses a response which was formerly evoked by the stimulus. "Overinclusive thinking" may be the result of a disorder (failure) of the process whereby "inhibition" is built up to circumscribe and define the learned response (the word or "concept"). In short, it could be an extreme degree of 'stimulus generalization."

The same theory can be expressed in different terms. All purposeful behaviour depends for its success on the fact that some stimuli are "attended to" and some other stimuli are ignored. It is a well-known fact that when concentrating on one task, normal people are quite unaware of most stimuli irrelevant to the task. It is as if some "filter mechanism" cuts out or inhibits the stimuli, both internal and external, which are irrelevant to the task in hand, and thus to allow the most efficient "processing" of incoming information; overinclusive thinking might be only one aspect of a general breakdown of this "filter" mechanism.

The term "overinclusiveness" has now been superseded by others, such as "allusive thinking," or "looseness of cognition," but the underlying idea is the same—a shallow associationist gradient, mediating novel combinations of ideas. The word association test is perhaps the most widely used test of this concept, and we have already seen that it groups creative persons with schizophrenics and manic-depressives. If "overinclusiveness" is the common link between psychosocial creativity, at least as far as the originality and unusualness of associations is concerned, and if it is due to a failure of inhibition, as suggested above, can we measure directly this process of inhibition? And is it true that it fails in the case of psychotics and creative people? The answer seems to lie with the concept of *latent inhibition*.

This concept is defined in terms of the experimental processes used to measure it. This involves two stages. In the first of these we present the subject with a task that is quite irrelevant to what we are really trying to measure, but which will engage his attention. Let us say we make him learn a list of word pairs, so that he can say the second word of each pair when the first word of the pair is presented. At irregular intervals during this learning process we present some completely irrelevant stimulus, say, a soft bell sound. Subjects disregard it, and concentrate on their appointed task. Now according to conditioning theory, this irrelevant stimulus, call it S_1 serves as a link in a conditioning process—it is not followed by any sort of response, so it signals to the subject the association: S_1—no response. Unknowingly this is what the subject learns; S_1 does not mean anything, and we need not pay any attention to it.

We now come to the second part of the experiment. In this we try to condition the subject to link S_1 with some response, let us call this R. We sound the bell (S_1), and follow it with a puff of air to the eyeball, which leads to closure of the eyelid (R). After a while, our subject blinks to S_1, even before the puff of air is administered. This is the so-called eyelid conditioning paradigm. But theory says, and experiment shows, that the preexposure phase in which S_1 had no effect (no R of any kind) has made S_1 more difficult to use as the conditioned stimulus for eyelid closure; compared with the effects of some other stimulus (S_2) that had not been used in a preexposure trial: *conditioning to S_1 takes significantly longer.* In other words, cognitive inhibition has been built into S_1 through our procedure, and if the theory linking such inhibition and *normal* associative functioning is correct, then high P scorers and schizophrenics, who appear to have little such inhibition, should show less of an effect when S_1 is used, than do normal low P subjects.

This is precisely what has been found in a number of experimental studies. *Latent inhibition,* as the phenomenon is called, is much weaker, and may be completely absent, in schizophrenics and high P scorers as compared with normals and low P scorers. Thus overinclusiveness is explained by the low inhibitory potential of psychotics and creative people; they fail to form the appropriate conditioned responses of S_1, and hence this stimulus fails to have the correct inhibitory properties. Extended to the field of association of ideas, we may say that *latent inhibition prevents the formation of remote associations,* and leads to a person having a steep associative gradient. Poor latent inhibition leads to a shallow associative gradient, and the production of many unusual, remote associations, and hence creativity in the genius, word salad in the schizophrenic. This, in brief, is the theory accounting for the similarities in cognitive functioning between creative people and psychotics. The major deduction from such a theory is of course that both psychotics and high P scorers should show little latent inhibition, and as already mentioned, that is precisely what has been found. Another prediction, namely that people who score high on creativity tests should do poorly on tests of latent inhibition, has not yet been tested, but should be decisive in evaluating the theory.

Can we go one step further? Theories of schizophrenia have emphasized its cognitive dysfunction in recent years, and there is much agreement with the notion that schizophrenia has a major attentional deficit component. This of course links up with the major theory associated with latent inhibition, namely that the absence of latent inhibition is due to attentional failure to S_1. There is further much agreement that schizophrenia is mediated by a dopamine system dysfunction. Dopamine of course is one of the major neurotransmitters, and has recently been associated experimentally with P, as well as with schizophrenia. Perhaps we can link dopamine directly with latent inhibition? Such a link would strongly support the theory here developed. The experimental evidence does indeed bear out this deduction. It has been found that dopamine agonists, such as amphetamines, attenuate or abolish latent inhibition, while dopamine antagonists, such as heloperidol or chlorpromazine increase latent inhibition. In other words, these drugs act on latent inhibition in much the same way as they act on schizophrenia. Those that increase severity of schizophrenic symptoms attenuate or abolish latent inhibition, while those that reduce or abolish the severity of schizophrenic symptoms increase latent inhibition. Again, we await a direct experimental study of the relation between creativity and dopaminergic activity.

As a final argument relating to our theory, consider the notion of "relevance." Scientists tend to consider in their theorising only data that are judged to be "relevant." But this is an elusive concept; difficult problems often find their solutions in terms of data and ideas not considered relevant by experts. It has often been remarked that great creative advances are frequently made by outsiders, precisely because they are not prevented from creative thinking by notions of orthodox "relevance." Wegener was not a geologist, but a meteorologist when he proposed his theory of continental drift. Pasteur was not a medical man, but his discoveries were fundamental for modern medicine. Mendel was not a geneticist, but practically created single-handedly modern genetics. Pavlov was not a psychologist, but was probably more important for its development than any other person. The list is endless.

Now Jeff Gray has drawn attention to a large empirical literature when he says, of schizophrenia, that "there is a weakening of the capacity to select for cognitive processing only those stimuli that, given past experience of similar contexts, are relevant." This might be regarded as a statement of schizophrenic deficit, but it also fits in perfectly with our view of creativity. If we select for cognitive processing only those stimuli that, given past experiences of similar contexts, are relevant, then clearly we are not going to use those stimuli in a novel, original, creative manner! The formulation of "normality" implicit in it would condemn us to forever do the customary, ordinary, accepted, familiar, habitual, regular, traditional; never the novel, adventurous, imaginative, inventive, visionary, or stimulating sort of thing we call "creative." Perhaps here we have the essential link between genius and madness, creativity and psychoticism, originality and cognitive impairment. The influence of past experience can be useful for everyday living, but may be a dead hand for the creation of novel experiences and difficult problem solutions. Perhaps plotting the importance of past experiences against mental health gives us a curvilinear regression; too much leads to rigidity, fixed behaviour, lack of flexibility, intransigence, undeviating courses of action, while too little leads to gross abnormality, as in schizophrenia. Best is a middle position, making use of prior experience, but not being a slave to it.

We end up with a general model of creativity that goes from DNA (heredity) to creative achievement (figure 14.1). Heredity determines the working of neurophysiological structures, in particular the hippocampal formation, and the neurotransmitter receptors, in particular those associated with dopamine and serotonin. Their activity leads to cognitive inhibition, as determined by latent inhibition and negative priming (a somewhat similar process that has been linked experimentally with creativity). Failure of cognitive inhibition leads to psychoticism (when counteracted by traits related to ego-strength), and to schizophrenia, and manic-depressive illness when not so counteracted. Psychoticism, in turn, leads to (trait) creativity, which when joined synergistically with motivational and cognitive traits, and sociocultural variables, may under favourable circumstances, result in the outstanding creative achievement we attribute to genius. Much remains to be filled in in this model, but there is also much support for it. Perhaps *ars invendi* can be studied scientifically, after all!

FIGURE 14.1

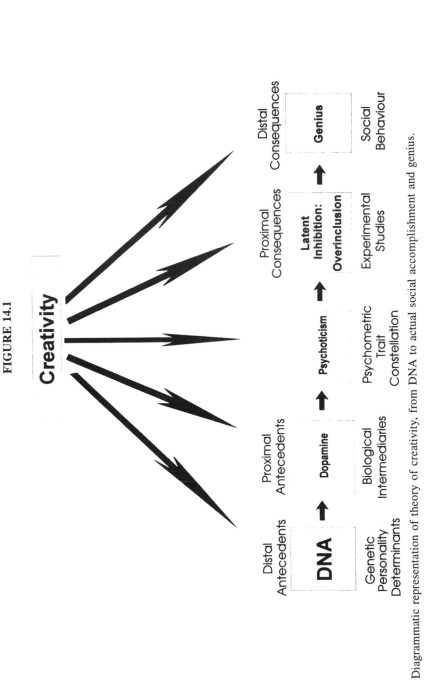

Diagrammatic representation of theory of creativity, from DNA to actual social accomplishment and genius.

It would not be right to stop here. Psychoticism, dopamine and latent inhibition play a role on the cognitive side, but something more is needed. The genius, and even the less elevated creative scientist or artist, is usually opposed by the orthodox majority—inevitably so, because what is *new* challenges established truth, and must therefore be destroyed. Does P and dopamine throw any light on the fighting qualities the creative person has to develop in order to survive? It may be useful to document the "fight for survival" of the creative person a little further.

Bronowski once wrote a paean to scientists, which is as naive as it is stereotyped:

> By the worldly standards of public life, all scholars in their work are of course oddly virtuous. They do not make wild claims, they do not cheat, they do not try to persuade at any cost, they appeal neither to prejudice nor to authority, they are often frank about their ignorance, their disputes are fairly decorous, they do not confuse what is being argued with race, politics, sex or age, they listen patiently to the young and to the old who both know everything. These are the general virtues of scholarship, and they are peculiarly the virtues of science.

In my experience scientists are no different from other human beings. Many of them (not all!) do make wild claims, appeal to prejudice and authority, claim omniscience, fight like Manx cats, and are jealous of their peers. To help potential young rivals, more creative and more original in their thinking, would certainly go against the grain. There are exceptions, but to deify scientists is factually quite wrong and historically incorrect; Newton is a much more likely role model—cheating, constantly engaged in underhand battles about priority, insanely jealous of others' achievements, trying to do rivals down, seeking authoritative office—a poor human being, yet one of the greatest scientists ever! If the budding genius had to depend on older peers, he would be in a sorry state!

Why is this so, and why, mutatis mutandis, does it apply to artists just as much? The creative scientist has had three mortal enemies in the past. One was religion; it is only necessary to name Galileo or Darwin to illustrate the constant interference in scientific affairs that has been characteristic of religion. Even now, "creationism" is fighting the theory of evolution in American schools, a state of affairs to make you laugh or cry, depending on your disposition. The second enemy was the state. As I have already pointed out, Stalin banned relativity theory and IQ testing, because they were bourgeois, Hitler banned both because they were Jewish! These sources of interference are too well known to deserve detailed discussion, and although "political correctness" (p.c.) has had a powerful influence in enforcing agreement on many issues when the scientific evidence contradicts the p.c. edicts, and prevented important social issues from being investigated properly, I doubt if these forces are as strong now as they have been in the past.

Much more likely to make scientists (and artists) so contumacious, willful, aggressive, bloody-minded, and altogether unruly has been the simple fact that in both cases we are dealing with an authoritative orthodoxy against which the creative mind of the genius has to battle constantly for acceptance. As Swift said, "When a true genius appears in the world, you may know him by this sign, that the dunces are all in confederacy against him." John Milton pointed out that "truth...never comes into the world but like a bastard to the ignominy of him that brought her forth." And Roger Bacon listed the four main obstacles to understanding as: "Frail or unsuitable authority, long custom, uninstructed popular opinion, and concealment of ignorance in displays at apparent wisdom." Alas, these are still the main obstacles to advancement, and possibly more than ever orthodoxy has its dead hand on the levers of power, in science as in art. Genius has to fight, even fight dirty, to survive—after all, the opposition has all the power, and fights even dirtier!

The widespread notion that unlike lawyers, scientists are only concerned with the truth, and do not indulge in adversarial practices, is simply untrue. We need only recollect the battle of the giants, Newton and Leibnitz, as to who invented the infinitesimal calculus to realize what scientists are really like (with honourable exceptions, of course!) Here two outstanding geniuses accused each other of plagiarism and all sorts of other villainies, rigged committees, got colleagues to abuse the opposition, and indulged in behaviour so vicious that one can only wonder at their sanity. (Both are now known to have invented the calculus separately and independently.) The same principle is at work when a creative idea encounters the massed ranks of orthodoxy. As Max Planck put it in his autobiography, "An important scientific innovation rarely makes its way by gradually winning over and converting its opponents; it rarely happens that Saul becomes Paul. What does happen is that its opponents gradually die out, and that the growing generation is familiarised with the ideas from the beginning." Much the same could be said about novel ideas in the arts—creative artists are not always welcomed by their peers!

Many writers have drawn attention to this combined hostility of religion, state, and orthodox scientists to new and creative ideas.

Kierkegaard pointed out that "genius is like a thunderstorm, it rushes against the wind, frightens the people and cleans the air. The status quo has in defence invented the lightning conductor." Or as Oscar Wilde said, "The public is wonderfully tolerant. It forgives everything except genius." Quite generally, as Burkhardt stated: "Mighty governments have a revulsion against genius"—and that includes the mighty governments of science, made up of councils and elected representatives of mediocrity. And common sense is no protection; in Einstein's words: "It is the collection of prejudices acquired by the age of eighteen."

All this contradicts Bronowski's statements quoted earlier, and such notions are incorporated in a book I once read as a young student, *The Religion of the Open Mind*. Scientists and artists are certainly very far from doing anything but giving verbal obeisance to the shibboleth of the open mind; reality is very different. Objectivity is far from being the characteristic of the typical scientist where serious, far-reaching new ideas are concerned. Michael Polanyi, himself a famous scientist, has drawn attention to the importance of the scientist's personality, and it is difficult not to conclude that scientists (and artists) are as emotional, quirky, self-centred, excitable, temperamental, enthusiastic, fervent, impassioned, zealous, bellicose, malevolent, rancorous, dishonest, and hostile to competition as anyone else.

To return to Newton, he behaved very badly not only towards Leibnitz, but also towards Hooke, Locke, Flamstead, and many others. As F.E. Manuel, his biographer, says: "Newton was aware of the mighty anger that smouldered within him all his life…many were the times when (his censor) was overwhelmed and the rage could not be contained.… Even if allowances are made for the general truculence of scientists and learned men, he remains one of the most ferocious practitioners of the art of scientific controversy. Genteel concepts of fair play are conspicuously absent, and he never gave any quarter." Anyone still doubting that this picture fits the facts better than Bronowski's vacuous and sanctimonious caricature is invited to read Richard Milton's *Forbidden Science*, which details many instances of neglect, persuasion, hounding, victimisation, and suppression of truly creative ideas, unwelcome facts, and disturbing theories, and their creators. And for the actual fraud, William Broad and Nicholas Wade gave many examples in their book, *Betrayers of the Truth*, as do David Muller and Michael Hersen in *Research Fraud in the Behavioural and Biomedical Sciences*. We are not talking about nonentities, there is good evidence to arraign Ptolemy, Kepler, Newton, Mendel, Freud, Pasteur, and many more.

Why bring up this shadowy side of genius and of orthodoxy? It is not done to libel an honourable profession; of course many scientists do behave as Bronowski says, look at problems objectively, and do show an open mind. However, it is impossible to understand the nature of genius, and of the creative mind generally, if we do not understand the glacial lack of interest or understanding that fellow scientists show when confounded with the new, the original, the creative. Planck made a discovery that originated one of the most important developments in physics, particularly sub-atomic physics, giving rise to quantum theory. This is how it was received. "None of the professors of the University had any understanding of its contents," he said after submitting his Ph.D. thesis containing the experimental account of his discovery. "I found no interest, let alone approval, even among the very physicists who were clearly connected with the topic. Kirchhoff expressly disapproved. I did not succeed in reaching Clausius. He did not answer my letter, and I did not find him at home when I tried to see him in person at Bonn. I carried on a correspondence with Carl Neumann, of Leipzig, but it remained totally pointless." He was lucky: Wegener was persecuted mercilessly when he proposed his theory of continental drift, now universally accepted. Pasteur's theory of the fermentation process was found unacceptable, with Liebig and many others defending the traditional chemical theory of these processes long after the evidence in favour of Pasteur was conclusive. His microorganism theory of disease, too, caused endless strife and criticism. Lister's theory of antisepsis was also long argued over, and considered absurd. Priestley retained his view of phlogiston as the active principle of burning, and together with many others opposed the modern theories of Lavoisier, with considerable violence.

It might be said that these were revolutionary theories the support for which was not all that strong at the beginning, and which in any case were complex, difficult to understand, and required a lengthy period of testing. This is partly true, but it does not explain the strong *emotional* quality of the reaction, the hatred heaped upon the unfortunate originator, or the way he was despised, derided, reviled, and practically drummed out of the scientific community altogether. The appropriate reaction would have been "Here is an interesting theory that would seem to explain lots of things the existing theories fail to explain. Let's see how it stands up to serious examination, to further experimentation, to theoretical scrutiny." But that was not done; there was an active attempt to throttle the new theory at birth, without giving it a proper hearing—and to throttle its originator into the bargain, if possible! And this was done when the evidence was incontestable, obvious, and palpable.

A good example is the success of the Wright brothers in building and flying a heavier-than-air machine in the early years of this century. Experts were so convinced, on purely scientific grounds, that powered heavier-than-air flight was impossible that they rejected the Wright brothers' claims without troubling to examine the evidence. Their claims were derided and dismissed as a hoax by the *Scientific American*, the *New York Herald*, the U.S. Army and most American scientists. Simon Newcomb, the professor of mathematics and astronomy at Johns Hopkins University, published an article showing scientifically that powered human flight was "utterly impossible"—just weeks before the Wright brothers actually flew! The chief engineer of the U.S. Army, Rear Admiral George Melville, wrote to say that attempting to fly was "absurd." Long after the success of the venture was attested by thousands of spectators, scientists and reporters refused to go and see for themselves; they knew it couldn't be done!

The Wright brothers were young bicycle mechanics, without any scientific credentials. But Edison was already well known as a scientific genius when he announced that he had succeedcd in making a practical incandescant lamp, which he was demonstrating publicly in Menlo Park. What did his fellow scientists have to say? Sir William Preece, FRS, simply said that "Edison's electric lamp is a completely idiotic idea." And Sir William Siemens, who had been working in this field for some ten years, said that "such startling announcements as these should be deprecated as being unworthy of science and mischievous to its true progress." Professor Henry Morton, who lived nearby and was personally acquainted with Edison. did not even bother to go and see Edison's lighting, but wrote that he felt compelled "to protest on behalf of true science" that Edison's experiments were "a conspicuous failure trumpeted as a wonderful success. A fraud upon the public." At nightfall, we can witness this "fraud" when the electric lights come on all over the world!

These are just a few examples; I have given many others in my book *Genius: The Natural History of Creativity*, as has Richard Milton who has devoted a whole book, *Forbidden Science*, to an exploration of the topic. Here let me just give a personal example of the sort of thing that is happening all the time to new ideas in science. I was invited by the Royal Medico-Psychological Association, to give a paper at one of their meetings, something I had done many times before. I chose as my topic "Learning Theory and Behaviour Therapy," proposing to discuss an alternative theory and method of treating neurotic patients to the traditional psychodynamic methods which had failed to do any better than placebo treatments, or no treatment at all. We had been doing a good deal of experimental and clinical work on this topic in my department, and the time seemed to be right (this was in 1958) to discuss the results with a knowledgeable audience. (The RMPA was the official psychiatric society in Great Britain.) I delivered my talk, hoping for a critical discussion with the assembled experts, and receiving cautious approval of the new ideas of procedures. I should have known better!

The end of my talk was marked with an eruption of hostile emotion, pent-up anger, aggressive hostility. Revered professors of psychiatry jumped up and down in fury, waved their fists and shouted insults; it was truly pandemonium. The chairman had to tell the audience that this was no way to behave towards a visitor, and when the noise subsided a number of people asked questions—none of them, unfortunately, having any discernible scientific meaning. It was a salutary experience, made even more interesting by some of the events that followed. The professor of psychiatry at the Institute of Psychiatry, where my department was located, tried to make it impossible for us to obtain patients on whom to practice behaviour therapy, and failing that, reduce the importance of the department or even shut it down. Consultants queued outside his door demanding my dismissal. The RMPA never invited me again to address their members. Many psychiatric colleagues never talked to me again. I had ceased to be *persona grata*.

Consider how odd this emotional outburst really was. Psychiatrists were supposed through their training to avoid emotional reactions, and behave rationally. The theory was not all that new; having been proposed in embryonic form by J.B. Watson forty years earlier. It had good background in thousands of experiments, and modern conditioning theory. The clinical successes were undoubted, and usually obtained with patients with whom every other method had failed. Surely psychiatrists should at least have listened, and perhaps voiced any reasoned objection? To think this is to repeat the Bronowski error; people, even scientists and medical specialists, just aren't like that. They believe what they have been taught, and that anyone who puts forward new ideas is a heretic, a maverick, someone to squash with all means at your disposal.

Actually psychiatry officially adopted behaviour therapy as a useful technique later on. Some 3,000 empirical studies have found it much the most useful, least time-consuming and most outstandingly successful of the methods used to treat neurotic disorders. It is being used more and more widely. Why then the original reaction? I would say it was a perfectly general human, or even animal, response to something new, frightening, upsetting of old ways of doing things. Even a rat, if you cross-foster groups of bright rats to dull rats, will tend to kill the bright pups! I am sure my RMPA psychiatrists would have loved to lynch me; fortunately a civilized society frowns on such behaviour.

Faced with such truculent opposition, unreasoning at best, vehement at worst, creative people need personality traits that help them to cope with such opposition. Such traits are not always approved of by the majority. Persistence, bloody-mindedness, nonconformist behaviour, even asocial and antisocial behaviour—these are some of the protective devices needed by the creative person to cope with the obstacles society, and specifically the society of his peers, throws in his way. If you want to be creative, you must be prepared to fight; if you are a genius, the fight may be even more deadly. Sometimes genius shuns the fight. Copernicus did not publish his heliocentric theory till he was dying. Gauss did not publish his work on n-dimensional geometry; he knew how it would be received. (Lobachevsky, who was the first to actually publish his results in this field, was considered insane, and banished to remote parts of Russia!)

15

Much Ado about IQ

No other topic in psychology has ever given rise to as much controversy, debate, and downright calumny as the apparently simple and innocuous IQ. Some exponents of simple truths about it, and their families, have been threatened with bombs, and physically assaulted, they have had their lectures disrupted, been threatened with dismissal, had research grants withdrawn, and faced refusal to have their research papers printed. Many have been exposed to the most violent, and hostile press campaigns imaginable, usually based on quite erroneous and distorted accounts of their views. In Stalin's Russia, an editor was sent to the labour camps for publishing a translation of one of my books! Clearly the social implications of IQ testing arouse strong feelings—usually based on ignorance of what has been said, what the facts are, and what their social implications might be.

The recent publication of *The Bell Curve* by Richard Herrnstein and Charles Murray enabled unprejudiced readers to compare what the authors actually said, and what the *New York Times*, the *Washington Post*, the *Independent*, the *Guardian*, *Time*, the *Economist*, or the *New Yorker*, said they said. It is a chastening experience for anyone who believes that "quality" papers and journals check their sources, have reviewers with some expertise in the subject involved, and treat serious matter in a serious manner. Here I will only mention one typical point, made by Stephen J. Gould, a paleontologist with no background in psychology, whose wild criticisms of IQ testing in the book: *The Mismeasure of Man*, have been universally dismissed by experts in the field as instances of being economical with the truth. Having stated (in the *New Yorker*) that Herrnstein and Murray make it one of the two central arguments in their book that racial differences in IQ are mostly genetic in origin, he goes on to say that they "violate fairness by considering a complex case that can yield only agnosticism into a biased brief for permanent and heritable difference."

187

What did the book *actually* say? "If the reader is now convinced that either the genetic or environmental explanations (of ethnic differences in IQ) have won out to the exclusion of the other, we have not done a sufficiently good job of presenting one side or the other. It seems highly likely to us that both genes and the environment have something to do with racial differences. What might the mix be? We are resolutely agnostic on that issue; as far as we can determine, the evidence does not yet justify an estimate." Gould, as usual, completely misrepresents the clear position of the authors and then severely criticizes a man of straw put up specifically for the purpose. Greater love hath no man than that he should lay down his scientific integrity for his political correctness! Most of the other reviews were by people who never had a reputation in the first place, and made even worse errors and misrepresentations! Perhaps they should have kept in mind Sir Francis Bacon's famous words: "For what man had rather were true he more readily believes. Therefore he rejects difficult things from impatience...things not commonly believed out of deference to the opinion of the vulgar. Numberless in short are the ways, but sometimes imperceptible, in which the affections colour and infect the understanding." Let us reflect and remember.

In this book I have tried to put down the facts of the case. There is no doubt that intelligence is important in our society. It would be very peculiar if a very general mental capability that, among other things, involves the ability to reason, plan, solve problems, think abstractly, comprehend complexities, learn quickly, and benefit from experience, did not have very important implications. This ability, and the problems it creates because of its uneven distribution, is a biological gift; our attempts to measure it do not create the problems which are becoming more apparent as the advances of technology make high intelligence more and more important, and destroy the usual types of repetitive and brawn-requiring activities that used to give employment to below-average IQ men and women. This is a very real problem that will not go away because we choose to disregard it, and throw rotten eggs at psychologists who warn us of the developing danger instead. Psychology can do so much to help society in crises of this kind. It may not have all the answers, but it presents us with the factual knowledge that alone is likely to help us overcome our difficulties. It is not rational to prefer ignorance to knowledge, and surely the facts recounted in this book will suggest possible ways out of our dilemma. What we are doing at the moment is to make matters worse by adopting "progressive" methods of education that have produced a work force in which one-in-four is practically illiterate and innumerate. Children in England and America are some two years behind those in Germany and France. Yet our teaching unions make certain that the teachers who are being trained should remain as ignorant of IQ testing, which could help so much to redress the balance, as are present-day teachers. Political correctness has done its worst to censor all knowledge of advances in this field, and has filled the media with untrue and often libellous statements about the IQ in order to prevent the public from discovering the truth.

The tide may be turning, now that many people appreciate the harm that has been done by "progressive" education with its fake gods of "equality" and mixed-ability classes, its neglect of the really bright, and its contempt for competition and achievement. Dead uniformity is not the way to prosperity and a happy life for everybody, and nature's inexorable insistence on human diversity gives a hollow ring to egalitarian claims. Excellence, outstanding success, genius—these are the horses that pull the chariot. If we wish to remain in the vanguard of progress, we need all the help we can get, and psychology, in spite of its youth is already able to give us some valuable assistance. We would be foolish to reject it!

It is not argued that there are no social and even political implications and consequences of psychological investigations into the nature and inheritance of intelligence. But these are the consequences of biological reality; psychological study and measurement only tell us what nature ordained. Psychologists do not create the facts, they merely clarify them and make our knowledge more precise. As I pointed out earlier on, the Chinese knew pretty well what the major facts were concerning intelligence and its inheritance and measurement; we have made this knowledge more precise, and have added ideas about the underlying physiology. The social problems that arise, arise from the facts, not our investigation of these facts. And of course the problem that differences in IQ give rise to are not likely to be solved by sweeping the facts under the carpet, and refusing scientific investigation and scholarly discussion.

Two areas of virulent debate, centering on the issue of intelligence, have been concerned with *equality* and with *eugenics*. A few words concerning these issues may be useful because so much of the discussion is partisan and based on ignorance. Let us take equality first. Now like motherhood and apple pie, equality is the sort of concept most people readily take to their hearts. But what exactly does equality mean? The Greeks, as usual, had a word for it—indeed several words. *Isonomia* is equality before the law. *Isotimia* is equality of human diversity.

Isopolitia is equality of political rights. *Isokratia* is equality of political influence. *Isopsephia* is equality of the right to choose or elect representatives. *Isogotia* is the equal right to free speech. *Isoteleia* means equality of taxes and dues. *Isomoria* is equality of partnership. *Iskleria* is equality of possessions. *Isodaimonia* is equality of ability. And so it goes on—equality appears in many guises, some desirable, others not, some possible, others not. We would probably be in favour of equality before the law, free speech, political rights, but how about equality of taxes and dues? Does progressive taxation curtail our freedom and our equal rights? And how about equality of possessions? Equality of ability, as I have pointed out, was already dismissed as a chimera by Marx and Lenin, but it still raises its head among the more militant and less knowledgeable. You cannot be in favour of equality *tout court*; it is essential to specify which of many types of equality you are talking about.

Those who shout loudest for equality usually shout loudest against eugenics. Eugenics, the brainchild of Sir Francis Galton, is defined by the *Oxford English Dictionary* as "the production of fine offspring by improvement of inherited qualities." Similarly *Collins Dictionary*, which defines it as the study of methods of improving the quality of the human race. Clearly Galton called for both positive and negative eugenics—eliminate heredity diseases and further positive qualities in so far as they are inherited. Doing so would obviously further equality, by eliminating diseases and lessen the occurrence of debilitating and degrading psychological states, like imbecility. This does not seem an egregious, heinous or nefarious aim, and Galton emphasized that any application of his eugenic principles must be based on solid knowledge and refined measurement. Why have these seemingly highly desirable aims been attacked so furiously by those whose desire for equality would have been so well served by eugenics?

The main reason, of course, has been the absurd claims that Hitler pursued a eugenic policy when killing millions of Jews, as well as socialists, Gypsies, mental defectives, cripples, and others not living up to his idea of the *Herrenrasse*. (The leaders of the Nazi Party were hardly good examples of the Aryan type. As a frequent comment at the time went in Germany—the *Uebermenschen* is as blonde as Hitler, as tall as Goebbels, and as slim as Goering!) The idea of breeding Uebermenschen is a scientific absurdity, and has nothing whatever to do with Galton-type eugenics. To insist on a close association is a kind of inverted McCarthyism—guilt by association. Having been on the Council of the British Eugenics Society, I can state categorically that nobody on the Council, or in the Society, would ever have associated himself with any such Hitlerian ideas. It is unfortunately impossible to patent scientific ideas, and deny their use to people willing to employ them for the wrong ends. Does the scientist have responsibility for the way others misuse his ideas, his discoveries, his inventions? If he had, no scientific advances would be possible. From the earliest times, new inventions and discoveries have been used for the benefit of society, but also misused for malignant ends. The printing press brought knowledge to the people, but also enabled Goebbels to spread his foul lies, and Streicher to publish vicious attacks on the Jews. The discovery of atomic fission gave rise to the production of electric power without depleting our stock of nonrenewable coal, gas, and so on. It also produced the atom bomb!

But should the scientist not be cautious and predict the consequences of his discoveries? Unfortunately there is no way we can look into the future, and predict what will happen to our discoveries. In the 1930s, Einstein, the greatest theoretician, and Rutherford, the greatest experimenter associated with atomic fission, both declared quite clearly that there would never be any practical applications of the new discovery. A dozen years later the first atom bomb fell on Hiroshima! If the greatest theoretician and the greatest experimental scientist cannot predict the fate of their discoveries twelve years later, how can anyone? Decisions about the uses of new knowledge must be left to the democratic process, not to the inventor or discoverer; the will of the people is our only safeguard against misuse.

Thus misuse of great ideas is always possible. But does Hitler's absurd and completely unscientific bungling not inculpate eugenics as a movement? We may ask the same question about equality. Has Stalin's absurd and completely unscientific bungling not inculpated egalitarianism as a movement? I would deny any such argument. We know that Marx, Lenin, and Stalin have jointly and severally produced hell on earth under the guise of creating an egalitarian society. We know that the Soviet Union was in fact one of the least egalitarian societies that ever existed. We know that its leaders simply used the notion of equality to cover their ideological *nakedness*. All this does not begin to touch the genuine human desire for greater equality— before the law, the election of representatives, in social worth as human beings. In a similar way we must look at eugenics in the true spirit of what it is offering us, and not in the way the Hitlers of this world have maligned and misused it.

Why should we consider eugenics seriously? We should not dismiss the study of methods to improve the human race unless we were certain that there was nothing wrong with the human race; that it was in fact perfect as far as bodily and mental health are concerned, and that socially we are all behaving in an impeccable manner towards each other—no war, no crime, no exploitation of one human being by another. No racism, no sexism, no jingoism—all happy, healthy people living together in harmony! If that was the reality of life as we approach the twenty-first century, there surely would be no need for eugenics. Unfortunately, what we find is quite different—famine, war, racial and sexual discrimination, "ethnic cleansing," poverty, fanatical hatred, disease, unhappiness, and an overpowering fear of what the future may bring.

Consider muscular dystrophy, a cluster of diseases characterized by progressive weakness and wasting of muscles. It affects boys, beginning with leg weakness before the age of three, and progressing rapidly, with death often occurring before the age of twenty-five (Duchenne dystrophy). This is a disease where indeed heredity is destiny; there is nothing we can do to cure it. Would not eugenics, that is, attempting to find ways of studying the precise method of genetic transmission, trying to give sound factual advice to carriers of the disease, perhaps using advances in molecular genetics to alter the gene responsible, be welcome to potential sufferers and their parents? Would not such attempts justify the definition of "improving the human race"?

This is just one of the many diseases caused in whole, or in part by genetic factors. In Britain, about one child in thirty is born with a genetic problem of one kind or another. Those working in the field of genetic research may not know it, but they are eugenicists close to the heart of Galton!

Few people would oppose eugenics were it confined to the prevention and elimination of gene-carried diseases. How about such things as low intelligence? We know that this is partly inherited, with many genes implicated. We also know that men and women with low IQs have on the average many more children than those with high IQs. Should we look for ways of using advances in molecular biology to change or eliminate genes making for low IQ, and change them to produce high IQ instead? It cannot be done at present, but the possibility is there—we are just about to locate relevant genes in the genome. Eugenics does not *advocate* doing so; it simply states that we should collect all the information we can to come to meaningful conclusions. There are arguments for and against, but decisions can only be based on much sounder knowledge than we possess at the present time. But given a society that is needing high IQ more and more, and brawn less and less, we may have to think seriously about issues of this kind. Would we be doing our children a kindness if we left them at a low level of IQ if we had the means to raise it 30, 40 or more points? Decision would of course have to be left to parents; the idea of the state deciding on such issues is inherently undemocratic. But it might be useful to think about such issues; they may confront us suddenly, before we are ready.

Intelligence is fairly easy; few people would regard stupidity as preferable to high intelligence. But take criminality. Here, too, genetics plays a very important part. If we could modify the genes involved, should we do so? Here any decision would be even more difficult. Mankind has never succeeded in eradicating crime; would we be better advised to make use of recent psychological advances and try our hand at succeeding where everyone else has failed? Should we try genetics, and get rid of "bad" genes? The danger of course is that the same gene may have other effects than criminal, antisocial activity, and we might wipe out activities that are socially useful. As Claude Bernard said, "In ignorance, abstain." We would have to know far more than we do before even thinking about the problems in any but the most abstract terms.

How about the many neurotic disorders, the anxieties, depressions, phobias, obsessions, and other emotional illnesses human flesh is heir to? Here, too, there is a strong genetic component; should we try to change it? As with crime, "bad" genes may be linked to many other desirable consequences as well as to those that plague us. Creative writers suffer overwhelmingly from depression, but many refuse the available drug treatments because they fear it would compromise their creativity. They would rather suffer the depressive episodes (and that suffering is very real!) than lose the inspiration apparently linked with this emotional charge. We might in doing so also get rid of our geniuses!

I hope I have made clear that eugenics as a movement should be judged by what it proposes, namely the scientific study of our genetic equipment, and the possibilities of modifying it, with a view to improving humankind. To do any of this by genocide is not a serious proposal that would even begin to be considered by anyone other than mad fanatics like Hitler, ignorant of all the scientific principles involved (quite apart from the humane questions!). To use selective breeding is not a serious proposition in a democratic society either; we could never trust a government with the necessary powers. Attempts have been made in India and in China to bribe or coerce married couples to have fewer children, but their attempts have not involved selection; they have been motivated by the simple fact that population growth was outpacing the increase in the means of subsistence. Selection has been involved in Singapore, where the president tried to persuade female students to have more children, because their relative barrenness threatened a culture based on high IQ for survival. Results were disappointing. Again, there are strong arguments against selective breeding, but future developments may bring us face to face with the same problem that arose in Singapore. Above all, let us consider the problems of eugenics and egalitarianism in a spirit of scientific objectivity, rather than as an ideological punching bag; what Stalin and Hitler did has absolutely nothing to do with the case!

There is, however, one frequent error against which it may be useful to warn readers. Intelligence is important, but it is not all important. Even in the cognitive realm special abilities—verbal, numerical, perceptual speed, visuo-spatial ability, memory, creativity, etc.—play an important part, and general intelligence without special abilities is unlikely to lead to outstanding success. Indeed, success, even in moderation, owes a great deal to factors completely outside the cognitive field. Recall figure 5.1 which showed three kinds of intelligence—biological, psychometric, and social or practical. As I suggested in commenting on this figure, "practical intelligence," so-called, and identified with worldly success, is in part determined by IQ, but there are many other factors determining it. Even with a high IQ you may fail because you are an alcoholic, or a neurotic, or seriously ill. You may lack motivation, have the wrong personality for the job, or come from the wrong background. Your family connections may be important, or your old-school- tie networks—there are hundreds of factors that may determine your success. Lots of people make it rich *without* sound intellectual attainments: pop stars, athletes, prostitutes, actors and actresses, models, royalty, tennis, golf, and football stars—the list is endless.

But even worldly success is not the be-all and end-all of human life. Most value systems, whether religious or not, place the acquisition of riches very low; they give a much higher place to honesty, kindness, benevolence, empathy, altruism, trustworthiness, reliability, integrity: "To thine own self be true, and it must follow, as the night the day, thou canst not then be false to any man." These, moral philosophers and religious leaders tell us, are the important elements in life, not chasing after material possessions, hoarding money, or seeking power and influence. There is some slight correlation between intelligence and virtue, but not enough to mistake one for the other; for the crook, the villain, the malefactor a high IQ simply enables them to do more harm, cheat more successfully, amass more ill-gotten gains. Some of the greatest mass-murderers in history were far from dumb—Hitler, Stalin, Napoleon, Mussolini, Caesar, Frederick the Great, Alexander the Great spring to mind. They were not lacking in IQ, but in common humanity, and without that IQ by itself is of little value as far as society is concerned.

Consider for a moment, Edmund Emil Kemper III, a serial killer who grew up in a dysfunctional family in which his parents were constantly fighting, only to divorce eventually. His mother sent him to live with his grandparents. Edmund grew to be huge, and at age fifteen he shot and stabbed his grandmother because she insisted he help her with some job. Later he also shot his grandfather, and was committed to an asylum for the criminally insane. He was set free at the age of twenty-one, in spite of psychiatric objection, and placed in the custody of his mother, whom in due course he also killed, together with a friend. Before that, six foot, nine inches tall, and weighing twenty-one stone, he picked up two female students, took them to a secluded area, and stabbed them to death. The bodies he took to his mother's house, photographed them, dismembered them, and finally buried the remains. This he followed by murdering three other female students and a young girl. What was this monster's IQ? 145—he was a genius at serial murder. IQ surely is not everything! It certainly shows only a slight correlation with "goodness."

Nor is happiness, or contentment, highly correlated with IQ. As a famous saying has it, "Would you rather be a happy pig, or an unhappy Socrates?" A high IQ may enable us to see the worst in everything, to foresee disaster, to be discontented even with high achievement. A high IQ does not determine a man's value, nor a woman's; it does not make one person superior to another. Of the myriad things that make us valuable members of the human race, intelligence is but one, and no psychologist working in this field has ever pretended differently.

Finally, intelligence is not to be identified with common sense. Highly intelligent people often seem to lack common sense to a quite unusual degree. (High Court judges are a good example.) Common sense is difficult to identify, and even more difficult to measure, but for everyday living it is surely of considerable importance. The genius lives in an abstract world far removed from the sphere of our sorrows; these abstract concepts may not make contact with human life as it is lived by the great majority. Sidney and Beatrice Webb, famous for their scholarly achievements, went to the Soviet Union when Stalin's agrarian reforms caused millions to die of starvation, and summed up their findings by saying: "We have seen the future, and it works!" Bertrand Russell, eminent philosopher, went to prison for his pacifist beliefs during the First World War, only later on to advise the American president to destroy Russia by nuclear bombs if they didn't agree to give up their atomic arsenal! H.G. Wells and G.B. Shaw admired the dictators, Hitler and Mussolini. Intelligence does not guarantee common sense; alas, it just makes you able to put your crazy ideas in a more persuasive fashion—crazy ideas that are often grown from emotional roots, rather than rational ones.

For most people these warnings will not be needed. A measure of intelligence is just that—a measure of intelligence. It is not a measure of man—or, as the title of Gould's book asserts, a mismeasure of man. Much more would enter into that than just intelligence. But without intelligence man would be little better than a brute, so let us value it for what it is—an important part of man, but only a part. Carlyle's professor, dry-as-dust no doubt, had a formidable IQ but no originality or creativity, things we value more highly. Many members of Mensa, the high IQ society, have made little or no real contribution to society. Intelligence derives some of its importance from the fact that we can measure it, and in consequence know a great deal about it. Not enough, but research is constantly improving our knowledge, and making it more and more likely that we will be able to use our knowledge for the good of society. To pretend, as voluble writers often do, that psychologists are only concerned with IQ, and neglect other aspects of man, is absurd and untrue. It takes its place among the other absurd and untrue criticisms I have discussed earlier. No psychologists ever put forward such notions, and only the ignorant would imagine that anyone ever did.

As Thomas Arnold of Rugby once said, "What we must look for is, 1st, religion and moral principles; 2ndly, gentlemanly conduct; 3rdly, intellectual ability," In other words, *moral* behaviour is most important; only slightly less important is the quality of being cultured, courteous, and chivalrous; intelligence only comes in third. In other words, what is needed is intelligence in the service of morality and decency. Would anyone disagree?

Endnotes, References, and Comments

Introduction

The book, *Intelligence*, by Nathan Brody was published by Academic Press in 1992. Mark Snyderman and Stanley Rothman's *The IQ Controversy* was published by Transaction Publishers in 1988. The article on "Mainstream Science on Intelligence" was published in the *Wall Street Journal* of December 13, 1994, and has since been republished in the scientific journal, *Intelligence*. Because of its interest and importance, it is reprinted here in the appendix, so readers can compare my view with those of some fifty experts.

The APA Task Force article, entitled: "Intelligence: Known and Unknown," was published in the *American Psychologist*, February 1996, pages 77–101. Political criticisms of IQ testing are well presented by Leon Kamin's *The Science and Politics of IQ*, published by Lawrence Erlbaum in 1974, and by S.J. Gould's *The Mismeasure of Man*, published by Norton in 1981, and a second edition in 1996. *The Intelligence Controversy* by H.J. Eysenck and L. Kamin was published by John Wiley in 1981, and may still illustrate the arguments put forward by those adhering to the orthodox opinion of strong genetic predisposition for IQ, and those rejecting any such predisposition, and taking a 100 percent environmentalistic line. Rushton's review of Gould's book was published in *Personality and Individual Differences*, 1994, under the title "Special Review of S.J. Gould's 'Revised' Edition of *The Mismeasure of Man*."

Finally, my book on *The Structure and Measurement of Intelligence* and *A Model for Intelligence*, published by Springer Verlag in 1979 and 1982 respectively, present in textbook form the arguments popularized in this book. For readers keen to consult an alternative popular presentation to mine, David Seligman's *A Question of Intelligence*, published by Carol in 1994, has received much professional praise, although the author is essentially a journalist; he is unusual in that his account is accurate as well as well-written.

Chapter 1

A good introduction to the paradox of IQ testing is given in my book *The Inequality of Man*, published in 1973 by Maurice Temple Smith. The genetic problem is discussed in detail by Robert Plomin and Gerald McClearn in *Nature, Nurture, and Psychology*, published in 1991 by the American Psychological Association. More recently, there is David Rowe's book, *The Limits of Family Influence*, published by the Guilford Press in 1994. More general discussions of the whole topic of intelligence are available in the *Handbook of Intelligence*, edited by Benjamin Wolman in 1985, published by John Wiley, and the *Handbook of Human Intelligence*, edited by Robert Sternberg and published by Cambridge University Press in 1982.

The best introduction to Chinese theories and measures of intelligence is a chapter by Jimmy Chan, "Chinese Intelligence," published in 1995 in the *Handbook of Chinese Psychology*, edited by M. Bond and published by Oxford University Press. A good introduction to the concepts of fluid and crystallized ability is given by Raymond Cattell in his *Abilities, Their Structure, Growth, and Action*, published by Houghton, Mifflin, in 1971.

The apparent ramification of conceptions of just what is intelligence is discussed in a book by the name, *What is Intelligence?*, edited by Robert Sternberg and Douglas Detterman, and published by Ablex in 1986. Readers may enjoy sorting out what are genuine definitions, what mere listings of applications of implied definitions, or the particular aspect of intelligence (biological, psychometric, applied) that catches the writer's fancy. Few of the apparent differences are real, as I have tried to point out in "Intelligence: The One and the Many", a chapter in a book *Is Mind Modular or Unitary*, edited by Douglas Detterman and published in 1992 by Ablex, and in an editorial on "The Concept of Intelligence: Useful or Useless?", published in *Intelligence*, 1988, 12, 1–16. Many relevant issues are discussed in another book edited by Douglas Detterman, *Theories of Intelligence*, published by Ablex in 1994.

Chapter 2

The origin of IQ testing, and the controversies attending it, are presented in personalized form by Raymond Fonder in his book on *The Intelligent Man: Makers of the IQ Controversy*, published by

Norton in 1985. Galton's views are expressed in his *"Inquiries into Human Faculty and its Development*. For Binet, there is a translation of much of his work in A. Binet and T. Simon, *The Development of Intelligence in Children*, published by Arno Press in 1973. See also Theta Wolf's *Alfred Binet*, published by the Chicago University Press in 1973.

Detailed data on the relation between social status and earnings on the one hand, intelligence on the other, are given in *The Bell Curve* by Richard Herrnstein and Charles Murray, together with an extended discussion of the social implications of the observed correlation. This is the most recent summary, and the most inclusive. The psychometric argument between Spearman and Thurstone is well reviewed by John Caroll in *Human Cognitive Abilities*, published by the Cambridge University Press in 1991.

The similarity of physical and psychological measurement has been discussed at some length in my *Structure and Measurement of Intelligence*, which also deals with the problem of theory and hypothetics-deductive argument, as opposed to simple inductive reasoning. Spearman was well ahead of the field in his insistence on the discovery of *laws* in psychology. He, like Galton, wanted to go beyond descriptive statistics and discover the causal factors behind g; psychophysiology was not then advanced enough to make this possible. It is only in recent years that we have been able to give real meaning to his concept of "energy" underlying g. His major publications are *The Nature of Intelligence and the Principle of Cognition*, and *Abilities of Man*, both published by Macmillan, in 1923 and 1927 respectively.

Chapter 3

It is difficult to pretend that there is still an argument between "nature" and "nurture"; in scientific circles there is no such argument, and there never has been. There are no psychologists who would suggest that IQ was *completely* determined by heredity, and I know no serious scientists who would contend that environment was *totally* responsible. From the beginning it was recognized that *both* were essential for any phenotypic behaviour to emerge, the only question remaining was a *quantitative* one—how much of each. As explained in the text, this is much more complex than is often realized, but there is growing agreement on the major issues.

I have already referred to two recent books that review the available evidence and may be regarded as the voice of orthodox science, namely the *Nature, Nurture and Psychology* book edited by Robert Plomin and Gerald McClearn, and David Rowe's *Limits of Family Influence*. They contain all the references needed for a full understanding of the present position.

It is *interesting* to note that behavioural genetics always underestimate the heritability of intelligence, personality, or whatever; I have pointed out the random errors encountered in zygosity diagnosis and an unreliability of the measuring instruments. Both lead to a serious underdiagnosis of genetic causation, and ought to be corrected statistically, (Spitz, E., et al. (1996). "Comparative diagnoses of twin zygosity by SSLP variant analyses, questionnaire, and dematoglyphic analysis" in *Behaviour Genetics*, 26, 45–63.) It seems socially desirable to try and minimize genetic influences, as if environmentation was the natural state, and heritability somehow unclean and to be avoided as far as possible. In a similar vein, many authors mention 50 percent genetic determination as the agreed average, without mentioning that this is the figure for young children, and that for adults it is nearer 80 percent! Scientifically speaking we could disregard social demands of this kind, and be concerned simply with the optimum estimates to be made with our present methods and results, always acknowledging possible weaknesses and criticisms.

Adoption studies are well reviewed by Charles Locurto in his book on *Sense and Nonsense About IQ*, published by Praeger in 1991. The Rowe book already mentioned is also a well-argued summary of this important area. Good adoption studies are as important as good twin studies; it is the agreement between them that is particularly valuable because they are subject to quite different types of criticism.

Molecular genetics is too recent to have been treated in detail in book form; the best introduction is perhaps an article by Robert Plomin et al., "DNA markers associated with high versus low IQ: The IQ quantitative trait loci (QTL) project," which appeared in *Behaviour Genetics*, 1994, 24, 107–118. Be warned—it does not make for easy reading! Briefly put, the project in question uses an *allelic association* strategy. High and low IQ groups are established, and then allelic frequencies are compared, using DNA markers in or near genes that are likely to contribute to neural functioning. Permanent cell lines, established for low IQ, middle IQ and high IQ groups, made up of Caucasian children, were replicated on another sample of even more extreme high-and-low-IQ children. Two markers yielded significant allelic frequency differences between high-and-low IQ groups in the combined sample. One of these was a new HCA marker for a gene unique to the human species, while the other was a new brain-expressed triplet repeat marker. As the authors point out, "It seems clear that the field of behavioural genetics is at the dawn of a new era when molecular genetic techniques will be used to identify specific genes that contribute to the ubiquitous genetic influence found for behavioural dimensions as well as disorders." Recommended readings are Peter McGuffin and Richard Murray's *The New Genetics of Mental Illness*, published in 1991 by Butterworth-Heinerman, and Robert Plomin's article on "The role of inheritance in behaviour," published in *Science*, 248, 183–88.

For details on multivariate genetic analysis, the studies by A. Thapar, S. Petrill, and L. Thompson (1994), "The heritability of memory in the Western Reserved Twin Project"; *Behaviour Genetics*, 24, 155–160; R. Plomin (1988), "The nature and nurture of cognitive abilities." In R. Sternberg (ed.), *Advances in the Psychology of Human Intelligence*" (vol. 4, pp 1–33), Hillsdale, N.J. Erlbaum; R. Plomin & S. Petrill (1996), "Genetics and Intelligence: What is New?" *Intelligence*, in press; these studies relate to the heritability of special abilities. Overlap is documented in various studies discussed in detail by Plomin and Petrill in the references given above. The major study showing the decline of shared environmental influence on intelligence, is one by J. Loehlin, J. Horn, and L. Williamson (1989), "Modeling IQ change: Evidence from the Texan Adoption Project," *Child Development*, 60, 993–1004.

Chapter 4

The topic of ECTs, and reaction time and inspection time in particular, is well-reviewed in a book edited by Philip Vernon in 1987, and published by Ablex—*Speed of Information-Processing and Intelligence*. Eysenck's edited book, *A Model for Intelligence* also has a summary of work on reaction time. More recent work will be found in the pages of the journal, *Intelligence*, and in *Personality and Individual Differences*, the other major journal in this field. Inspection time is well reviewed in an article by I. Deary, P. Caryl, and G. Gibson, published in 1993: "Nonstationarity and the measurement of psychological response in a visual inspection time task" (*Perception*, 22, 1245–1248). See also J. Kranzler and A. Jensen, 1989, "Inspection time and Intelligence: A Meta-analysis." (*Intelligence*, 13, 329–47). For discrimination tasks, see D. Vickers, A. Pietsch, and T. Hemingway (1995), "Intelligence and visual-auditory discrimination" (*Intelligence*, 21, 197–224).

Chapter 5

A good recent introduction to this field is a book edited by Philip Vernon, entitled *Biological Approaches to the Study of Human Intelligence*, published by Ablex in 1993. This contains an introduction on "The Biological Basis of Intelligence" by myself, and excellent chapters on genetics by Tom Bouchard, physical correlates of intelligence by Jensen and Sinha, nutrition and intelligence by Richard Lynn, EEG and evoked potentials by Ian Deary and P.G. Caryl, cerebral glucose metabolism and intelligence by Richard Haier, and biochemical correlates of human information processing by Hilary Naylor. This is the best available summary of a large body of evidence, and should certainly be consulted by readers of this chapter who want to go into the biological field in some more detail.

The question of brain size and intelligence has given rise to many heated discussions. The present knowledge base is well reviewed by Philippe J. Rushton and Davison Aukney in an article on "Brain size and cognitive ability: Correlation with age, sex, social class, and race," in *Psychosonomic Bulletin and Review*, 1996, 3, 21–36. In an interesting reflection, Rushton and Aukney mention Stephen J. Gould's charge that S.G. Morton, one of the pioneers in this field, writing in 1849, doctored his results to show Caucasian superiority. A random sample of the Morton collection was remeasured in 1988, and it was found that not only were there very few errors, but that these were not in the direction that Gould had asserted. Instead, errors were found in Gould's own work! This curious episode should warn readers to be highly suspicious of anything asserted by Gould, whose political convictions often seem to cloud his judgment.

The rat studies on brain size and intelligence are reported in an article on "Evidence from the rat for a general factor that underlies cognitive performance that relates to brain size and intelligence," by Britt Anderson that appeared in *Neuroscience Letters*, 1993, 153, 98–102. Neuron numbers, for reasons given in this chapter, were not correlated with intelligence in rats (Individual variation in cerebral cortex size and neuron number does not predict behavioural abilities in the rat) in another study by Britt Anderson, which appeared in *Personality and Individual Differences*, 1995, 18, 205–11.

The results of the most recent study of intelligence and brain structure in normal individuals, published by Nancy Andreasen et al., which appeared under that title in the *American Journal of Psychiatry* in January 1993, 130–34, are perhaps representative of current orthodoxy. They found full-scale IQ to be significantly correlated with intracranial, cerebral, temporal lobe, hippocampal, and cerebellar volume, using magnetic resonance imaging scans. Correlations for full-scale, verbal, and performance (nonverbal) IQ were found for overall gray matter volume but not for white matter or CSF volume—shades of Hercule Poirot and his "little gray cells"!

The data on intracellular pH are presented in an article by C. Rae et al., 1996, entitled: "Is pH a biochemical marker of IQ?" which appeared in the *Proceedings of the Royal Society London*, B, 263, 1061–64. It contains a good deal of supporting evidence.

Not yet recorded in any book are some recent studies of the averaged evoked potential theory that have attempted to explain some of the experimental anomalies encountered. These studies have undergone peer review before publication, but until they have been replicated cannot be regarded as being firmly established. In one study by Paul Barrett and myself, it was shown that for some people the positive correlation between IQ and complexity of the evoked potential breaks down. It proved possible to define this group of people independently. Those who did not behave in the predicted fashion had AEP P180 component amplitudes that were less than a specified target value. This failure was noted in several samples, and extended to the inspection time—IQ correlation, which also failed to appear in this small group of people. A possible explanation may be that low P180 component amplitude is related to low attention; there is some evidence in the literature for this. This study appeared under the title: "The relationship between evoked potential component amplitude, latency, contour length, variability, zero-crossings, and psychometric intelligence" in *Personality and Individual Differences*, 1994, 16, 3–32.

Also related to possible attentional differences are two studies which showed that the nature of the task involved in the AEP measurement might be crucial to the type of result found. Tim Bates and I suggested that while the string length-IQ correlation might be positive when there were no task requirements, it might turn negative when subjects were required to carry out some complex mental task (*Personality and Individual Differences*, 1993, 15, 363–71: "String length, attention and intelligence: Focussed attention reverses the string length-IQ relationship"). Tim Bates et al. replicated in essence this finding in an experiment reported in *Intelligence*, 1995, 20, 27–40, under the title of "Intelligence and complexity of the Average Evoked Potential: An attentional theory."

Readers may consider the notion of a comparator as a kind of homunculus in the brain that does all the dirty work, but has no scientific status. Originally postulated by Y. Sokolov, it has been carefully researched by E. Zubary, P. Hileman, and S. Hochstein in an important article on "Time course of perceptual discrimination and single neuron reliability," published in *Biological Cybernetics*, 1990, 62, 475–86. As the authors point out, "The reliability of identification of a visual target increases with time available for inspection of the stimulus. We suggest that the neural basis of this improvement is the existence of a mechanism for integrating a noisy firing rate over some period, leading to a reduction in mean firing rate variance with available processing time." This corresponds in principle to Sokolov's notion, and the experimental data presented by the authors support their analysis.

Chapter 6

There is such an abundance of tests dealing with this topic that only a few of the more important will be mentioned. Jensen deals with education. *Educability and Group Differences*, published by Methuen in 1973, and *Genetics and Education*, published by Harper & Row in 1972, give an excellent view of what the measurement of intelligence can do for education, and what has already been achieved. Brody's *Intelligence* gives an excellent summary of the most recent empirical studies.

Brody also gives an excellent summary of the most recent studies on the relation between intelligence and occupations. He quotes a table giving the connection between IQ, perceptual ability, and psychomotor ability with predicted success in different job families, corrected for criteria unreliability and for range restriction. To quote a few, for "manager" the three correlations are .54, .43 and .26. For "sales person" they are .61, .49, and .29. For "vehicle operator" they are .28, .31, and .44. For "service worker" they are .48, .30, and .27. Much important information is given in Herrnstein and Murray's *The Bell Curve*.

It is worth noting that intelligence is related to criminality, with criminals about 10 points below noncriminals on IQ tests. Of course there are some very bright criminals committing white-collar offences, but their number is very small compared with the much more common type of villains committing mugging, stealing, burglary, and violent offences. Nor is it true that "only the stupid are caught." Even with a clear-up record of 20 percent or less, repeat criminals are nearly always caught in the end. And of course there are alternative methods of getting at actual rates of offending, as I have pointed out, together with Gisli Gudjonsson, in *Causes and Cures of Criminality*, published by Plenum Press in 1989.

Use of tests in the Armed Forces is well described by Philip Vernon and John Parry in *Personnel Selection in the British Forces*, published by the London University Press in 1949. If you are willing to spend the rest of your life reading about the topic, you may wish to consult the numerous reports by the Army Air Forces. And these deal only with the Aviation Psychology Program! The Army and the Navy also published numerous lengthy reports of varying accessability containing tens of thousands of correlations. If you love correlations, this is your diet!

It is often interesting to dissect socially important correlations, such as those between IQ and educational achievement, into a genetic and an environmental part. Lee Thompson, Douglas Detterman, and Robert Plomin have done this in a paper entitled "Associations between cognitive abilities and scholastic achievement : Genetic overlap but environmental differences," which appeared in *Biological Science*, 1991, 2, 158–65. Eventually what they found was that genetic correlations among the cognitive and achievement tests ranged from .57 to .85, but shared and specific environmental correlations were very low or nonexistent. "Performance on ability measures differs from that on achievement measures largely for environmental reasons." So much for the popular notice that schooling caused IQ differences!

Chapter 7

Herman Spitz, *The Raising of Intelligence: A Selected History of Attempts to Raise Retarded Intelligence* is the volume to read. The book was published by Lawrence Erlbaum, in 1986. Also, well worth consulting is Charles Locurto's *Sense and Nonsense* mentioned earlier. These books clearly demonstrate the widespread fraudulence that pretended to advance IQs of deprived children by up to 40 points, and the complicity of the media that praised studies before publication because they once and for all proved environmentalism triumphant—to fall silent when the fraud was demonstrated.

The effect of micronutrients are discussed in detail by myself and Stephen Schoenthaler in a chapter on "Raising IQ level by vitamin and mineral supplementation," which appeared in *Intelligence, Heredity and Environment*, edited by Robert Sternberg for the Cambridge University Press, 1996.

Chapter 8

The major advocates for "many intelligences" are J.P. Guilford, whose *Nature of Human Intelligence* was published in 1967 by McGraw-Hill; see also the book by him and R. Hoepfner, *The Analysis of Intelligence*. The major points of criticism were contributed by Johan Undheim and John Horn in *Intelligence*, 1977, 1, 65–81, in an article entitled "Critical evaluation of Guilford's Structure of Intellect Theory," edited by John Horn and John Knapp, in the *Psychological Bulletin*, 1973, 80, 33–43, in a paper entitled "On the subjective character of the empirical base of Guilford's Structure of Intellect Model." I also contributed in my book, *Structure and Measurement of Intelligence*, already referred to.

Guilford's work, of course, is truly academic, and has given rise to a great deal of valuable test construction, although its central core is now recognised as essentially incorrect—the supposedly separate tests are in fact highly correlated. Later "many intelligences" writers like Gardner and Golman have little scientific support. Howard Gardner wrote *Frames of Mind* in 1984, and *Multiple Intelligences* in 1993, published by Heinemann and Basic Books respectively; both rely entirely on assertions ("What I say three times is true"), and give no evidence for the alleged independence of his alleged "frames of mind." David Golman published *Emotional Intelligence* in 1996, Bloomsbury being the publisher, and his major error, namely combining two separate factors, intelligence and neuroticism, in one shotgun marriage, has been discussed in the text.

While Gardner and Goleman are both wrong, and it is interesting to note that they are wrong in opposite ways. Gardner argues for *separate* and *multiple* intelligences, disregarding the fact that there is no evidence for these "intelligences" to be uncorrelated. Golman argues for one single "emotional intelligence," although the evidence strongly suggests a complete *lack of correlation* between the two traits. The argument for g is simply that all cognitive abilities correlate together in a specific pattern, a fact demonstrated countless times.

The notion of "practical intelligence." as advocated by Robert Sternberg and Richard Wagner, in a book by that title edited by them in 1986 (Cambridge University Press), makes another kind of mistake. Science advances by *abstraction*, reducing complex totalities to constituent elements. Sternberg and Wagner take the opposite course, as does Golman; they use elementary concepts, like *g*, drive, motivation, etc., to build up a complex total they call practical intelligence, as if that had any scientific meaning. But you cannot do anything useful with such a base of unrelated notions. The best you can do is to measure all the constituent parts, but of course that is where we come in; that is what science has been doing all this time!

Chapter 9

I have treated the topics of "genius" and "creativity" exhaustively in my book on *Genius: The Natural History of Creativity*, published by Cambridge University Press in 1996, and all references in these last chapters will be found there. Extremely valuable in this connection are several books written by the doyen of writers on the subject, Dean Simonton. *Scientific Genius* was published by Cambridge University Press in 1988; *Genius, Creativity and Leadership* by Harvard University Press in 1984; and *Greatness* by the Guilford Press in 1994. All are well worth reading. Arthur Koestler's *The Act of Creation* was published in 1964 by Macmillan.

The paper by Felix Post is entitled "Creativity and Psychopathology: A study of 291 world famous men," and appeared in the *British Journal of Psychiatry*, 1994, 165, 27–34. Sir Francis Galton's *Hereditary Genius* was republished in 1978 by Julius Friedman in New York. The paper by E. Folgmann is entitled "An experimental study of composer-preference of four outstanding symphony orchestras," and appeared in the *Journal of Experimental Psychology*, 1933, 16, 709–24. The work of IPAR is well presented by Frank Barron in his *Creativity and Psychological Health*, published in 1967 by Norstrand.

Chapter 10

Catherine Cox wrote her book entitled, *The Early Mental Traits of Three Hundred Geniuses* in 1976, and Stanford University Press published it. The latest follow-up of the Terman gifted children is published under the title *The Gifted Groups in Later Maturity* by Carole Holaban and Robert Sears in 1995, also by Stanford University Press. J.P. Guilford's famous article on "Creativity" appeared in the *American Psychologist*, 1950, 5, 444–54. The Barron-Welsh Art Scale is introduced and discussed in detail by George Welsh in *Creativity and Intelligence: A Personality Approach*, published in 1975 by the University of North Carolina Press. Work on intuition is discussed by M. Westcott in *Toward a Contemporary Psychology of Intuition*, published by Holt, Rinehart and Winston in 1968.

The work of IPAR is discussed by Frank Barron in *Creative Person and Creative Process*, published by Holt, Rinehard and Winston in 1969, and in *Creativity and Present Freedoms*, published by Norstrand in 1968.

Chapter 11

The model for genius is discussed at length in my book, *Genius: The Natural History of Creativity*. The concept of emergenesis is discussed by David Lykken in "Research with twins, the concept of emergenesis," *Psychophysiology*, 1982, 19, 361–73, and by Lykken, Nja Gue, Tellegen, and Bouchard in "Emergenesis" in the *American Psychologist*, 1992, 47, 1565–77.

Conditions for excellence and achievement are discussed in detail in the Dean Simonton books already mentioned. For age and creativity, see G. Beard's *Legal Responsibility in Old Age*, published in 1874 by Russell under this rather misleading title. H. Lehman's *Age and Achievement* is somewhat more appropriately named; it was published in 1953 by Princeton University Press.

Chapter 12

Galton's *Hereditary Genius* is of course the *focus et origo* of this branch of study. I have given a detailed account of George Washington Carver's career in my book, *Psychology is About People*, published in 1972 by the Library Press in New York. Colin Martindale's *The Clock-*

work Muse was published in 1990 by Basic Books. Scientific multiples are discussed by Simonton in his books, already mentioned.

Chapter 13

Psychoticism as a dimension of personality was published in book form under that title by myself and Sybil Eysenck, in 1976 by Hodder and Stoughton. A later update is my article on "The definition and measurement of psychoticism," published in *Personality and Individual Differences*, 1992, 13, 757–85. For the question of the unitary nature of different functional psychoses, see R. Kendell and I. Brockington's article, "The identification of disease entities and the relationship between schizophrenic and affective psychoses" in the *British Journal of Psychiatry*, 1980, 137, 324–31. The method of statistical analysis I have worked out to decide between the dimensional and the categorical approach to diagnosis is described and applied in my article on "Criterion Analysis: An application of the hypothetico-deductive method to factor analysis," published in the *Psychological Review*, 1950, 57, 38–51.

The study by Erik Woody and Gordon Claridge, "Psychoticism and thinking" was pubished in the British *Journal of Social and Clinical Psychology*, 1977, 16, 241–48. My own study, "Creativity and personality: Word Assdociation, Origence and Psychoticism," was published in the *Creativity Research Journal*, 1993, 7, 209–16. The work of K.O. and K. Goetz, "Personality characteristics of successful artists," and "Personality characteristics of professional artists" was published in *Perceptual and Motor Skills*, 1979, 49, 919–24, and 227–34.

Chapter 14

Robert Payne's work on overinclusiveness is contained in his chapter on "Cognitive Abnormalities" in my *Handbook of Abnormal Psychology*, published by Pitman in 1960, and a chapter co-authored by him and J. Hewlett, "Thought disorders in psychotic patients," in a book I edited, *Experiments in Personality*, published in 1960 by Routledge and Kegan Paul. For N. Cameron's own work, see his *Psychological Behaviour Disorders*, published in 1947 by Houghton Mifflin, and his book with A. Magaret, *Behavior Pathology*, 1951, same publisher. For latent inhibition, R. Lubow and his book on *Latent Inhibition and Conditional Attention Theory*, published in 1989 by Cambridge University Press, is the prime source. The theory of schizophrenia mentioned by Jeffrey Gray et al., is in an article entitled "The neuropsychology of schizophrenia," which appeared in *Behavioural and Brain Sciences*, 1991, 14, 1–84.

Richard Milton's *Forbidden Science* was published by Fourth Estate in 1994. Also relevant is B. Barber's essay on "Resistance by scientists to scientific discovery," published in *Science*, 1961, 134, 596–602. M. Planck's *Scientific Autobiography*, published in 1949 by the Philosophical Library, is also well worth reading. For my adventures with the rampant psychoanalysts at the RMPA meeting, see my autobiographical note, "Maverick Psychologist, in *The History of Clinical Psychology in Autobiography*, edited by Eugene Walker and published in 1991 by Brooks/Cole.

Chapter 15

The Snyderman and Rothman book on *The IQ Controversy* should be familiar to anyone discussing the astonishing things the media dish out as informed comment on matters psychological. It may also explain why books on psychology, particularly on intelligence, are seldom, if ever, reviewed by psychologists familiar with the field, but usually by politically motivated outsiders with no qualifications in the field, and apparently no desire to discover what genuine psychology actually has to say. Also interesting in this context is the book *Social Scientists Meet the Media*, edited by Cheryl Haslam and Alan Bryman, and published by Routledge in 1994. The numerous social scientists assembled to voice their complaints about the lack of accuracy, lack of care about checking facts, and general search for sensational rather than accurate presentation of research outcomes. A general advice to readers of newspapers might be that whatever the papers say, the opposite is probably true! Political correctness is no lover of truth; whatever is counter to PC must be either suppressed, misrepresented, or turned into its opposite.

One favourite trick is to turn a perfectly true statement into an objectionable untruth, and then accuse the original author of insensitivity and racism/sexism/ageism. I may say, truthfully, that with age g_f slowly declines, with a more rapid decline after sixty or so, while g_c remains at the same level, or may even increase. A typical headline might be: "Professor says the old are stupid." Now the original statement was factual, and referred to hundreds of studies using a variety of IQ tests. The journalistic statement does several things: (1) it neglects to mention the large and solid factual basis of the statement, and makes it appear one person's subjective notion; (2) it neglects the vital distinction between g_f and g_c; (3) it cues an emotion-laden word—stupid—which has many meanings not identical with g_f.

There is no doubt that my IQ (g_f) has deteriorated over the years, but I don't think anyone would call me "stupid" at eighty! People with high IQs often do very stupid things; low IQ and stupidity are by no means the same things.

There are many other tricks. The more I know about a subject, the less accurate I find newspaper accounts to be. The only advice I can give the reader is to disbelieve anything he reads in the newspapers about science, particularly social science and medicine. If you are interested, try and get a copy of the original report, or talk to someone knowledgeable in the subject. If any newspaper should review this book favourably, itself a contradiction in terms, I would know that I have finally reached too low a level of g to continue writing! Fortunately there is little danger of that happening.

Appendix: Mainstream Science on Intelligence

Under the title: Mainstream Science on Intelligence, the following document was published in the Wall Street Journal on Tuesday, December 13, 1994, under the names of over 50 of the leading experts in the study of intelligence. It has since been republished in the pages of "Intelligence", the leading academic journal in the field. The document was drafted to set the record straight after the media's onslaught on the Herrnstein and Murray book, "The Bell Curve", which showed little appreciation of the fact that the book represented mainly orthodox thinking, and gave a very accurate picture of the views held by mainstream academics. Its publication may redress the view, frequently expressed by newspapers, on TV, and in popular journals that psychologists like Herrnstein, Jensen or myself are mavericks, lone voices, rebels isolated from the great majority. The document drafted for the American Psychological Association by a special Task Force to state majority opinion of experts is too long to be reproduced, but does not essentially differ in any important way from the Wall Street Journal document. The document is reproduced by permission of Dow Jones & Co.

Since the publication of "The Bell Curve," many commentators have offered opinions about human intelligence that misstate current scientific evidence. Some conclusions dismissed in the media as discredited are actually firmly supported.

This statement outlines conclusions regarded as mainstream among researchers on intelligence, in particular, on the nature, origins, and practical consequences of individual and group differences in intelligence. Its aim is to promote more reasoned discussion of the vexing phenomenon that the research has revealed in recent decades. The following conclusions are fully described in the major textbooks, professional journals and encyclopedias in intelligence.

The Meaning and Measurement of Intelligence

1. Intelligence is a very general mental capability that, among other

things, involves the ability to reason, plan, solve problems, think abstractly, comprehend complex ideas, learn quickly and learn from experience. It is not merely book learning, a narrow academic skill, or test-taking smarts. Rather, it reflects a broader and deeper capability for comprehending our surroundings—"catching on," "making sense" of things, or "figuring out" what to do.

2. Intelligence, so defined, can be measured, and intelligence tests measure it well. They are among the most accurate (in technical terms, reliable and valid) of all psychological tests and assessments. They do not measure creativity, character, personality, or other important differences among individuals, nor are they intended to.

3. While there are different types of intelligence tests, they all measure the same intelligence. Some use words or numbers and require specific cultural knowledge (like vocabulary). Others do not, and instead use shapes or designs and require knowledge of only simple, universal concepts (many/few, open/closed, up/down).

4. The spread of people along the IQ continuum, from low to high, can be represented well by the bell curve (in statistical jargon, the "normal curve"). Most people cluster around the average (IQ 100). Few are either very bright or very dull: About 3% of Americans score above IQ 130 (often considered the threshold for "giftedness"), with about the same percentage below IQ 70 (IQ 70–75 often being considered the threshold for mental retardation).

5. Intelligence tests are not culturally biased against American blacks or other native-born, English-speaking peoples in the U.S. Rather, IQ scores predict equally accurately for all such Americans, regardless of race and social class. Individuals who do not understand English well can be given either a nonverbal test or one in their native language.

6. The brain processes underlying intelligence are still little understood. Current research looks, for example, at speed of neural transmission, glucose (energy) uptake, and electrical activity of the brain.

Group Differences

7. Members of all racial-ethnic groups can be found at every IQ level. The bell curves of different groups overlap considerably; but groups often differ in where their members tend to cluster along the IQ line. The bell curves for some groups (Jews and East Asians) are centered somewhat higher than for whites in general. Other groups (blacks and Hispanics) are centered somewhat lower than non-Hispanic whites.

8. The bell curve for whites is centered roughly around IQ 100; the bell curve for American blacks roughly around 85; and those for different subgroups of Hispanics roughly midway between those for whites and blacks. The evidence is less definitive for exactly where above IQ 100 the bell curves for Jews and Asians are centered.

Practical Importance

9. IQ is strongly related, probably more so than any other single measurable human trait, to many important educational, occupational, economic, and social outcomes. Its relation to the welfare and performance of individuals is very strong in some arenas in life (education, military training), moderate but robust in others (social competence), and modest but consistent in others (law-abidingness). Whatever IQ tests measure, it is of great practical and social importance.

10. A high IQ is an advantage in life because virtually all activities require some reasoning and decision-making. Conversely, a low IQ is often a disadvantage, especially in disorganized environments. Of course, a high IQ no more guarantees success than a low IQ guarantees failure in life. There are many exceptions, but the odds for success in our society greatly favor individuals with higher IQs.

11. The practical advantages of having a higher IQ increase as life settings become more complex (novel, ambiguous, changing, unpredictable, or multifaceted). For example, a high IQ is generally necessary to perform well in highly complex or fluid jobs (the professions, management); it is a considerable advantage in moderately complex jobs (crafts, clerical and police work); but it provides less advantage in settings that require only routine decision making or simple problem solving (unskilled work).

12. Differences in intelligence certainly are not the only factor affecting performance in education, training, and highly complex jobs (no one claims they are), but intelligence is often the most important. When individuals have already been selected for high (or low) intelligence and so do not differ as much in IQ, as in graduate school (or special education), other influences on performance loom larger in comparison.

13. Certain personality traits, special talents, aptitudes, physical capabilities, experience, and the like are important (sometimes essential) for successful performance in many jobs, but they have narrower (or unknown) applicability or "transferability" across tasks and settings

compared with general intelligence. Some scholars choose to refer to these other human traits as other "intelligences."

Source and Stability of Within-Group Differences

14. Individuals differ in intelligence due to differences in both their environments and genetic heritage. Heritability estimates range from 0.4 to 0.8 (on a scale from 0 to 1), most thereby indicating that genetics plays a bigger role than does environment in creating IQ differences among individuals. (Heritability is the squared correlation of phenotype with genotype.) If all environments were to become equal for everyone, heritability would rise to 100% because all remaining differences in IQ would necessarily be genetic in origin.

15. Members of the same family also tend to differ substantially in intelligence (by an average of about 12 IQ points) for both genetic and environmental reasons. They differ genetically because biological brothers and sisters share exactly half their genes with each parent and, on the average, only half with each other. They also differ in IQ because they experience different environments within the same family.

16. That IQ may be highly heritable does not mean that it is not affected by the environment. Individuals are not born with fixed, unchangeable levels of intelligence (no one claims they are). IQs do gradually stabilize during childhood, however, and generally change little thereafter.

17. Although the environment is important in creating IQ differences, we do not know yet how to manipulate it to raise low IQs permanently. Whether recent attempts show promise is still a matter of considerable scientific debate.

18. Genetically caused differences are not necessarily irremediable (consider diabetes, poor vision, and phenal keton uria), nor are environmentally caused ones necessarily remediable (consider injuries, poisons, severe neglect, and some diseases). Both may be preventable to some extent.

Source and Stability of Between-Group Differences

19. there is no persuasive evidence that the IQ bell curves for different racial-ethnic groups are converging. Surveys in some years show that gaps in academic achievement have narrowed a bit for some races,

ages, school subjects and skill levels, but this picture seems too mixed to reflect a general shift in IQ levels themselves.

20. Racial-ethnic differences in IQ bell curves are essentially the same when youngsters leave high school as when they enter first grade. however, because bright youngsters learn faster than slow learners, these same IQ differences lead to growing disparities in amount learned as youngsters progress from grades one to 12. As large national surveys continue to show, black 17-year-olds perform, on the average, more like white 13-year-olds in reading, math, and science, with Hispanics in between.

21. The reasons that blacks differ among themselves in intelligence appears to be basically the same as those for why whites (or Asians or Hispanics) differ among themselves. Both environment and genetic heredity are involved.

22. There is no definitive answer to why IQ bell curves differ across racial-ethnic groups. The reasons for these IQ differences between groups may be markedly different from the reasons why individuals differ among themselves within any particular group (whites or blacks or Asians). In fact, it is wrong to assume, as many do, that the reason why some individuals in a population have high IQs but others have low IQs must be the same reason why some populations contain more such high (or low) IQ individuals than others. Most experts believe that environment is important in pushing the bell curves apart, but that genetics could be involved too.

23. Racial-ethnic differences are somewhat smaller but still substantial for individuals from the same socioeconomic backgrounds. To illustrate, black students from prosperous families tend to score higher in IQ than blacks from poor families, but they score no higher, on average, than whites from poor families.

24. Almost all Americans who identify themselves as black have white ancestors—the white admixture is about 20%, on average—and many self-designated whites, Hispanics, and others likewise have mixed ancestry. Because research on intelligence relies on self-classification into distinct racial categories, as does most other social-science research, its findings likewise relate to some unclear mixture of social and biological distinctions among groups (no one claims otherwise).

Implications for Social Policy

25. The research findings neither dictate nor preclude any particular social policy, because they can never determine our goals.

They can, however, help us estimate the likely success and side-effects of pursuing those goals via different means.

The following professors—all experts in intelligence and allied fields—have signed this statement:

Richard D. Arvey, University of Minnesota
Thomas J. Bouchard, Jr., University of Minnesota
John B. Carroll, University of North Carolina at Chapel Hill
Raymond B. Cattell, University of Hawaii
David B. Cohen, University of Texas at Austin
Rene V. Dawis, University of Minnesota
Douglas K. Detterman, Case Western Reserve University
Marvin Dunnette, University of Minnesota
Hans Eysenck, University of London
Jack Feldman, Georgia Institute of Technology
Edwin A. Fleishman, George Mason University
Grover C. Gilmore, Case Western Reserve University
Robert A. Gordon, Johns Hopkins University
Linda S. Gottfredson, University of Delaware
Robert L. Greene, Case Western Reserve University
Richard J. Haier, University of California at Irvine
Garrett Hardin, University of California at Berkeley
Robert Hogan, University of Tulsa
Joseph M. Horn, University of Texas at Austin
Lloyd G. Humphreys, University of Illinois at Urbana-Champaign
John E. Hunter, Michigan State University
Seymour W. Itzkoff, Smith College
Douglas N. Jackson, University of Western Ontario
James J. Jenkins, University of South Florida
Arthur R. Jensen, University of California at Berkeley
Alan S. Kaufman, University of Alabama
Nadeen L. Kaufman, California School of Professional Psychology at San Diego
Timothy Z. Keith, Alfred University
Nadine Lambert, University of California at Berkeley
John C. Loehlin, University of Texas at Austin
David Lubinski, Iowa State University
David T. Lykken, University of Minnesota
Richard Lynn, University of Ulster at Coleraine
Paul E. Meehl, University of Georgia

R. Travis Osborne, University of Georgia
Robert Perloff, University of Pittsburgh
Robert Plomin, Institute of Psychiatry, London
Cecil R. Reynolds, Texas A & M University
David C. Rowe, University of Arizona
J. Philippe Rushton, University of Western Ontario
Vincent Sarich, University of California at Berkeley
Sandra Scarr, University of Virginia
Frank L. Schmidt, University of Iowa
Lyle F. Schoenfeldt, Texas A & M University
James C. Scharf, George Washington University
Herman Spitz, former director E.R. Johnstone Training and Research
    Center, Bordentown, N.J.
Julian C. Stanley, Johns Hopkins University
Del Thiessen, University of Texas at Austin
Lee A. Thompson, Case Western Reserve University
Robert M. Thorndike, Western Washington University
Philip Anthony Vernon, University of Western Ontario
Lee Willerman, University of Texas at Austin

Index